FINALLY!

SOMEONE SAID IT!

PART ONE

ROCKY FAIRFAX

Finally! Someone Said It! Part One
Copyright ©2025 by Rocky Fairfax

PB ISBN: 979-8-9931151-0-8

Book design by Variance Author Services
www.varianceauthorservices.com

FINALLY!

SOMEONE SAID IT!

PART ONE

DEDICATED TO:

SAMUEL ADAMS,
CHARLES CARROLL, AND
CHARLIE KIRK!

TABLE OF CONTENTS

SECTION 6- SHUT YOUR PIE HOLES LIBERALS!

SECTION 1

THE MEDIA

CHAPTER ONE

MEDIA CORRUPTION

I should clarify what I mean by "the media." Media can mean anything. In air conditioning and refrigeration, the media can be the filters on the air conditioning unit. In print photography it can be the specialty paper needed to transfer an image from the negative. The truth of the matter is when we use the term "media" these days, our minds instantly think of Fox, CNN or CNBC. Calling these news shows the media is both correct and incorrect. The best way to think of the media is by realizing that the word media, aside from what the word has come to mean, is the plural form of the word medium. Medium, like the spirit *medium* your great, great grandmother would invite to her house for a séance. The spirit medium was the vessel through which spirits would speak to those attending the séance. Fittingly, the medium at a séance in almost all instances was a fraud at the head of the table stealing money from the gullible attendees. Just as the mediums in the media are the frauds sitting at the table in front of television cameras claiming that they are, truthfully, telling you the news.

A medium is the object required to do something. It can get complicated. For the purposes of this book, when I use the word media, I am referring to the *information media*- The objects or organizations used to pass on information. The News Media, the Movie and Television Media and the Data Media (Silicon Valley) and they have all been corrupted!

The problem with me saying they have been corrupted is that it doesn't differentiate between **corruption** and **bias**. If a member of the media highlights the liberal viewpoint of a story and nothing else, that is a bias. If they get paid by an outside organization to report what the organization wants said, they are **corrupt**. If they allow an outside organization to unduly influence their reporting, purposely skewing the reporting towards the views of that alien organization, they are **corrupt**. If they get paid either through commercials or a specific contract requiring such behavior, they are **corrupt**. If it is company policy to highlight one side of the story and downplay the other, **corrupt**! The purpose of the information media is to pass on information. Notice I did not say they pass on specific information. I have left it as a general statement.

Is it okay for a media organization to focus on information that favors the Democrat Party? The short answer is yes! But if they do, they must tell people as much. In the news media, when a news anchor or pundit owns stock in a company, they always or should always, inform the viewers of the fact that they do own shares in the company they are about to discuss. I think the current jargon used by those in the know is to say they *"···hold positions in the company."* This is to alert the viewers of possible bias in the reporting, and that they may be trying to influence the stock price. It's also to protect the news organization from lawsuits filed by people who take everything that is said on television as gospel, who because of what they hear end up losing their life savings.

The same should happen for people who blatantly support one side of the argument or another. If a guest pundit on CNN is a diehard Republican who is about to comment on a politics, they should be required to state their affiliation, as should Democrats. A pundit should not be allowed to spew forth the Democrat Party talking points without a warning to the consumer that they are about to hear the daily Democrat Party talking points. That is vile corruption! This includes the news anchors.

News anchors should be required to preface every story with a phrase similar to, *"I am a diehard Democrat, and I hate all things not Democrat."* Not only that, but they should also be required to say it again every 15 minutes until the segment ends. Should they fail to do so, they should be punished, and I don't mean a spanking in the breakroom. For every time they forget, a $10,000.00 fine payable to the company's shareholders. They can afford it.

As a lead-in to the next section, here is a news story that was broadcast on Fox News on 9 March 2023. Tucker Carlson's "C" block was about a journalist who would no longer be allowed to sit in on the White House press briefings. Over the course of the story, it was brought to the audience's attention that this person was the only journalist in the room routinely asking White House Press Secretary Karine Jean-Pierre questions about newly released videos of the January 6th "Insurrection." This journalist, at the time, was working for Today News Africa. This journalist's name is Simon Ateba, and he is a member of the White House Correspondence Association (WHCA).

According to the story, Mr. Ateba will no longer be allowed to attend White House Press Briefings. The decision was made by the President of the White House Correspondents Association. That the decision was made after the White House Press Secretary called the President of the WHCA and requested it. So, what is the issue?

First, who decides who is allowed to attend White House Press Briefings? I've always assumed it was open to all people possessing the proper credentials on a first-come/first-served basis. My assumption was wrong. And not just wrong, but seriously wrong. In fact, I could not have been more wrong. I hope people can follow these next few paragraphs. It shows the corruption of the information media in a perfect light.

According to the story, only members of the WHCA are allowed to attend the briefings. Which means any person who wishes to attend the briefing must first *bribe* the WHCA by becoming a member of the WHCA. After having read the requirements for admission into this self-proclaimed, exclusive club, I can tell you straight up, it is a corrupt organization. Not only are they deciding who gets to attend Press Briefings, but they hide behind a false veneer of having an unassailable reputation by touting that their members have been "credentialed" by a Congressional Standing Committee.

So, if you wish to attend a briefing to ask questions of *your* elected representative- the President of the United States via his Press Secretary- you *must* be a journalist and you *must* work for a "proper" news organization. The WHCA apparently owns the seats and leftover standing room in the White House briefing room, and news organizations pay the WHCA for their seats. Or as is stated on the WHCA website:

> *"Applicants for Red membership must provide verification that either the applicant or the applicant ' s employer has a share of a seat in the briefing room, or an assigned workspace, or participates in one of the pool rotations …"*
>
> *White House Correspondence Association Website*
> *https://whca.press/for-members/*

I emphasize the part where it says, *"share of a seat."* Your access to factual information directly from the White House is being controlled by an unaccountable, non-profit organization. And this organization takes millions of dollars each year in dues from members and in grants from the federal government.

Second, how is the WHCA's ability to deny people access to the White House not corruption. In the news report, it was said that Ms. Jean-Pierre asked the president of the WHCA to revoke Mr. Ateba's credentials. This is corruption. Essentially, this is the ***President of the United States*** denying 1st amendment rights. This is illegal. The journalists in that room would be screaming bloody murder if this happened to any of their troupe had it happened during an administration that is politically at odds with the WHCA and its other members. To recap, the Biden Administration called over to the WHCA and told the WHCA to keep a person from ever again attending a press briefing. This is collusion! This is the government telling a Non-Government Organization (NGO) to do something which is forbidden by law. It's not just morally wrong, it is legally wrong. It's not wrong by the standing rules of the federal government, or by the operating rules of the Department of Justice. It is wrong by law.

It isn't wrong by a simple, run-of-the-mill law. It is wrong by the highest law of the land which specifically says it. The US Constitution specifically states that the government cannot do this. The Press Secretary *cannot* call the WHCA and have a person banned. Karine Jean-Pierre needs to be slapped in handcuffs; perp walked out of the White House Press Briefing Room and charged with violating the U.S. Constitution. End of story! 'Nuff said! The fat lady is singing! Nope! Wait! She's done singing!

Hey, all of you lawyers out there, I don't want to hear about how my interpretation is wrong. It is because of you and your ilk that we the people are in this situation. Lawyers such as yourselves, cherry pick words from sentences, then cherry pick the most obscure definition ascribed those words to assign meaning in legal briefs. Your kind will take the word "sell," for instance, use the definition for the word, "sail," and hope no one notices, as you hope to start a precedent and establish "case law."

By the way, enforcing case law is not the same as enforcing the law. Case laws are laws of interpretation, not laws of legislation. Laws are made by legislators who have hopefully debated those laws before passing them. Case law is made by lawyers and judges who are too cowardly to admit the law as written will cause the victim to be punished. Here's a thought, maybe instead of enforcing case law to ease your conscience, let's enforce actual laws. The greater the number of victims that are punished as a result of the law, the sooner the law will be changed or, heaven forbid, repealed. The sooner that happens, the sooner victims will no longer be punished for the crimes of the criminal. Case law is what didn't happen in terms of the abolition of slavery. Holier-than-thou lawyers and judges didn't suddenly grow a conscience and begin emancipating people in a courtroom. Had they done so, other judges and lawyers would have sued to have that verdict overturned as being unconstitutional. Case laws are unconstitutional because they are laws passed by judges and attorneys, not legislators.

The News Media

Yes, the news media is corrupt! Don't let them fool you. They want you to believe they are paragons of truth when they are really the righthand of Beelzebub. They are corrupt and have been for a very long time; probably from the point when their profession was invented. Even Benjamin Franklin was printing corrupted "news". Much of his stuff was misinformation. The question is, "Did he use his ability— his positional power— to influence a narrative and to influence people's opinions and gain support for his political stance?" The short answer is, "Yes, he did!"

With that in mind, it is time we hold the media and liberals in general, to the exacting and excruciatingly high standards to which they hold the US military and police forces across the country. Deep down everyone knows today's media distributes false information. They distribute false information and deceptively edit stories so frequently, they are in reality, propagandists. They would make Joseph Goebbels proud.

In fact, if today's American news media were to time travel back to Nazi Germany, Goebbels would begin a love affair on par with Romeo's and Juliet's with today's media. If he liked the American media during Hitler's rise to power in the 1930's, he would be lovestruck about it today. Goebbels in his most satisfying wet dream could not have fantasized about our current American media- Hollywood included. If today's media existed back then, even after the liberation of the Nazi's extermination camps was made public, the New York Times would still publish a Goebbels OP-ED. And to make matters worse the pundits on NBC would start calling the OP-ED a work of literary genius worthy of a Nobel Prize.

Speaking of the Nazi extermination camps, after the camps were liberated, the New York Times continued to deny their existence even though,

"Most scholars agree that the truth about the Holocaust was established when the 11 allied countries confirmed the Final Solution in December 1942."

Buried by the Times, Laurel Leff, page 4

And if the *Times* did acknowledge the existence and purpose of places like Auschwitz, Dachau, and Nieder Hagen, the story wasn't printed on the front page, above the fold, in the righthand column. It was printed in parts of the newspaper where people were less likely to see the story.

"The story of the Holocaust- articles that focused on the discrimination, deportation, and destruction of the Jews- made the Times front page 26 times and only in six of these stories were Jews identified on the front as the primary victims."

Buried by the Times, Laurel Leff, pages 2-3

Ladies and gentlemen, in Europe World War Two lasted 2,079 days. Three years after it began and almost 2 1/2 years before its end, the Allied Forces acknowledged what was happening, but the NYT did not change its coverage. During the whole of World War Two, only 1,186 stories about the Holocaust were printed. That is roughly 17 per month. Most stories were buried deep in the paper and camouflaged by other stories of supposed greater importance. Begrudgingly being mentioned, in many cases, as afterthoughts and footnotes of other stories. This was the actions of "The Bible of Journalism" during the largest conflict ever fought on the planet.

Today's media has convinced half the U.S. population that the people calling for the government to restrict other people's free speech *aren't* the fascists. They have convinced them instead that the real fascists are the very people whose lives are being destroyed and whose speech *is* being regulated. The media truly believes their fascists foot soldiers are the saviors of free speech. According to the American information media, the people that are literally repeating Kristallnacht, the Night of Broken Glass, and the Nacht der Langen Messer, Night of the Long Knives, are the new heroes of society.

Not to insult the Jewish community, or to minimize their pain or to minimize the experiences of their ancestors, but the enemies of today's U.S. information media are the "New Jews." And they aren't even Jewish. I purposely make this comparison because for years the phrase, "Never Again," has been wantonly bandied about by the information media. Yet, the phrase is rarely, and then with great reluctance, assigned to those for whom it was created— The Jewish People!

Whenever possible, the news media co-opts the phrase, "Never Again!" As I mentioned above it was coined to refer to the Jewish Holocaust. As in we will "never again" allow the wholesale or attempted extermination of a group of people. If it did start to happen, society resolved to rally around the phrase and stop it immediately. However, the media uses the phrase as a rallying cry for everything regardless of the degree of actual injury to the purported victim. It has become the civil rights talking point of every contemporary college student. If they are currently talking about gay marriage, someone always says something along the lines of *"Never again! We will never again be subjugated by the Christian orthodoxy."* One of the most recent examples of the co-opting of this phrase by the media was a pundit using it to mean all of World War 2.

The news media is always intellectually dishonest. To them it is about money and prestige. That's it! They covet the glory attributed to battlefield heroes, but they don't want the risk. In short, they are cowards. If you come up with a catch phrase that gets people's attention, they will try to steal it, and claim they invented it. I direct your attention to the use of the term, "snowflake." Originally, it was used to describe crybaby liberal college students who can't handle living in a world where people who don't agree with them on everything also exist. Now liberals are using it to describe people who work for a living and don't believe in the same false gods worshiped by liberals. To the Jewish people, standby. Soon it will be taught that the phrase, "Never Again," was really the rallying cry shouted by people to precipitate the formation of the United Nations!

If you don't believe the media is corrupt, answer these questions.

Why do the election-altering surprises only occur in October?

There is never a March surprise. It only happens in October. Are we to believe that election altering incidents only occur in October because of the divine hand of providence?

Have you ever noticed that? It ALWAYS happens in October, and it ALWAYS happens three weeks before an election. Not only that, but it NEVER happens in non-election years. It's as if the gods and goddesses worshiped by liberals are only awake for three weeks in a two-year period, and only at the end of October. No wonder liberals worship these gods, they are lazy. *Hey, no one tell them about the Greek god Dionysus, they'll ruin Greek mythology for everyone. They'll say it isn't diverse enough. Pre-emptive strike: Having a god for* literally *everything is the epitome of diversity.* Are we to further believe that in a country of 350 million people no one is capable of explaining:

1) Why did a particular year's Immaculate Prognostication occur when it did, and not immediately following the discovery of the subject thereof?

2) How is the Prognostication *not* an attempt to change the outcome of the election occurring three weeks thusly?

3) Why the people who dare to offer contrarian views to the prognostication are dummkopfs, rubes, or are people with waning mental faculties?

4) Why is everyone else expected to treat those with contrarian views as neo-heretics, and shun them from society?

5) Why do the surprises that gain traction only benefit the liberal orthodoxy?

Explain to me how those questions in themselves don't prove the corruption of the news media. Those are questions the media should be asking, but they never ask them.

Get these next few sentences through your heads, journalists and news anchors. Your job is to investigate for ***facts*** and to report those ***facts*** to the populace.

Did you catch that? You- members of the media- go in search of <u>facts</u>. You dig through dumpsters looking for facts. Your whole life should be fact-based because a fact is the Holy Grail of journalism. Facts! Facts! Facts! Facts, ***not*** truth. Why not truth you ask? Because truth is subjective. What I believe is the truth of the matter may not be the truth of the matter for someone else. We may look at the exact same facts, but because we have had different experiences in life, the truth- our *separate* "truths"- may be on opposite ends of the spectrum. That is why in a court of law, the jury consists of more than one person. By having multiple people on a jury, it purposely creates a debate. The more people on the jury, the greater the chance of a debate breaking out. The more people, the better the chance will be that there will be someone who will *not* submit to popular opinion.

FYI, when someone says they are "speaking their truth" they are not having a religious epiphany. Saying something is "their truth" is not an ultra-righteous way of stating a fact. It is only a vainglorious way for them to voice their opinion. According to them, if they are telling you, "their truth" you are to take that to mean it is a gospel from on high. They want other people to believe their opinion is the purest definition of truth.

Here are some examples to illustrate the difference between truths and facts.

Fact: Both McDonald's and Burger King sell hamburgers.
Truth: The Big Mac is better than the Whopper.

Fact: The price of oil spiked during the presidencies of George Bush and Barrack Obama.

Truth: During their respective tenures, both presidents did all they could to lower the price of oil.

Can you see the difference? The media is *not* reporting facts to the populace. They discover the facts of a story; They interpret the meaning of those facts; They report *their* interpretation.

Using hurricanes as an example, for the better part of fifty years the media has been trying to get people to believe that when more than 3 hurricanes develop in one season it is unprecedented. They do this so they can panic people into believing the cause of the hurricanes is global warming. They can never let a simple statement of fact stand alone. They never say, *"Three hurricanes made landfall in the United States in one season."* They never tell you the other facts because those facts are inconvenient and disprove their narrative. They leave out facts such as:

- Hurricanes form every year.
- Some hurricanes fizzle out before making landfall

- Some make landfall in the United States
- Some make landfall somewhere outside the United States.
- Sometimes five hurricanes make landfall in a single year and sometimes zero hurricanes come ashore.

They also conveniently leave out the fact that hurricanes and typhoons are the same thing. They just happen to be in different hemispheres.

It is not the job of the media, as I have heard multiple media figures say, "…to hold truth to power." It is not the job of the media to be a check on power. It is not the job of the media to bring people to justice. It is not the job of the media to hold the powerful accountable.

That is the job of the voters! And in the case of justice, justice is the job of the jury!

The voters will hold truth to power at the ballot box. If the media are withholding facts from the American people, the media should share in any blame attached to the failures resulting from their lack of integrity. For example, during the 2020 election cycle the news media blatantly lied to the American people about Hunter Biden's laptop. Therefore, all the woes being suffered by the American people should be blamed on the media. You can't necessarily blame President Biden or his staff. Why, because it was the media's job to report to the American people facts about the candidates. The media lied however, and it caused people to vote for Biden. They should never be allowed to forget it. Just as they will never allow other members of society to live down their failures, the media should never be forgiven for theirs.

Some people have stated to pollsters that had the media done its job and reported on Hunter's laptop with integrity, they would not have voted for Joe Biden. Further, because the media's lies resulted in Biden being elected, and Biden being elected resulted in the Afghanistan pullout fiasco, it is the media's fault that 13 U.S. soldiers were killed unnecessarily. At Trump rallies the chant should be,

"The media lied, and people died!"

Or,

"The media lied, and 13 soldiers died!"

There is however, a silver lining to this particular cloud. It is being shown, regarding Hunter Bidens' laptop, that the media was *purposeful* in its deception and dishonesty. Because of this deception, the families of the 13 soldiers killed now have standing and should file a lawsuit against the media. The media are accomplices to the murder of their loved ones! If the media hadn't overtly and knowingly lied, their loved ones would still be alive. But because they purposely ignored the story- An October Surprise by the way, one that for once did not favor liberals- people who wouldn't have voted for Biden did vote for him, and it was enough to change the outcome of the election. *The media conspired to affect the outcome of a presidential election.* Had Joe Biden lost the election, he would not have been Commander in Chief of the U.S. Armed Forces and as such, he could never have ordered the abandonment of Afghanistan. Again, the media is 100% to blame for the fiasco in Afghanistan!

The media has decided their job is to be king makers. They have decided they need to protect their preferred candidates and politicians. The media has decided that they are better than the people whose daily toil results in them getting dirt under their fingernails. The media has decided they know better than greasy mechanics. This is not a new occurrence. One person held in high esteem by members of high society is Joseph Pulitzer. But, gentle reader, do you know anything about this person- the namesake of the award given to journalists for their *prized* compositions? Time to burst some bubbles…

As it is stated in not one, but two biographies on Joeseph Pulitzer, one written by W.A. Swanberg, *Pulitzer,* the other *Pulitzer: A Life,* by Denis Brian, he once got so bent out of shape in a debate, he went back to his room and retrieved his gun. He then returned to the debate and when he again began to lose the argument, he pulled his gun and pointed it at his opponent. Just as he did back then, Antifa does today. He saw he was losing the fight, one which he started, and then escalated the fight. Had Pulitzer's opponent backed down in fright, Pulitzer would have proclaimed it a victory. As it stands, his opponent attempted to disarm him, so Pulitzer shot him in the knee. This is attempted murder! Joseph Pulitzer was an attempted murderer. The investigation that followed had him indited on charges of attempted pre-mediated murder, and in the subsequent trial he was found guilty by a jury of his peers.

In another event completely separated by time and distance, Pulitzer showed his disdain for civil discourse again. He became the political activist owner of a newspaper, the St. Louis Post-Dispatch. During campaign season Pulitzer allowed his managing editor to use the Post-Dispatch to malign, not the candidate, but an innocent third party. The managing editor began to libel and slander a person known by the candidate, calling him a coward. When the person came to the newspaper offices and confronted Pulitzer's editor, Pulitzer's editor killed the person.

Ladies I give you the hero of modern journalists and news anchors everywhere. The person with many writers, not just journalists, strive to equal. I give you Joseph Pulitzer- Attempted murderer and accomplice to murder.

Wait! There's more!

Pulitzer spent most of his adult life condemning rich Republicans, or the rich in general. However, he was a rich Democrat. He socialized with rich Democrats. In fact, he joined the Manhattan Club. He used his newspaper to support rich Democrat candidates. I tell you this not because I can find no fault with other newspapers at the time, I tell you this because no one else will.

Think of how things happen today. During campaign season, Democrats and the media will jump up and down screaming about how Republican candidates take money from the Koch brothers, rich billionaires. What they won't do is jump up and down screaming that Democrat candidates take money from Bill Gates and Warren Buffet- richer billionaires. I tell you this because the media's hypocrisy will not allow them to tell you. You are supposed to believe that because a journalist or news anchor or writer was awarded the Pulitzer Prize, they are telling you everything and you are supposed to believe that you aren't being sold a bill of goods.

In what may have been the first "October Surprise," Joseph Pulitzer put his thumb on the scale for *his* preferred candidate. It is eerily reminiscent of the 2020 election between Donald Trump and Joe Biden. In 1884, two men wanted to be President of the United States. As you might well have deduced, one was a Democrat, the other a Republican, Grover Cleveland and James G. Blaine respectively. In March of that year, Pulitzer discovered that Blaine held a fundraiser which was attended by many wealthy Republicans. Blaine was running on an "anti-rich" platform. Instead of reporting this news to the public as soon as he found out, he waited. He waited until October.

Surprise!!

Grover Cleveland became the 22nd President of the United States.

Joseph Pulitzer- attempted murderer, accomplice to murder, hypocrite, fraudster, and liar.

Another notable American Journalist held in high regard by liberals and the media is Karl Marx. Yes, that Karl Marx! In 1848, Marx published his pamphlet *The Communist Manifesto*. Yes, Karl Marx was an American journalist. He never made it to the United States, but he was a renowned journalist for a well-known American newspaper- The New York Daily Tribune. He was a foreign correspondent in London and worked for the Tribune for 10 years. His work for the New York Daily Tribune began 10 years *after* his Communist Manifesto was published. While he lived in London, Marx became active with a group known as the German Workers' Educational Society. This is starting to sound familiar, too. I wonder what the German Workers' Educational Society morphed into…

A couple other works of Karl Marx were *Das Kapital* and *On the Jewish Question*. Yes, a hero of the left was advocating for the Holocaust 75 years before Adolf Hitler came to power. His essay, On the Jewish Question was published in 1844, and it makes a person wonder where did Hitler get some of his ideas? Forty-six years before Hitler was born, and six years *before* he became a correspondent for a major New York newspaper, On the Jewish Question was published. This guy is a hero of democrats, socialists, and college students worldwide.

With all the breakthroughs in "philosophy" credited to Marx, he never made a dime. He was always poor. Noble? You be the judge. He was constantly asking people for *their* money. He came from a wealthy family, but he never had money. Most of the money he "made" was given to him by his *rich* friends. All the studies which Karl Marx is credited with "studying," were recent studies within

Europe. Studies made by his contemporaries; the so-called academics who much like today's, ignored 99% of western history. Had Karl Marx been a true student of history, instead of being a disgruntled rich kid, he would have realized his ideas were not original to him.

The ancient Athenians tested the theories of Marx almost 3000 years- yes, THREE THOUSAND YEARS- before Karl Marx was even born. This next part will come as a shock to some people, but not even Athenians could get collectivism/communism/socialism/fascism (pick your poison) to work. Twice the Athenians tried it and twice it failed! The only good thing to come from the Athenians' attempts at collectivism is the evolution in their philosophical thinking and their new economic format. Economically, the result of collectivism failing were the reforms of Draco. You know, as in "That is so Draconian!"

Karl Marx- Plagiarizer, disgruntled rich kid who didn't inherit any of daddy's money, instigator of riots, hero of college graduates, influencer of Adolf Hitler. (Oh, did I mention Marx only wrote his Manifesto because he didn't believe it to be fair that his eldest brother was the inheritor of the Marx fortune and upon his father's death he wouldn't get anything.)

Why did the media, including Fox News, find it necessary to show Senator John McCain's funeral procession?

I'm not against the media broadcasting the funeral of a Senator. I am turned off by the idea of it though because it reeks of one-upmanship. This is how the gladiatorial games of ancient Rome came into being. A person of note would die, and his family would put on a big spectacle, complete with men fighting to the death in honor of the recently departed. Then someone else would die and that family, feeling their family was more important, would put on an even larger spectacle. Then the gladiatorial games became something for Emperors to honor themselves. Oh, they said it was to honor their predecessor, but it wasn't. If Titus put on 100 days of Games, Caligula would put on 120 days of Games. Hadrian would follow with 140, on and on it would go. (Don't quote me on the number of days the games lasted or who paid for the games, I was only making a point.)

If we aren't careful, this is what will happen when future politicians die. In some regards it is already happening. Every time a politician dies, someone tells us to lower the flag to half-mast. No matter how horrific the politician is, the flags must be lowered so as not to offend anyone. It's as if in death, the person was somehow absolved of all their mortal sins. No one has the courage to not order the flags to be flown at half-mast.

Before long, it won't be enough to have the entire funeral procession shown on television. It will evolve into not only the procession being shown, but the wake, the embalming process, the autopsy, and the person's last breath. Everyone will be required to stop and watch the procession. The size of the processions will grow. They will be 100 miles long and will be driving in a circle at 25 miles per hour. A custom will develop where social importance of the deceased will be demonstrated by the speed of the procession- The slower the speed of the procession, the greater the person. To add insult to injury, the huddled masses will be forced to endure the prognostications of actors and actresses; These actors having been *hired* to attend the funeral because in life the deceased politician was hated and reviled. So much so that no one who isn't paid will be trusted to say anything nice about the newly departed.

I'm not against portions of the processions being broadcast to the world, I'm against the news media thinking we need to watch it *all*. Senator McCain's funeral procession was shown on Fox News. I don't know who made the decision, but they need to be kicked in the groin- Twice! This person needs to be interrogated to find out why they deemed it necessary for them to show cars driving down the road at 25 mile per hour the entire trip. The entire trip from the U.S. Capitol building to the U.S. Naval Academy is a trip of 31 miles. At normal speeds *on a Saturday,* it's a 43-minute drive. At 25 miles per hour this trip would take 1 hour, 45 minutes. It is an unwritten fact that funeral processions have to drive slowly, therefore, the drive time is even greater. Yet, for some reason, those masochists in the news media thought us peons needed to watch the entire trip.

Every mile was shown. Every mention of his military service was amplified. Our "betters" in the media did give us a break though and showed us videos of his family crying. Honest to God, there were so many videos of his relatives crying, the Potomac River was in danger of flooding. I'm not trying to take away anything from John McCain, or his legacy. I'm not trying to take away anything from his family. Yes, he had died, and his family was mourning and suffering through the pain of his loss. I get that! But I didn't need to see everything that transpired. Get a clue News Media! You are as bad with "good ideas" as are the arrogant computer programmers who think they are making things easier for everyone with their "good ideas".

Here are some more examples of just how useless and corrupt the media has become.

During his Reign of Ignorance and Incompetence, whenever something happened which did not exponentially magnify his other-worldly magnificence and further confirm his status as a living deity, President Obama was always absolved of responsibility by all forms of the media, by stating the following phrase in one way or another,

"I found out about it the way you [the American people] found out about it, through the media."

It doesn't matter what the scandal- Fast and Furious, Benghazi, IRS targeting conservative groups- if it would make him look bad, he always found out about it through the media. In fact, sometimes he was notified of it by the White House Press Corps during the press conference. How is that possible? The President of the United States found out about national issues by a journalist telling him? That means President Obama was incompetent to say the least. If he wasn't incompetent, then his National Security Council was incompetent. Here's another way to look at it. The President of the United States has 23 of the absolute best intelligence gathering organizations in the universe, but they missed a major national security issue not once, not twice, not thrice, but at least four times.

Twenty-three intelligence agencies were so incompetent, so useless, the President of the United States was blindsided on multiple occasions. Did you hear that CIA, FBI, NSA, every time President Obama said he found out about something because he read about it in the newspaper, *he, not me, he* was telling the world that you are so incompetent you can't count your balls and get the same number twice!

Here are some quotes proving he was truly incompetent, and he did find out stuff from the media, not his incompetent government.

Note: I added the **bold** as emphasis to call out when Obama was talking about himself.

> "…He's [Eric Holder] indicated he's not aware of what was happening in Fast and Furious **certainly I was not**, and I think both he and I would have been very unhappy if somebody had suggested that guns were allowed to pass through that could have been prevented by the United States of America…"

White House press briefing
https://www.youtube.com/watch?v=iETmDoRvSkc
7 October 2011

> "There have been problems, you know. **I heard on the news about this story** that fast and furious, where allegedly guns were being run into Mexico and ATF knew…"

Interview on CNN Espanol
22 March 2011

And on the IRS scandal,

> "…let me make sure that I answer a specific question. I can assure you that **I certainly did not know** anything about the IG report before the IG report had been leaked through the press."

Rose Garden Press Conference
On 16 May 2013

Again, are we to believe that the most powerful man in the world had no clue about what was happening in his own administration? That he was ignorant of what was happening in his administration, an administration that would bend over backwards to heed his every word? The same members of his administration who would have had naked pillow fights on top of the Washington Monument had he ordered- nay, even remotely suggested, and yet somehow, they couldn't be bothered to keep him informed about what was happening. How is that possible? Again, it's because either he, Obama, was incompetent, or all the agencies that are supposed to keep him informed were incompetent.

How do these stories and other stories relate to the media? Because they failed to ask the follow up question. If Obama told them the sky is purple, they would blindly accept the answer. In these cases, and in *all* the other scandals that plagued his administration, the press blindly accepted his answer. When he told them he found out about it from the media, they never asked, *"Mr. President, are we to believe that you, arguably the most powerful man in the world, found out about this from us? Mr. President if that is the case, then you need to fire the entire Executive Branch and hire only journalists."* But the corrupt media did not. Corrupt!

But it isn't only them giving President Obama a free pass. There are other examples of their corruption.

The media's hatred of President Reagan was so great they could not stop talking about how he was a cowboy; That he was going to start World War 3; That he had no business being the President. They talked about how unstable President Reagan was so much *the Soviets* started to believe it. The Soviets believed it so thoroughly, President Reagan and the leaders of other western nations had to call the Soviets to let them know that Reagan had no intention of launching a nuclear first strike. The media, the irresponsible children that they are, with their daily hissy fits, damn near started World War 3. The media! Not a rogue admiral or general as is *always* depicted in movies- the news media almost started a nuclear war.

Here is another example of the media not doing their job. In June 2022 the U.S. Supreme Court overturned the controversial judgement Roe V. Wade. Everyone who was pro-life at the time was celebrating. Everyone who was pro-abortion was lighting their hair on fire and screaming the world was going to end.

The media showed which side of the abortion controversy they support. Most of them support killing little babies. That's ironic because during the Vietnam War, the media was okay with soldiers returning home being called baby killers with no proof other than what the Soviet propagandists told them when they were, "In country." Now, they are *literally* advocating for babies to be killed, and somehow the media is comprised of noble creatures.

As you probably are aware, following the ruling of Dobbs V. Jackson, the news media started interviewing democrat politicians as if they were all about to go extinct. One such politician was Stacey Abrams the Georgia gubernatorial candidate. Here is what she said about the ruling which did *not* outlaw abortion; this is what she said in the first 30 seconds of a 10-minute interview.

> "In 2019, Brian Kemp the current governor signed an extreme 6 weeks ban on abortion that's 6 weeks often before women know they are pregnant and in Georgia where half of our counties don't have an OB-GYN it can be that they won't find out they are pregnant until after it's too late to have this medical opportunity…"
>
> CNN interview with Jake Tapper
> https://www.cnn.com/videos/politics/2022/06/26/abrams-full.cnn

Did you catch the problem which Jake Tapper decided to let ride? Stacey Abrams just said that of the 159 counties in the State of Georgia, only 79 counties have OB/GYNs. Really? Are you sure? Do you really want to continue that thought? I'm not referring to an abortion now being called, "…this medical opportunity…"

Stacey Abrams said in the State of Georgia there are no obstetricians in 79 counties. She said that in 79 counties there are also no gynecologists. If this is the case, I have a business proposition for half the hospitals and clinics in Georgia; open OB/GYN departments in your hospitals and clinics. You already have a customer base if Stacey Abrams is correct. I will bet somewhere in the same interview she also said something along the lines of women not being able to get other types of "woman only" healthcare if abortion clinics are run out of business. If she did, I would like to restate my idea for hospitals in Georgia to expand their customer base. I only ask for a small stipend for coming up with the idea of having OB/GYNs in medical facilities across the state of Georgia, and the country as a whole. You can send the compensation to www.navy.mil.

Cleary, if we are to believe Ms. Abrams, the only place a woman can get medical attention for "woman" issues is Planned Parenthood. A woman apparently cannot go to a regular medical clinic. Apparently, hospitals in Georgia forbid women from coming to the hospital if they feel a lump in their breast. And only Planned Parenthood can definitively tell whether or not a woman is pregnant. Women can go to a hospital if they break their leg, but the doctors and nurses working in hospitals are too stupid to know how to treat a yeast infection. That is what Stacey Abrams and by omission, Jake Tapper are saying.

Why did you not ask that very important follow-up question, Mr. Jake Tapper? Yes, it is an important follow-up question. It's important because there are people who now think there are no places for women to have their "girl" problems tended to in half of Georgia. This is how riots start. First, some idiot ideolog puts out a set of talking points, and because no one pushes back, listeners believe it is true. Over time frustration builds up until someone gets hurt. Usually, the people who are hurt are those who need the help most. Further, how can the media stand by and let places get firebombed whose purpose is to help women who don't want to have an abortion? The short answer is because the media is corrupt! They don't care about reporting facts. They only wish to sensationalize. If babies get killed in their quest for high ratings, they will not lose any sleep. Corrupt!

Another example of media corruption...

Hillary Clinton once bragged that she knew Supreme Court Justice Thomas in Law School. However, they never met. Hillary claimed that when she would see him, she realized, "...he was a person of grievance." That is what she said on Gayle King's show on CNN. Gayle King, just as Jake Tapper did previously, failed to ask the obvious question. That question being,

So, Secretary Clinton, 60 years after you left law school, can still remember seeing Justice Thomas at law school. Not once did you interact with him, but your memory is so good you managed to pick him out of the thousands of other students on campus that one fateful day.

You managed to see, *and remember,* someone who, up until your husband's first State of the Union Address, was never within 100 yards of you. Also, at that distance, and without ever talking to him, you figured out he "…was a person of grievance." You managed to find a *black* "person of grievance" in the early 1970s. Not only that, but you found it weird that a black man was holding a grudge. Were you that out of touch in the 1970s? I'll ask it again, in the 1970s, you felt there was no reason for an African American to have grievances. During law school you believed African Americans had no reasons to complain about anything?

If you did believe that African Americans in the 1970s did have reasons to be aggrieved, you miraculously managed to recognize how the grievances held by one African American were different from the grievances of other African Americans. You realized with a quick glance from afar that you were experiencing a moment which required you to consciously tell yourself to "make a memory." You remember that quick split-second glance from 50 years ago, but you can't recall anything about the Benghazi tragedy that occurred six weeks prior to your statement about Justice Thomas. How is that possible? You must really think people are that stupid. Do you really think people will believe that you somehow knew he was going to be a Justice on the Supreme Court? Are we to believe you are clairvoyant?

Yes, there are a lot of examples of media corruption of late, but it extends over time. The media is constantly making excuses for their masters in the DNC. By contrast, they demonize the accomplishments of Republicans. If a Republican president claims something, the media goes out of its way to prove him wrong. Just look at the 2009 financial crisis. Dubbed the Great Recession by the media, when it comes to the Clinton-Bush-Obama trifecta, the media placed all blame on Bush. They ignored the true cause of the collapse. They gave all the credit for recovery to Obama.

All the remedial actions taken by Bush and the Republicans, *while Bush was still president and I don't mean as a lame duck President,* the media attributed to Obama. When it was obvious Obama's policies were not working as promised, that they were making the situation worse and prolonging the Great Recession, the media continued to blame President Bush. On national television, when asked about the anemic recovery, the media allowed Obama to claim that the crisis he had inherited was worse than originally thought. The media will invent evidence or ignore it altogether if it means the Republican looks bad.

FYI, the true cause of the financial collapse of 2008 were the laws passed by a democrat Congress and signed into law by President Clinton. These laws _ordered_ banks to give mortgage loans to people who had no business getting a loan because they couldn't afford the loans for one reason or another. The media, being the corrupt idiots they are, immediately started telling the public the reason those people couldn't get loans was due to their skin color. They never told anyone the real reason the loans were denied. Those people who were denied the loans because they were applying for a loan that would require a monthly payment that was greater than what they made every month. But the forever bleeding-heart liberals in Congress passed the laws, and then Clinton enacted them; President Bush paid for them along with all republicans. I focus your attention on the landslide election of President Obama and the next set of Democrats that would control Congress and make the next financial crisis possible. And it is here!

Here is another blatant example of it happening six years prior to the Great Recession!

In March 2003 then President George W. Bush- a Republican- ordered the invasion of Iraq. He didn't give the order by throwing darts at a dart board. President Bush gave the order based on information given to him by the 23 world renowned intelligence agencies that were under his control. Did you catch that? Twenty-three- 23- of the world's greatest intelligence agencies told the President of the United States that Saddam Hussein had weapons of mass destruction. Those 23 intelligence agencies - whose sole job is to keep the President of the United States informed of what is happening - failed in their primary job of keeping POTUS informed. Yet, no blame has been attached to those incompetent ignoramuses. It's solely Bush's fault. Ten years later, when Hiliary Clinton and the DNC needed them most, these same 23 agencies would have current and former employees make multiple appearances on multiple news shows to blather on for a decade that President (then President-elect) Trump was somehow a Russian spy.

WMDs for those of you who only know, the abbreviation stands for Weapons of Mass Destruction. In this case, the narrative was focused solely on nuclear weapons. At first the media supported the invasion. As time went on however and no weapons were found, the media began to turn on President Bush. Yes, originally, they were supportive, but that was the façade they always front. They had to hype it to make the downfall more delectable. I don't know why I said, "They began to turn on him." There wasn't a "begin to turn!" It was an ambush! The media were waiting for the opportunity to completely obliterate him and his credibility. So, when the order from On High came, from head of the Democratic National Committee, being obedient paid operatives, the media acolytes spent a whole five seconds making the transition. It would have been an instantaneous transition, but some news anchors had earpiece issues and didn't understand the garbled order.

Weapons of Mass Destruction *were* found in Iraq while President Bush was still in office. A British unit found a cache of WMDs. CNN reported it. CNN spent about 15 seconds reporting on it, and they only talked about it once. How do I know this? Because I was sitting at a bar watching CNN. I spent the next 6 hours waiting for the story to be played again to see if what I heard was what they said. But the story was never repeated. I was able to watch the stories they talked about on either side of that story multiple times, but I never saw that story again. Why? It exonerates President Bush! It shows them to be purveyors of hysteria and I don't mean they were selling copies of the Def Leppard album.

When did the story air, I hear you asking? Sometime between 2004 and 2007. That is the best I can tell you. I have tried to locate the broadcast. But Al Gore had only recently invented the internet, and YouTube was still in its infancy. Any proof of that find would have to be made by going through after-action reports and hoping they aren't classified to keep the *"Bush Lied; People Died"* narrative alive. Or by sitting in a chair for hours and watching news clips from CNN for months on end.

What WMDs were found? Chemical weapons! The very weapons that when Obama was President, would be a major story themselves. If you recall, there was a big to-do about Russia volunteering to take chemical weapons from Syria. From where do you think Syria got those chemical weapons? Gee let's see, in the 1980s Saddam Hussein is known to have- without a doubt in anyone's mind- used chemical weapons against his own people on multiple occasions, and evil men don't simply build or buy one or two weapons. Yes, weapons of mass destruction include chemical weapons. The classification includes nuclear, biological, and chemical weapons. At the time the media wanted us to believe nuclear weapons are **"the"** weapon of mass destruction. That was the narrative at the time. However, the definition which is used to classify a weapon as a WMD is:

"A weapon of mass destruction is a nuclear, radiological, chemical, biological, or other device that is intended to harm a large number of people."
Department of Homeland Security
https://www.dhs.gov/topics/weapons-mass-destruction

Or, as per the UNRCP, United Nations Regional Centre for Peace and Disarmament,

"Weapons of mass destruction (WMDs) constitute a class of weaponry with the potential to:
- Produce in a single moment an enormous destructive effect capable to kill millions of civilians, jeopardize the natural environment, and fundamentally alter the lives of future generations through their catastrophic effects.
- Cause death or serious injury of people through toxic or poisonous chemicals.
- Disseminate disease-causing organisms or toxins to harm or kill humans, animals or plants.
- Deliver nuclear explosive devices, chemical, biological or toxin agents to use them for hostile purposes or in armed conflict."
https://unrcpd.org/wmd/

The definition from the UN is particularly interesting. According to that definition it is not the warhead which makes a WMD, a WMD. A weapon only needs to be capable of *delivering* the warhead to be classified as a WMD. That means every warship, every airplane, and every tank around the world is a weapon of mass destruction. How so? They all have the ability to, "...Deliver nuclear explosive devices, chemical, biological or toxin agents."

But the media will conveniently ignore that if doing so would prove them wrong and George W. Bush right. In the case of WMDs in Iraq, if I remember correctly, the British unit that found the cache found warheads capable of delivering chemical weapons. FYI, the news report came with video proof; it wasn't simply a lone reporter regurgitating what was told to him. PRESIDENT BUSH DID NOT LIE! THE MEDIA LIED! Would the media and all its lapdog activists care to retract their "Bush lied; People died," statement everyone is still being forced to endure?

In yet another example of how long the media has been corrupted at all levels. Think of our current President, Joseph R. Biden.

Before he became President of the United States, and was constantly watched at ceremonies and other gatherings, then Senator or Vice President Biden always found a way to stand behind some woman with his hands on her shoulders. Sometimes he would sniff their hair. Sometimes he would whisper stuff in her ear. These were women he had never seen before and never had any prior interactions. In another news report, *while he was the Vice President of the United* States, there was a video of him in a restaurant with a woman sitting on his lap. Prior to his arriving at the restaurant, this woman's existence- to him and his enablers in the media- was merely a philosophical exercise.

And yet, there he is on national television with a complete stranger sitting in his lap. A woman whose husband would have kicked the crap out of any other person attempting to be that familiar with his wife. But because of the title bestowed upon him, that of Vice President of the United States, no one in the restaurant did anything. The media not once condemned him; they only exclaimed it is proof that he is truly is an "ordinary Joe". Yet, if you look at it from the other side of the Grand Canyon, this is just one of the many reasons why one of his nicknames is, "Creepy Uncle Joe!" The corrupt media are protecting him. He's a democrat and therefore scrutiny is not allowed. If anyone dares to question his behavior, the media excuses said behavior by claiming it to be proof that he is a passionate man. Or the media claims it is a show of how much he cares about women. Even more repugnant is the media enabling him by claiming his behavior is somehow representative of his generation.

Let's discuss the caring and passionate excuses first. Does this mean I can stand behind a strange woman and sniff her hair? And if I do and if she calls the cops, will the police let me go if I tell them I am demonstrating my passion? No and no! At the very least, I would be given a warning not to do it again. If I did it again, I would be arrested and charged with assault. But not Creepy Uncle Joe, he does it again, and again, and again, with no consequences.

His being born in a different generation is no excuse either. His generation also grew up using a certain six letter word that begins with "N" in normal conversations. A good portion of his generation also grew up believing a woman's place was in the kitchen. His generation witnessed their dads leaving every morning to go to work while mom stayed home. To his generation, mom was the home maker. The first generation of children to be part of a two-income household as a normal occurrence would be the next generation. It was rare, but the baby boomers did see mom and dad go to work. It usually only occurred in the restaurant industry, but it was there.

Why? Because up until the 1960s, when a woman married, she, not necessarily by law, was required to quit her job, and run the household. This was how society functioned for eons and eons. The man went to work; the woman looked after the kids. I know this for a fact because not only did my mom believe this, but she also attempted to pass this on to her children as well. I can still iron a shirt the way my mom taught me. When I asked, grandma didn't hesitate to teach me how to knit.

The difference between the generations is stark. My grandmother was told by her employer at the time she would be fired if she didn't "do the honorable thing" and quit. Both mom and grandma were housewives. It was my dad and granddad who earned the money for food, rent, etc. When my dad lost one job, he *immediately* looked for another. Mom continued to raise us kids. A few times she did get a job to supplement the household income, but those were temporary jobs, not careers. This was the social convention when Joe Biden was growing up in Scranton, PA as well. Being from an older generation is no excuse for Creepy Uncle Joe's behavior.

Furthermore, Creep Uncle Joe Biden is my dad's senior by two years. So, when some moron in the news industry ignorantly proclaims Creepy Joe's perversions are okay because that's what Creepy Joe's generation did, I must throw down bullshit flag. No one in my dad's orbit, hell, no one in my granddad's orbit would blatantly stand behind a strange woman with his hands on her shoulders. Hell, they wouldn't do what Joe does to women with whom they are friendly. That is a learned behavior. Biden acquired that behavior because he was allowed, in that no one ever punched him in the nose. He figured out early in his 50-year stint as a US Senator that he could be as perverted as he wished and no one would even think about slapping him. They were still- by societal standards of the time- taboos. If Biden were not a Senator, the Vice President of the United States or the President of the United States, and he tried doing that, he would have gotten his ass kicked.

If you don't believe me, try it. In front of a woman's husband or boyfriend, stand behind her, place your hands on her shoulders and sniff her hair. You won't because you know what will happen. If the woman didn't put to use her Krav Maga, her significant other would. But the media is corrupt and is protecting him. They refuse to call him what he is because of who he is. They like him and protect him. He is a predator! He should have been shamed into quitting his job years ago. Hell, he should have gotten his ass kicked decades ago. But because he's public figure of the democrat persuasion, he is unassailable.

Here's something that might frustrate people on a daily basis and yet they don't realize it is proof of media corruption as well. How many "news" stories do you see when you first go to Yahoo.com? I see very few. When I say, "news stories," I mean *news* stories, not gossip. I see tons of advertisements and tons of gossip stories. I did a screen grab of the homepage every day for a week while

Trump was president, and the results aren't surprising if you look at it through the lens of corruption. Not even Yahoo wants you to be informed of what is truly happening. Everyday half the "stories" were advertisements, or "click bait." One third of the remaining "stories" were about sports stars or other celebrities. That means less than one fourth of the "news" stories were truly news stories. And guess what, many of those stories were old stories, meaning they have been posted for multiple days.

The number of actual news stories has dropped even lower since Joe Biden became President. It appears that Yahoo is trying to keep people from realizing or at least finding out how utterly incompetent the Biden-Harris administration truly is. So, what do they do? Yahoo adds more stories about celebrities and sports stars hoping people won't notice.

Let's discuss something other than how the media is protecting people. Let's talk about how *they* don't want you to know certain things!

On 19 July 2011, the U.S. House of Representatives debated a Republican sponsored bill that would begin fixing Congress' massive spending problem. It was commonly referred to as the "Cut, Cap and Balance Act." The actual debate was totally partisan! There was no debate. The democrats, not wanting their blatant, out of control spending practices to be outlawed, opposed it. They opposed this so vehemently they, with poisonous contempt for truth, stood on the floor of the House of Representatives and lied. Every time a democrat was recognized to speak during this debate, they stood in front of the American people and lied their asses off. They would claim the bill would not protect veterans, even though it did. They would go on record claiming it would discriminate against the disabled, which it did not. Everything they claimed it would or wouldn't do was a lie.

I remember this bill because I decided it was high time I did a better job of keeping up with the happenings of Capitol Hill. I watched the debates on television- LIVE! I sat through the 3 hours of debates and watched them lie. How do I know they were lying? Was it because someone told me they were lying? No, I knew they were lying because I had recently bought a phone capable of accessing the internet, so I downloaded the bill. I read the bill as it was being debated. I read the entire bill 3 times as it was being debated. With my own eyes I was able to see these slimy politicians repeatedly lie. These people had no intention of debating the bill. Whenever a democrat stood up claiming the bill would be a detriment to one group of people or another, I flipped to that section of the bill and verified there was an exemption for that group of people. Lie after lie after lie. I listened to these criminals for 3 hours non-stop.

Yes, they are criminals! They were actively- even intentionally- committing fraud against the people they **represent**. They have no excuse for what they did! The whole bill was eight pages long. When I say eight pages long, I mean it in terms of an editor. The official copy was double spaced. That means if it were formatted as someone would a personal letter, the Cut, Cap, and Balance Bill would have been four pages. It was the double-line spacing that made it eight pages long. In reality, the actual meat of the bill was less than eight pages long. When one considers the fact there was only one paragraph on the first page because half of the first page was taken up by headings and standard speak, "Be it known that one this day, ___ July, 2011...," it's down to being seven pages long. It's shorter still when you realize the last page of the eight pages too, only had one paragraph on it. In short, I was able to read this bill multiple times while watching the debates live on CSPAN because it wasn't that long- 6-1/2 pages max.

Most bills that Congress votes on are hundreds of pages long. This bill was less than eight. The PDF version I just downloaded is 12 pages long, with a whooping 24 lines per page. I have seen newspaper articles longer than this bill. But the democrats couldn't be bothered to read the damn thing. And the media would not talk about this bill. It's the media's fault!

It was decided by faceless news program producers that the House of Representatives "debating" this not-so-lengthy bill, designed to stop wasteful spending by congress and force them to balance the budget, wasn't the most important story. In their minds, there was a story whose importance to the American electorate was orders of magnitude more important. So much so, that *all* the major news networks shifted into 24-hour non-stop mode. That mode being the one they reserve for dire emergencies where they try to be the first to break the story. Many times, they don't show commercials for this type of story. That shows how important this story was, it superseded commercials. Yes, this story was so important that the money losing media companies decided to tell their cash-cows to pound sand. This bill was that unimportant to them. They didn't mention it once. It wasn't even an afterthought.

What was this all-important story the media conned people in to believing was more important than the United States Congress reigning in their out-of-control spending? A woman had just been acquitted of murder and was about to walk out of the courthouse a free woman. That was the emergent story! Even though, this woman's trial was not unique since there were at the time a couple dozen other women were on trial for the same thing with the same outcome, every news network had to be the first to get video footage of her leaving the courthouse. I think at one point in their incessant coverage one network called it, "The trial of the century!"

Hey, everyone, I recently found a message written on a Post-It note. It's from something that happened on Wednesday, January 2, 1935. The message is for journalists and news anchors everywhere. Because on that day in history, the high paid, over educated members of the media then put their bachelor's degrees in creative writing to use and came up with a new dramatic headline "Trial of the Century," for something that happened then. Not every trial can be the "Trial of the Century." Especially since most "Trials of the Century" only qualify as such because the media spent a year sensationalizing the story. (A century is 100 years long; therefore, the Lindbergh trial still reigns as the *true* "Trial of the Century.")

Do people realize that every time a celebrity goes on trial, or a crime against a celebrity is being tried, the media immediately dubs it, "The Crime of the Century?" Off the top of my head, I can think of two times when this happened in the previous century. The Lindbergh Baby trial and the OJ Simpson trial. Both were separately deemed by the media to be, "The Crime of the Century!" And those are just the stories I can recall without doing a Google search. I would be willing to bet that every year witnesses a crime so heinous, or one which involved someone so famous, it was christened, "The Crime of the Century!"

The last thing I will talk about before moving on to my ideas on how to fix the problem with the corrupt media, is to hold a class to teach the media the difference between a child and an adult. Allow me to correct myself and to use the current media parlance. Here's a Master-Class on the difference between an adult and a child. Hopefully, this discussion will get the media to stop using a person's age or lack thereof, to downplay a crime in the court of public opinion. This usually happens when the suspect is of certain protected group of people, and the media wants the public at large to feel sorrier for the perp than the accused's victim.

Here's the lesson. It is very simple. I encourage the reader to routinely quiz journalists on these very simple legal philosophies. If the media isn't quizzed regularly, they will forget. The difference between an adult and a child is a difficult concept; too complicated for the average reporter to understand. The definitions are so complicated, not even the overpaid news anchors can understand their meanings; With all their aides, assistants, and yes-men, the talking heads cannot grasp the meaning of these two words. In fact, the concept is so difficult a disclaimer of sorts is needed, and here is the disclaimer- Don't worry journalists, I am typing really slow because I know you can't read very fast. Here are the terms: adult and child.

Adult- ANY PERSON WHOSE AGE IS GREATER THAN OR EQUAL TO 18 YEARS.

Child- ANY PERSON WHO HAS NOT YET REACHED THE AGE OF 18. Yes, this includes a person who is 17 years, 364 days old.

Standby, for now is the time the know-it-all liberals of the world will suddenly reveal they are comedians, smart-asses, and *not* vainglorious dolts who know all there is to know about nothing. Believing they are the most cleaver people in the world, they will probably begin trying to use February 29th as a loophole and fallacy in my definition. This is how you know they have no business getting paid millions of dollars each year to sit in front of a camera. Keep it up morons! If you do, I'll simply call a person an adult based *not* on the number of times the day on which they were born comes around, but on the number of days they have lived.

I can't make it any simpler. This concept is needed because the media has an unhealthy habit of calling 18- and 19-year-olds "teenagers." While technically it is correct, as a matter of law, it is incorrect. When the term teenager is bandied about by the media, the mental image our superiors in the media want people to see in their mind's eye is of someone who has not yet graduated from high school. Why? Because they have a narrative to promote. Normally people consider teenagers to be people who have almost physically matured, but their cognitive abilities leave much to be desired at times. They think of teenagers as innocent children experimenting and still learning to be adults; People think of teenagers as people who should be held responsible for their actions, but the punishment imposed should be merciful and based primarily on the fact that they are cognitively somewhat "immature."

Follow me on this unlearned journalists. Anyone above the age of 18 who commits a crime is an adult and should be held accountable as an adult. Anyone who has not yet reached the age of 18 and who commits a crime should be held accountable based on the seriousness of the offense. Shoplifting, they go to a juvenile court. Murder, they go to adult court- regardless of age. If a "teenager" commits a serious crime, they should be held just as accountable. There should be no debate about whether the person will be tried as an adult or as a child. It should depend on the seriousness of the crime, nothing else.

When a person commits such a crime, they knowingly do so, in many cases they commit crimes as a way of showing maturity, as an initiation ritual into a criminal organization. Law enforcement knows this. Not only do the police officers investigating the crimes know this, but the district attorneys know this as well. Yet, there is always a debate about whether the kid should be tried as an adult, or as a juvenile. The leaders of the gangs whose membership these children are hoping to join know this too! That is why they enlist the help of children. If a child goes to juvenile court and is found guilty of murder, in most cases they will be set free on their eighteenth birthday. Why? Because they are no longer children, *and* they were put on trial as children not as adults. When they reach the age of 18, the law considers them to now be adults. And since an adult can't be incarcerated with children, they are released, and their records are sealed. Many times, if they commit new crimes as adults their juvenile records remain sealed and are not allowed to be admitted as evidence in other trials. There are exceptions to this. In recent years there have been a couple instances when a child was convicted of murder and was sent to adult prison on their 18th birthday, but those instances are few.

The media calls the person a teenager, to elicit sympathy. They are trying to get people to think of the mass murderer, the rapist, or the thief as a child to promote an ideology. They are trying to garner sympathy for that person not because they are children, but because the person ISN'T white. They have been so thoroughly indoctrinated into the Marxist way of thinking, the media can't stop thinking an African American criminal is only a criminal because they are African American. The same goes for a Hispanic criminal. The media conveniently forgets, in most cases, the person was either convicted by a jury of *their* peers, or they pled guilty to a *lesser* charge. That is why they are considered convicts. Not because they are black or brown. The media *would* do the same thing for Asian criminals, but because Asians overall are successful in life, in the eyes of the media Asian people are white people with slanted eyes. (Hey, don't condemn me for what the media thinks. I am just pointing it out.)

My frustrations are continuous. While I was writing this book, I was not living in isolation. And just when I thought the news media couldn't provide any additional direct evidence of how utterly useless they have become, China opened a police station in New York City! Why is this yet more evidence of the uselessness of the news media? Because they completely ignored it, aside from a quick twenty-second telling during off-primetime hours, and a ticker tape headline at the bottom of the screen. Useless. If the NYPD would have opened up a station in Mexico City, the media would be livid. The media would parade legions of academics in front of the camera; all of whom would drone on and on about American colonialism, white supremacy, and how the NYPD is the embodiment of evil. But when China does it in New York City- crickets!

Here is another illustration of how the news media is not concerned about the facts of a story. I noticed this story scrolling on the ticker-tape headlines at the bottom of the screen about a week ago. There were actually 2 separate headlines. Crap like this must stop if the media hopes to get back their credibility. These headlines were written to elicit drama and clicks on the internet only. This is media malpractice. Everyone who is paying for commercials on news media needs to demand a 50% rate reduction or a 50% rate refund from the news outlets who had these headlines. The companies are paying good money to advertise their products on <u>News</u> outlets, not as part of local drama queen gathering. Just so you know, these headlines were so accurate *NO* news program talked about it. *NO* news program mentioned it in passing. The headlines were so misleading that if someone not associated with a news organization had started talking about this, no one would ever again listen to them once the ***actual facts*** were made known. People would forever be known as the town liars. At the very least for the rest of their lives they would be considered the town drama queen who is always seeking attention.

These are the paraphrased headlines. I wish I had written them down, but at the time I first read them I figured they were such big stories someone would discuss them on-air soon enough. One of these days I will learn my lesson. Neither headline was ever discussed. To find out what was happening I had to get out of my recliner and log on to the internet. To find out what was really happening I had to spend 2 hours doing what multiple journalists deemed to be too difficult. Again, I am paraphrasing, but they are close to what was scrolling across the screen. (Notice, no quotation marks.)

Headline #1:

Astronaut and two Cosmonauts stranded with a leak in their spacecraft.

Ticker tape headline on either Newsmax, Real Americas Voice, or Fox News
20-27 February 2023

Headline #2:

Russia launches rescue ship to search for Astronaut and two Cosmonauts

Ticker tape headline on either Newsmax, Real Americas Voice, or Fox News
20-27 February 2023

Those headlines are serious! The first headline suggests that somewhere in space three people are in a life and death struggle, and their chances of survival are not good. The second headline suggests that those three human beings, assuming they are the same human beings, have made it back to earth, but no one knows where they landed.

If you were someone related to the astronauts, you would be freaking out. Your first freak out would be because your loved one may be suffocating due to the leak and that their death was excoriatingly painful as their blood started to boil as part of being exposed to the vacuum of space. The second headline would freak you out because now even though they are back on earth, no one knows where they are or if they are even still alive.

Before I go further, I am going to use the word astronaut to describe all the space travelers. Please understand the stories are centered around one person from the USA (an astronaut) and two people from Russia (cosmonauts). I am doing this simply for the sake of simplicity.

Obviously, if you were directly related to the three individuals, NASA and the Russian Space Agency (RSA) would be keeping you up to date. But what if the three people were dead, and the two agencies were trying to cover up their mistakes. Would they be forthcoming or would the next of kin be stonewalled under the guise of it being a national security matter. The deception by the news media does not end. Here is the *actual* headline which led me to believe this story was only a way to generate clicks on the internet.

> *"Two minutes before liftoff, NASA and SpaceX scrub launch of 4 crew members due to ground systems issue."*
> *USA Today*
> *27 February 2023*

Just before I began the log-on process to check my email, I noticed this headline. It struck me as odd because, after seeing the two other headlines, someone is possibly endangering four other people by sending more people up to the ISS knowing that it has a leak. Then, I began to think how maybe it was a capsule heading to the ISS earlier in the week which began leaking, which then caused the three astronauts mentioned earlier to abort their mission. Now I was really confused. If I wanted to find out what was happening with the "stranded" astronauts, I knew I would have to be the investigator. Here are actual headlines I discovered which deal with the "stranded" Astronauts.

"Russia launches unmanned rescue ship for NASA astronaut, two cosmonauts after spacecraft leak".
Yahoo!news
25 February 2023

"Russia launches rescue ship after spacecraft leak strands astronaut crew"
USA Today
24 February 2023

"Russia launches mission to give stranded space station crew members a ride home."
NPR
24 February 2023

"Russian replacement spacecraft for astronauts stranded by coolant leak docks with space station."
CNN
25 February 2023

Here is what really happened. Most of this could be found out by simply reading the first two paragraphs. In fact, most of the situations which the media was hyping to create angst in the general populace happened **three months prior to the above headlines.** Again, they were written in such a way to get people to think there was a life-or-death situation happening. The leak was discovered in December. Contrary to what the media would have us believe, NASA and the RSA don't operate as is depicted in movies and television. The "rescue" mission wasn't suddenly thrown together in a week. As soon as the leak was discovered on 14

December 2022 (three months prior to the headlines), NASA and the RSA began planning and assembling the "rescue". In this case, the rescue mission didn't require additional astronauts to go to the ISS, just a new capsule.

- Yes, the spacecraft had a coolant leak.

The coolant leak was caused by a micrometeorite punching a hole in the spacecraft. Specifically, it punched a hole in a radiator. With a coolant leak in a spacecraft, it may become unbearably hot causing computer systems to overheat or increase the danger to the crew. The craft was still functioning, and in an emergency could have been used as a re-entry vehicle. I won't speculate on how hot the interior of the capsule might get when it returned to earth the following March without passengers. However, I will bet dollars to donuts that somewhere in the capsule is a thermometer. And it wasn't a thermometer that was recently installed.

- The spacecraft with the hole was the Soyuz capsule designated MS-22, not the International Space Station (ISS).

MS-22 launched to the ISS in September 2022 and, as with all previous launches, the capsule they rode to get to the ISS was also their ride home. It's the same as anyone going anywhere really. When we go somewhere, unless we are on our way to buy a new car and get rid of the old one, we return home driving the same car. Yes, they were stranded, but only in the sense that their ride home *might* not be safe as a re-entry vehicle. However, if a situation were to develop into a life-death situation, the capsule could be used as a re-entry vehicle. Again, the damage to the astronaut's re-entry craft occurred 3 months prior to the stories and their fraudulent headlines were written.

- The mission the astronauts were on was a long duration mission.

When the astronauts launched on 29 September 2022, they were planning to be at the ISS for 6 months with a return date in March. They weren't in a desperate situation like a person shipwrecked on a deserted island with no supplies. They took supplies with them. On several occasions after their arrival, NASA and the RSA sent additional supplies. This was not a situation where the astronauts were surviving on half a fun-size Snickers bar each day. They were in no danger of starving to death or dying of thirst. In terms of the mission timeline, the micrometeorite hit the Soyuz capsule when the mission was 4 months away from being completed- 2/3 of the mission was still to come. I can pretty much guarantee that the astronauts did not have to worry about how they would get home.

- They weren't physically stranded at the ISS with no hope of getting home in the event of a dire emergency.

This will really piss off people, so let's get to it. That bullet point by itself should tell you something. Yes, the space capsule that brought them there was damaged and they couldn't use it as a *normal* re-entry vehicle. But there was a SpaceX capsule concurrently docked to the ISS. The astronauts could have used the SpaceX capsule to get home. Stranded my ass!

- The 3 astronauts were not the only 3 people on the ISS

There were 7 people living on board the ISS at the time the Armageddon-type headlines were written, not 3. The media once again is making a fraudulent claim to scare people. They wanted people to believe 3 people were about to die in space after a life-and-death struggle. And it was a load of BS. If you go to the grocery store, you return home in the same car, but if your car is destroyed while you are shopping you can always call someone to come pick you up. In this case, there was a second passenger capsule docked to the ISS. It was a SpaceX Dragon Crew capsule, and it was the primary re-entry vehicle for the other 4 people- The same 4 people it brought to the ISS on 5 October 2022.

What I am about to tell you will, without a doubt, show the level of fraud being perpetrated upon the general public by the media. This level of fraud is appalling and journalists should be held to task whether they had anything to do with the story or not. Yes, there were 3 people on the ISS whose designated re-entry vehicle was damaged and deemed unsafe for passengers. Yes, there were 4 other people on the ISS with them, and their re-entry vehicle was *not damaged and was not deemed unsafe for passengers*. Why not put all 7 astronauts in the SpaceX capsule? No one in the media asked this question. I know what you are thinking, screaming.

"You can't put all 7 astronauts in that capsule it's not big enough."

Well, according to the SpaceX website,

"…The Dragon spacecraft is capable of carrying up to 7 passengers to and from Earth orbit…"

According to stories solely focused on the Dragon Crew Capsule, the capsule is only designed for 5 passengers. But who are you going to believe, the spacecraft designer or someone who may think it is too difficult to do research. Either way, in a dire emergency- an actual emergency- all members of the ISS would find a way to squeeze into the SpaceX capsule. It may be extremely cramped, and it may present another danger, but they would have sat on each other's laps. Why? Because of the other alternative.

If the ISS had to be evacuated for such an emergency, the decision-making process would consist of two questions.

Question 1:

Do I cram myself into a re-entry vehicle designed to accommodate 5 people not 7, and fall to the earth and risk being stranded in the middle of the ocean 1000 miles from anything or anyone for a couple days while every rowboat, houseboat, super yacht, crude oil tanker and aircraft carrier look for me?

OR

Question 2:

Do I stay on board the ISS while an out-of-control fire consumes all the oxygen, burns through the skin of the ISS instantly depressurizing it. Causing me and the other 2 people to think our lungs are being sucked out of our bodies, while our blood boils in the vacuum of space and the minus 400-degree F temperature of space instantly freezes us like a TV dinner?

Ask the astronauts on the ISS at the time the headlines were published what they would have done. Ask them to see if they would have drawn straws to see who stays and who goes, or if they would have crammed themselves into one capsule. The residents of the ISS at the time were (the names in bold are the 3 "stranded" people):

Frank Rubio
Nicole Mann
Josh Cassada
Koichi Wakata
Sergey Prokopyev
Dmitri Petelin
Anna Kikina

At the time of the headlines, 20 to 25 February 2023, here is a list of all the capsules that were docked with the ISS. Some are re-supply capsules, and some are for occupants

Crew-5 Dragon
Cygnus-18
Soyuz MS-22
Progress 83
Soyuz MS-23

https://www.nasa.gov/feature/visiting-vehicle-launches-arrivals-and-departures/

If you would like to see all the different capsules that docked with and undocked from the ISS since August 2022, go to the NASA website (nasa.gov) and look up Expedition 68. In fact, this shows the utter dishonesty and laziness of the reporters who wrote the numerous stories. I found out this information over the course of a 3-hour intermittent research period. I didn't sit down to do research on a story. I was only trying to get basic information.

CHAPTER TWO

FIXES TO THE NEWS MEDIA!

How does a concerned person fix the media if you also have a corrupt government?

Capitalism!

Go full-blown, in your face, capitalist pig-dog on them.

There are two possible capitalist pig-dog fixes that would get the arrogant newsrooms to be humble and to be subservient to their audiences instead of preaching to them.

The first fix is to make it illegal for the parent company of a news organization to comingle earnings with the news division. There should be a law passed by Congress, an Amendment that codifies this would be better. If an organization wishes to call itself a "news organization" or have the word "news" in the title of the show- radio, television, internet, or otherwise- they need to adhere to this. If they decide to call it, "The 8 O'clock Opinions Show," and not the "8 o'clock News," then they can comingle funds. If a news organization loses 100 million dollars every quarter and has not been profitable for decades, the parent company should not be allowed to take money from their aerospace division to make up for the losses.

In other words, the overpaid news anchors would literally be required to earn their money. If the news division is losing money, they don't get paid. There must be a downside to not giving the customers what they are expecting. If a restaurant's patron orders a 12-ounce ribeye, and they bring them a bowl of coleslaw, the patron won't pay for the ribeye. He might pay for the coleslaw if he eats it, but the patron won't come back to the restaurant. And, if it happens to every customer, bad reviews will keep other customers away. Why are we allowing the news organizations to do otherwise?

Think about this for a minute. Unless the show's premise runs counter to upper management's ideology, religious or otherwise, television shows live and die by ratings. All television companies, cable providers and streaming services decide which shows to air based on ratings. If one show has 10 people watching it every day, and a second has 10 million, the least popular show will *not* be shown. Why? Advertising. No company wants to spend millions of dollars advertising to an audience of 10 people. They will, however, spend that much money to make a commercial which will be seen by 10 million viewers. Advertising companies don't see the viewers as viewers. They see the viewers as potential customers for their product. People see ads and might be persuaded to buy the product being advertised. This too is capitalism.

Broadcasting companies get most of their revenue selling airtime to "product and service" companies. So, much of their money comes from advertising, they probably don't need to charge their customers for their cable plans. They do that because they are greedy capitalist pig-dogs. Which air is worth the most money? The airtime associated with the most popular shows. Unless the show is "the news".

News programs are weird programs in terms of profitability. They can be the least popular shows in a network's line-up and they still won't get canceled. By its nature "the news" is not entertaining. It's simply there to pass on information. This is why many people don't watch the news; it can be boring and frustrating. When news anchors spend hours talking about a hurricane that won't make landfall for days, people living in the mountains change the channel. And yet, the advertisers still continue to spend obscene amounts of money on a time slot.

People do want to know about what is happening around the world, but they don't have time to do the research themselves. Investigating a news story is not a Do-it-Yourself job. It never has been a DIY project. Sure, a person can give a first-person account on television about the crime, but that is not the whole story. Someone still needs to find the guy on the grassy knoll, so to speak. The difficult part about getting the information to the masses these days is getting the anchors and reporters to state the pros <u>and</u> cons of the story not just tidbits which support their world view. But why must news anchors be the ones to tell people boring things? Because left to their own devices, most people will only read juicy gossip.

Believe it or not, a person learning to read will learn to read faster if their practice material is salacious- dare I say pornographic- in nature. Think about it. Do the research! It is widely known that women post better scores on the SAT/ACT than do men- especially in the verbal portion. There is also a thriving romance novel industry. Might there be a correlation? I believe so.

Growing up while today's men were playing football in the street, their sisters locked themselves in their rooms and read pornography. We just can't call what their sisters were reading pornography because when they finished reading the book, mom would read the book. It's art. It's an erotic expression of love. It's what the patriarchy has reduced women to in their quest for pleasure. And because there are no pictures in those "novels," women are also learning to use their brains analytically. How else does one explain a woman's innate ability to make a man believe he is angry at himself and not her for wrecking the car.

The reason people don't watch the news is because they have no reason to watch the news. They can now go online and look at news stories. If they decide to watch the news it is because they don't want to sift through the multiple lines of garbage looking for a story that affects or interests them. And now the "news" has become groups of people crying on television. They should rename news programs, "The Real Housewives of RKO Studios," or something similar. If I wanted to be entertained by a bunch of cackling hens, I only need to remember last Thanksgiving's dinner. I can guarantee the conversations between my mom and my sisters were more substantive than what passes today as news.

It's the difference between, *"I didn't leave Bill because I love him that much."* And *"Hey mom, did you just say Mrs. Jones in the big purple house is a whore?"* That is how much of the news just isn't news. It has become a bunch of people sitting around a table crying about something out of their control. If news anchors were responsible for revenue generation, it would force them to report the news instead of voicing their opinions and passing on gossip. If the news anchors did that the news divisions would suddenly turn profitable.

Members of the media take note of this. One day your psychotic thirst to promote narratives and gossip over facts will result in a jury pool's contamination. This media induced contamination will be so poisonous, an innocent person will be sent to prison for a very long time. This will happen! It will happen because you could not be bothered to confirm the truthfulness of an exposé before releasing it into the cosmos. It will happen because you put your real job second to your inextinguishable envy to be part of the ruling class. You long to be called, "Elite!" You want people to recognize you as being part of the elite so badly, a malodorous ether precedes your arrival. It will happen because your self-worth is directly linked to how you believe other people perceive you. Your ego is based on what you think other people think and feel about you personally, and not on your accomplishments or merits of action. Your desire to be beloved results in an aura that is fetid, foul, and nauseating to those in your general vicinity.

To be clear, the media is not the fourth estate. The media is not the fifth estate. The media is NO ESTATE. Meaning you have no power over people. You have no vote in government. You have no say in the passage of law. None! Get off your high horses. You, just as auto mechanics, plumbers, and electricians, are one component in a properly functioning society. Society does not exist to support you. You exist to support society. The really, really sad part is even after reading the previous paragraphs, you will attempt to renderer yourselves guiltless by prefacing all stories with the phrase, "We haven't verified the story, but…"

I'm going to go off topic for a minute. A few paragraphs earlier I brought up hurricanes. Someone please tell the news producers, editors, or whoever decides which stories are broadcast, that if the story has been front and center for a week it has long since ceased to be "Breaking News." It stopped being "Breaking News" after the first 8 hours. Not only that, if there is nothing new to report, the story is not being updated. Having a rotating panel of "experts" whose composition changes at every commercial break discussing the same situation is not "updating the story." It is called beating a dead horse. Do you know what the phrase means? You love using sayings and quotes so much, why don't you take heed?

I'm being serious. Every year there are multiple two-to-three-week periods when I stop watching the news. Sometimes there are three of these periods, sometimes there are six or seven. I do this because the "news" has long since ceased to be "new." It's old, regurgitated crap that has been scrapped up off the floor, put through a blender, and nuked for five minutes just to make it seem freshly cooked. The really sad part is when I start watching the "news" after my hiatus, many times I realize I haven't missed anything. The anchormen are still talking about the same things. There might be a new talking head espousing their "expertise" on the subject, but usually, absolutely nothing has changed. So, why do I bring up hurricanes, I hear people asking? Because some of the most idiotic news broadcasts of the year occur during hurricane season.

Here is the second possible way to fix the media. But there are a few things you need to understand:

First, _you_ may lose money.

When I say that, I'm not talking about millions of dollars. I mean you may lose some or all of the money you invested. The amount you invest is the maximum amount you might lose. If you invest $1000 purchasing shares of a media company, and it declares bankruptcy, you will lose your $1000. If you invest $10,000 and the company goes bankrupt, you will lose your $10,000. Don't worry, though, if you invest $1,000 and the company goes bankrupt, you won't lose $10,000. There are ways it is possible for you to lose money in that fashion, but if you make a simple purchase, you won't lose any more money than you originally invested. Stay away from the Options Market. If you don't buy on a margin, and don't do Puts and Calls, you will be okay.

Second, if you are willing to do this, you must also understand it is going to take a very, very long time for your efforts to bear fruit.

You will not know immediately if you are having any effect. You must be patient! This endeavor will not end in a year. It might not end a decade later. And, if you do attain the goal, you can't quit. You must continue!

You cannot stop! You must be vigilant! This is a generational fix! You need to be in this fight for multiple decades. The corruption of the media by communists (I mean that literally) started a century ago. They are already indoctrinating the next generation of news reporters to continue the work of the current generation. And it is the current generation of reporters who are continuing to advance the causes of the boomer generation. This means you will need to pass this on in your Last Will and Testament! Yes, it may take that long.

Third, the job isn't over once the original goal is attained. There is a follow-on goal, and you must see it through as well. What are the goals?

> **Initial Goal:** Keep the self-appointed gate keepers of power, the news media to be specific, from being the propaganda arm of political organizations and get them to start reporting _all_ the facts- Not the truth- to the American people and to the world.

> **Follow-up Goal:** Keep the achievement from being wiped out a couple months or years after the initial goal is met.

If you follow the standing Republican Party playbook, the original goal will never be completed. Playing devil's advocate, if you do happen to attain the initial goal, using the Republican playbook will cause you to immediately go back to square one. All will be for naught; Your accomplishments washed away with no memorial for the subsequent generations look upon in awe and wonder if the standing republican party order of battle is followed. Why? Because the current Republican Party modus operandi is to attain the goal- or come close- then quit. Republicans have yet to figure out that they must be _eternally_ vigilant. They can't simply stand watching for a couple of hours then go home.

To attain the follow up goal, you must act as though you never achieved the initial goal. You cannot change your behavior after the initial goal has come to pass. Don't disarm, so to speak. You must understand that though the battle appears to be over, it is not. Your adversaries are waiting for you to let down your guard so they can pounce, again. They will do everything they can to return to the "good old days" when *they* were close to power. No matter how much time has elapsed since they lost the power over you, they will always long for the days when everyone worshipped them because their face was on television. You must be forever vigilant! The forces which you fight will *always* try to destroy what you have built.

A RINO-type republican will tell you that after the original goal is accomplished, you can go home and never worry again. It will be the end of World War One all over again. *We don't have to remain vigilant. We can downsize our army to manning levels so low, even before the war, they would have been considered insanely low levels. We just fought the Great War. If someone does wish to go to war again, we only have to point to the carnage of the Great War to get them to stop. That will stop them in their tracks. Hey, I just bought a painting from a street artist in Munich, I think he said his name was Adolf! I can't remember. I couldn't stop wondering if he was a big Charlie Chaplin fan, though. He must have been, he was sporting the Tramp's mustache.*

Fourth, most news media are either a division of a publicly traded company, or a publicly traded company in their own right. They have thousands if not millions of owners. These people- people and organizations- own millions of shares in the companies.

Fifth, if a company is a publicly traded company, it must follow rules set out by the Securities and Exchange Commission. You must not hesitate to drop a lawsuit if you feel the company is doing something they should not be doing. The actions taken by the company may be designed to make it impossible, or at least more unlikely, for you to attain your goal. The easiest way for the company to thwart you is for them to issue additional shares, making it necessary for you to purchase even more shares.

In case you haven't figured it out already, here is what needs to happen to hold the media accountable. You are going to buy shares of these **publicly** traded companies.

Instead of donating to political campaigns, buy a couple hundred shares of a media company or its parent company. If you truly wish to do something "for the children," buy a couple hundred shares of a media company. If you can afford to purchase shares in a company whose shares are more expensive than the other companies, you should purchase the more expensive shares. This will allow those who can't afford the more expensive shares to purchase the cheaper shares, and it will advance the cause faster. But be careful. There is such a thing as a **non-voting share.**

There are also shares that have limited voting rights. Fox News, specifically the Fox Corporation, is one such media company.

The ticker symbols for the two types of shares are FOX and FOXA. Both are considered common stock shares as opposed to preferred shares. The major difference between the two types is shares of FOXA have _**limited**_ voting rights. One of the many things that shareholders of this particular stock _**cannot**_ vote on is whether or not to continue the employment of the CEO, board members, and other corporate officers. When you make your purchase, you will want to purchase voting shares that allow you to vote on the employment and/or compensation of corporate officers such as the CEO and members of the board of directors.

You can find which shares are considered voting shares and which are considered non-voting shares by reading the company's Articles of Incorporation. This document is also called:

1. The Certificate of Incorporation,
2. Corporate Charter, or
3. Business Incorporation Papers.

This information can also be found many times in a company's annual report. If you have problems finding the Articles of Incorporation, look in the annual report. They are required _by law_ to file an annual report so that the shareholders can know what is going on. The technical name for a company's annual report according to the Securities and Exchange Commission (SEC) is a Form 10-K. There is also the quarterly report- Form 10-Q- which may also contain the information.

Here's the plan, when you buy shares of the company of your choosing, do research on the corporate officers and the board of directors. It is these people who are refusing to hold their employees accountable for *purposely* libeling high school students to support a political narrative. They are the ones who inject themselves into your lives by telling you that you have no right to raise your children how *you* wish. If you feel like it, you can go to shareholder meetings and voice your opinion. I will remind you one more time, you cannot hesitate to initiate a lawsuit. If you attend a shareholder's meeting and politely express your concerns about the direction the Board of Directors is taking <u>your</u> company- and they have you arrested- sue them. File a complaint with the SEC. If you express your concerns and they ban you from future meetings, sue them. File a complaint with the SEC. Remember, when you own shares in a company, you are part *owner* of that company. ***The board of directors works for you.***

Here is the whole purpose of buying shares- <u>voting</u> shares- in a company. It will enable *you* to decide, by your vote who is a member of the board of directors. In many cases, if not all, as a voting owner *you* get final say on who becomes a corporate officer. This doesn't just pertain to the board of directors. You will have a say on the person who is installed as the company's CEO as well. The company cannot simply hire people to be on the Board in perpetuity without the *approval* of the shareholders. Why? Because the shareholders are the people who own the company. If, as a shareholder, you don't feel the people who comprise the Board aren't right for *your* company because you think they are using the company to support political causes to which you don't agree, the next time their continued employment is voted on by the shareholders, as a shareholder, you can vote to have them fired. If you feel they are wasting money by donating it to overseas charities, keep track of it and bring it to their attention. Many times, the board of directors is required *by law* to get shareholder approval for stuff like this. In which case, you can tell them not to send money to a charity whose values are suspect. If you feel their DEI policy is adversely affecting the bottom line of *your* company, you can vote them out of office. Don't boycott the company. Vote the board of directors, the CEO, the COO, the CFO out of a job.

You will need to keep track of all the actions of the Board. It is entirely possible the Board of a company will conspire to impede your progress. They may attempt to authorize more shares to be issued to increase the number of shares required to take control of the company. You may be required to vote on the issuance of new shares. If they do, you can vote no and keep the number of shares required to take control of the company the same. If they authorize a stock split, you may be required to vote on that too. This is why you need to buy voting shares. This is also why you need to read the Articles of Incorporation for the companies of which you have become a part owner- So they can't sneak anything by you. They can't hide documents from you. They are required *by law* to make them public. Even in cases where there is proprietary information, you, as a shareholder have a right to see these documents. If you didn't have a right to see these documents a company could hide documents from shareholders by simply saying they are proprietary documents.

At this point, I should caution the reader about when is the best time to buy the stock. If I knew that I would have bought my own private island by now, changed my name to Pelosi, and people would only visit me on an invitation basis. I can only give you this advice. Your friend does not know what he or she is talking about. Purchasing shares of a company is a gamble no matter how much time a person expends doing research. This holds true for stock market analysts, too. Yes, the analysts know more about how the stock market operates and what affects the different indices than most people do, but even they are guessing to some extent.

Here is how anyone who wishes to undertake this endeavor can minimize their chances of paying too much for a security. Look at the P/E ratio- The price to earnings ratio.

The greater the P/E ratio, the more the stock is overpriced. In one of the books I read on investing, Investing Smart from the Start, the author, Dick Goldberg, said that *he* would not invest in a company if the P/E ratio (he switches between calling it the P/E ratio and the stock's multiplier) is greater than 10. I believe that to be a good metric, but it may be a little low for our endeavor. Much of what affects a company's stock price is the public's perception of the company. Because the companies we are concerned with are entertainment companies, they are well known, and the price may be artificially high simply because the company is a household name. Also be concerned about how the P/E ratio has changed over time. These ratios will tend to remain relatively constant throughout the years, so a sudden spike may indicate that at the current moment it is not a good time to purchase shares.

On the next three pages you will find spreadsheets with information about the 5 major news media companies, in the year 2025. This information is publicly available. I do not have any top-secret information on these companies. If you use this information to purchase shares, it is a decision *you* will be making of *your* own accord. I am *not* responsible for your purchase. The information presented will most likely be outdated as it will have changed due to the passage of time. ***This information is only to give you an indication of just how devoted a person needs to be to hold the media accountable for their lies, and the propaganda they claim are facts.***

Chart 1 shows the basic information of the various media companies. As you can see most of the news outlets are owned by other companies- a conglomerate if you will. So, if you wish to affect how NBC does business, you need to buy shares of Comcast, and Comcast owns more than just NBC.

The "shares outstanding" figure is the number of shares the company has issued of that one type of stock. A few weeks after I first thought of this plan, I asked a friend for his input. After digesting what I had said for a couple days, he began to get excited about the plan and was ready to dive into it headfirst. However, as we were chatting about the plan the second time, I realized his elation was based on the "volume traded" figure, and not the "shares outstanding" figure. Do not confuse these two figures. They are two different things. The "volume traded (usually simply called 'volume')" is the number of shares that changed hands during that day's trading session. It varies from day to day. Sometimes the differences are stark. One day a company may see a million shares change hands, and the next day only a few thousand.

If a news report says a company is worth $35 billion dollars, what they are doing is multiplying the number of outstanding shares by the share price. In order to have a controlling interest in a company, a person or organization *must* own at least 50% of the shares outstanding - Of *voting* shares.

Quick disclaimer, as this book was being edited, the Paramount Corporation completed a merger with Skydance Corp to become the Paramount Skydance Corp. The information on the resulting company, while factual, isn't as accurate as I would like since the incorporation paperwork, annual reports, and other documents have not yet been made available to the public.

Chart 2 is a calculations spreadsheet, or rather a spreadsheet showing *resultant* calculations. It shows the number of shares needing to be bought and the number of people needed to buy enough shares to gain 10% control of the different companies. This is the number of people who are needed to purchase shares, where people only purchase shares in one of the many companies. Obviously, if everyone bought shares in multiple companies, the needed number of shares would be less.

At the very bottom of the spreadsheet, you will see the number of people required for a 10% takeover of the voting shares of *all* the companies. This is a 10% stake of the voting shares. We don't care about the non-voting shares because they don't vote. If you look at the numbers, it would be doable for all the people who voted for Donald Trump in the 2020 general election- All 74 million- to take control of all the companies. Even if each person only bought one hundred shares in only one of the companies, they could do it.

Chart 3 is the same as Chart 2 but for a 50% stake of the voting shares. I show both 10% and 50% for this reason, with 50% of the voting shares (actually 50.00000001%) you will effectively control the board of directors. It is required, in most cases, that changes in pay and other compensation for the corporate officers and the board of directors be authorized by the shareholders. If you voice your opinion of them allowing the company to become a propagandist arm of a political party and they ignore you, they will change their minds when you vote to deny them a pay raise. I guarantee it. If you stop their paychecks, they will stop giving partisan hack morons 3 hours every day to spew forth Marxist propaganda.

With a 10% stake you probably won't be able to stop their pay increases, but the board of directors will start to notice. When shareholders vote, most people vote as the board of directors recommends. How do you imagine a company's board of directors would respond if suddenly 10% of the shareholders started voting to remove them from their financially lucrative positions? Even if the shareholders were unsuccessful, imagine how the company's principal officers would respond. They might start noticing it happening with a 5% stake, but a 10% stake will be undeniable.

The most difficult part of this undertaking will be finding people to replace the board members. Who will replace them? There will have to be people waiting in the wings, so-to-speak. These people will need to be vetted, and they must have a strong disposition. The people waiting in the wings can't be afraid of litigation because a great number of lawsuits will be filed by the entitled elite shortly after they lose their position of power. If there isn't anyone waiting to take the reins, those who were voted out last week- or the other corporate officers- may decide to have a re-vote. Or somehow, they will use the lack of a replacement as an excuse for them to stay until "suitable" replacements have been found.

BASIC COMPANY INFORMATION

(All information is public and is most likely outdated.)

Note(s)	News Company	Parent Comp	Ticker(s)	Share name	Voting Shares		Shares Outstanding	Company Mkt Cap ($)	Recent Per Share Cost
					Yes/No	Ratio			
4	ABC	Walt Disney Company	DIS	Common	Yes	1 per share	1,810,939,306	$203,603,906,174	$112.43
6	CBS	Paramount Skydance Corp	PSKY	Class B Common	Yes	1 per share	633,500,000	$6,658,085,000	$10.51
7	NBC	Comcast	CMCSA	Class A Common	Yes	1 per share	3,771,578,226	$119,445,882,417	$31.67
3, 7	NBC	Comcast	Not Applicable	Class B Common	Yes	15 per share	9,444,375	$9,444,375	N/A
2	CNN	Warner Bros. Discovery	WBD	Series A Common Stock	Yes	1 per share	2,454,764,337	$26,781,478,917	$10.91
1	Fox	Fox Corporation	FOX	Class B Common Stock	Yes, Full	1 per share	235,581,025	$11,588,230,620	$49.19
1, 5			FOXA	Class A Common Stock	Yes, Limited	1 per share	209,954,934	$11,341,765,535	$54.02

Chart 1

Notes:

1. Company information retrieved from the company's SEC Form 10-K Filed on 6 Aug 2025
2. Company information retrieved from the company's SEC Form 10-K Filed on 27 Feb 2025
3. All Class B shares are owned by the CEO; currently these shares are not listed on a market.
4. Company information retrieved from the company's SEC Form 10-K Filed on 14 Nov 2024
5. **Cannot** vote for board of directors, et al. as per 2025 Annual Report, exhibit 4.1, page 1
6. Company information retrieved from the company's SEC Form 8-K filed on 7 Aug 2025
7. Company information retrieved from the company's SEC Form 10-K filed on 31 Jan 2025

Calculations for 10% ownership

News Company	Parent Comp	Ticker(s)	Shares Outstanding	Total # of Shares	# of people each with 100 shares	# of people each with 200 shares	# of people each with 300 shares	# of people each with 400 shares	# of people each with 500 shares
ABC	Walt Disney Company	DIS	1,810,939,306	181,093,931	1,810,939	905,470	603,646	452,735	362,188
CBS	Paramount Skydance	PSKY	633,500,000	63,350,000	633,500	316,750	211,167	158,375	126,700
NBC	Comcast	CMCSA	3,771,578,226	377,157,823	3,771,578	1,885,789	1,257,193	942,895	754,316
CNN	Warner Bros. Discovery	WBD	2,454,764,337	245,476,434	2,454,764	1,227,382	818,255	613,691	490,953
Fox	Fox Corporation	FOX	235,581,025	23,558,103	235,581	117,791	78,527	58,895	47,116
		FOXA*	N/A	N/A	N/A	N/A	N/A	N/A	N/A
		Number of people required to "take over"			8,906,363	4,453,181	2,968,788	2,226,591	1,781,273

For a 10% ownership (needs)

Chart 2

* Shares *cannot* vote for board members and company officers, therefore, no need to purchase these shares

Calculations for 50% ownership

News Company	Parent Comp	Ticker(s)	Shares Outstanding	Total # of Shares	For a 50% ownership (needs)				
					# of people each with 100 shares	# of people each with 200 shares	# of people each with 300 shares	# of people each with 400 shares	# of people each with 500 shares
ABC	Walt Disney Company	DIS	1,810,939,306	905,469,653	9,054,697	4,527,348	3,018,232	2,263,674	1,810,939
CBS	Paramount Skydance	PSKY	633,500,000	316,750,000	3,167,500	1,583,750	1,055,833	791,875	633,500
NBC	Comcast	CMCSA	3,771,578,226	1,885,789,113	18,857,891	9,428,946	6,285,964	4,714,473	3,771,578
CNN	Warner Bros. Discovery	WBD	2,454,764,337	1,227,382,169	12,273,822	6,136,911	4,091,274	3,068,455	2,454,764
Fox	Fox Corporation	FOX	235,581,025	117,790,513	1,177,905	588,953	392,635	294,476	235,581
		FOXA*	N/A	N/A	N/A	N/A	N/A	N/A	N/A
		Number of people required to "take over"		44,531,814	22,265,907	14,843,938	11,132,954	8,906,363

Chart 3

* Shares *cannot* vote for board members and company officers, therefore, no need to purchase these shares

CHAPTER THREE

HOLLYWOOD- THE ENTERTAINMENT MEDIA

When I say Hollywood, I include rock stars, comedians, and televisions stars, amongst the many. If your job is to entertain other people, this section is about you. If you don't like it, tough! You have several options. You can write a song about how I "wronged" you and get on with your life. You can go on the standup comedy circuit and cry about it to your audience. Or, you can make the millions of dollars you would have made anyway and get on with your life. Or you can spare us your dog and pony show hysterics and simply do the following:

Step 1: Stop what you are doing.

Step 2: Go home

Step 3: Get in the shower

Step 4: Turn on the water

Step 5: Curl up on the floor in the fetal position

Step 6: Stick your thumb in your mouth

Step 7: Commence sucking

Step 8: After 10 minutes of thumb sucking:

If you feel you can safely rejoin a world where 99.999999999999% of its inhabitants neither know you nor care about your feelings, you may return to your previously scheduled activity.

If after 10 minutes you can't think of what I just told you without bursting into tears again, continue sucking your thumb until someone comes to check on you. (Hint: No one is going to check on you for a very long time so get comfortable. They have better things to do than to wipe your runny nose, call you precious, and affirm your belief that everyone else is being mean.)

Hollywood in particular is dangerous. Left to their own devices actors and actresses will do everything they can to demonize everyone with whom they disagree. We'll talk about this later, but due to the incestuous relationship Hollywood has with the news media, many people in Hollywood feel they are a species of human being which is superior to all species which have come before. Is it the fault of the actors and actresses if they believe the hype? That depends on who you ask.

On the one hand, in the grand scheme of things actors and actresses are the pawns of Hollywood. The legendary director Alfred Hitchcock once said actors were a dime a dozen in Hollywood. It is still true. For every successful actor, there are thousands working menial jobs with a dream in their heart, while they await their big break. If it weren't for greedy studio executives wanting every movie to net over a billion dollars, there would be no reason to pay actors and actresses 20 million dollars to star in a single movie. Calling the studio executives greedy is a stretch, they are beholden to their shareholders, or at least they used to be. They are simply practicing the art of capitalism. If one actor refuses to do something, because actors are the pawns of the entertainment industry, a casting director can easily find another person to fill the slot. The actor who quits the role may find himself holding the door open for the person who replaces them as they enter the casting room.

On the other hand, actors and actresses are human beings with brains. They can think for themselves. They should be able to realize that when filming ends for the day, they are not the oil rig worker they are portraying. I think many people in Hollywood have a problem with this. Following filming, the actors should be competent enough to realize they need to "de-program." If their "method" sees them being horrifyingly consumed by the role to the point where it has messed up their brains and they don't realize they need to deprogram, their agent or someone should step in and immediately get them help. I bring this up because the world lost two great actors just as their careers were taking off. Simply because the roles they took on messed them up so much they turned to drugs and alcohol to cope- River Phoenix and Heath Ledger. And no one would step in to help them. I believe that had they been forced into a mandatory two-week deprogramming retreat, they would still be around astounding us with their talent. (You can't tell me that River Phoenix's portrayal of a young Indiana Jones wasn't totally awesome.)

There is a reason the golden age of Hollywood occurred prior to the 1960s. Look at the movies made then and compare them to those made today. Today's movies have tortured stories. Screen writers, believing they are Shakespeare reborn, seem to be twisting themselves into pretzels trying to tell the story using as few words as possible. The final cuts tend to rely heavily on special effects, and the music is so loud you can't hear what the actors are saying.

Watch a movie from the 1940s and listen to the soundtrack. You can actually hear every word spoken. Even if the actors are whispering, no one needs to ask their neighbor, "What did he say?". All actors and actresses want to be compared to Audrey Hepburn and Clark Gable, but the movie making magic has changed. Yes, there are great movies being made that aren't overly reliant on special effects, but those types of movies seem to be going the way of the dinosaurs. In fact, as computers become more capable, in the near future computer animation or AI may replace actors and actresses altogether. Hollywood is changing.

What hasn't changed about Hollywood is the fact that predators have taken up residence in Hollywood, too. They call themselves agents, producers and directors. Left to many of them, before getting a role in a movie or television show, women would first have to give themselves to someone. The same goes for men too! Guys don't for one second believe that girls are the only ones who want to have sex with you. There are people in the movie business that would like nothing more than to bend you over the armrest of the casting couch and go to town on your cute, "you-must-do-a-lot-of-squats" tushy.

Think about this too. Why is there a nude scene in most movies released these days? If there isn't a scene where someone, usually the woman, is bare chested, there is a scene that is heavily sexualized. The extent of the nudity is ever more expansive. In the 1960s, the definition of nudity according to the Motion Picture Association of American was considerably different than today's definition. At one time, wearing a skirt that showed the person's knees was considered not fit for anyone under the age of 18. The Raquel Welch movie, One Million Years B.C. was considered racy when it was released in 1966. Same with the movie Boy on a Dolphin with Sophia Loren which was released in 1957. If either of these movies were released in the 1940s, they would be called soft-core pornography.

Today most sex scenes and scenes with nudity are gratuitous. After watching the movie <u>Boogie Nights,</u> a movie about the pornography industry, I would say they are completely useless. In <u>Boogie Nights,</u> even though the story was about pornography, the movie was filmed with very little nudity of any type. It was left up to the imagination. Wrap your head around this. Every Disney cartoon movie has the same conspiracy attached to it- the subliminal sexual message. The sad part is, it seems that the Walt Disney Company is now shifting from covert sex scenes in children's movies, to overt scenes and suggestions. Do you still think Hollywood is innocent? Sex aside, here is an example of how dangerously influential Hollywood and other members of the entertainment media are on society.

Everyone knows that radioactive material glows and always gives off mist. Everyone knows that radioactive material can be readily identified by its florescent, light green color. Everyone knows this. This is a fact, right? No! It is not a fact. It is a myth created by Hollywood. At one point during the filming of a movie or TV show, there arose a need to present a visual representation of radioactivity in order to make the story more ominous. The audience needed to know just by looking at a puddle of water, that it is dangerous. How did the special effects crew do this? By making the water glow. Fast forward a few decades, everyone believes that radioactive water glows green.

This holds true for everything Hollywood. If a movie depicts the ancient Amazonian women to be extremely tall black women, that is how they will forever be envisioned. In a science fiction movie, if a nuclear spill is depicted and the nuclear waste is represented with a florescent green color. That is how people believe radioactive waste looks. Why? Because 99.9999% of the people in the world will neither see actual nuclear material, nor will they read a history book explaining the origins and beliefs of the ancient world

The truth of the matter is radioactive water looks just like other water. Radioactive water from the Mississippi River looks like normal Mississippi River water. A piece of irradiated steel looks as it did before it came into contact with the radiation. It is not glowing. It does not emit an eerie sound. It looks just as it did before it was irradiated. Or would you like to continue believing that absorbing copious amounts of radiation will give you superpowers? It's fun to think about, but that's not what would happen; people would just get dead! D*E*D dead!

The job of an actor is to entertain. That's it! End of sermon! The sooner Hollywood gets this fact through their heads, the sooner we can get back to having TV shows and movies that entertain. Most people don't truly watch television, they surf. They flip from channel to channel avoiding commercials or in a vain attempt to find a show which piques their interest. Believe it or not, most people really don't care what a superstar actor does at home. On some level it is interesting to see, but that is it. It is interesting to hear the story which led to an epiphany which in turn led to a movie to being made, but that is it. Most people couldn't care any less about a celebrity's personal problems.

Actors and actresses need to recognize that when filming stops, they aren't the people they were portraying. They need to understand that donning the costume doesn't magically transform a person into the expert they portray. When the filming stops, yes, they can still speak the lingo, but that is it. They are still only actors pretending to be someone they are not; That the people whose identity they usurped are the experts; That those people attained their experience over the course of decades of trials and errors, not through a two-week mini boot camp.

I get it, though. There are many reasons celebrities make appearances on television shows, radio shows, or podcasts. It could be to promote their latest work, or to promote a charity in which they believe. Many times, though the reason is more rudimentary. It's to ensure casting directors and others don't forget about them. We've all lived through a five-to-ten-year period when the same two or three actors seemed to be in every movie. Then one day they disappeared from the silver screen because Hollywood had moved on. So, in order to remain relevant as an actor in a town where there are millions of actors, a person can either make a public appearance: as a guest on a talk show, by getting drunk and doing stupid stuff, or spend the rest of one's life waiting tables just to keep a roof over one's head. Those guest appearances look pretty good no matter how degrading and taken out of context they end up being.

Does this mean an actor gives up the right to be called a subject matter expert even if they are truly an expert? No! It just means that people need to think about the qualifications and the background of the persons the information media are presenting as the "expert".

Here is another rhetorical exercise.

Let's use a couple of great actors, Tom Hanks and John Travolta, in this exercise. Tom Hanks portrayed an airline pilot in the movie <u>Scully</u>, and John Travolta played a stealth bomber pilot in the movie, <u>Broken Arrow.</u>

Imagine you are flying somewhere. You have boarded the plane; it has taxied away from the terminal and is heading for the runway. Suddenly, the pilot comes on the intercom and says,

"Hello ladies and gentlemen, this is the captain speaking, Captain Tom Hanks (or John Travolta). I will be flying the aircraft. Yes, I am *that* Tom Hanks (or John Travolta.) When we get up to cruising altitude, we will be showing an inflight movie that happens to be my most recent movie. Please sit back and enjoy the flight. Relax, I may not have stayed at a Holiday Inn Express last night, but I did portray a pilot in one of my other movies."

What would you do? If that announcement were made before the aircraft doors were closed, would you try to get off the plane?

What if following the announcement the pilot also said, "It's okay that I don't know how to fly the plane, because people are always asking me to weigh in on other issues of which I am equally clueless. Hey, while we are waiting for clearance to taxi, why don't I explain to you why *you* should be okay with having *your* paycheck taxed at 30%."

Just so everyone knows, John Travolta is a licensed airline pilot. He owns his own jet liner. He is qualified to fly and has flown a 747 many times. At one point he worked for Qantas Airlines as a pilot. No, I wouldn't mind riding in a plane piloted by John Travolta. Tom Hanks on the other hand, is not a pilot of any kind as far as I know. I would be one of the ones trying to get off the plane at double-time. It's not that I have anything against Tom Hanks, it's simply that he isn't a pilot. He's an actor. Now, if I were taking an acting class and Mr. Hanks was the visiting professor, I would take copious amounts of notes and do everything I could to impress him. (For the record, I would have the same reaction to Mr. Travolta teaching an acting class, too.)

The point here is that the information media has a very bad habit of hyping up people as experts when they are not. Having made a million dollars portraying a nuclear scientist does not bestow upon a person knowledge about everything. Prior to the start of filming, there isn't a knighting ceremony where the actor is touched on the shoulder with a branch from the tree of knowledge. If I were to make an appearance on television to talk about societal problems, the audience would demand that I produce my credentials and explain why they should listen to me. With actors however, even if they tell people they aren't experts, some members of the media still tout them as being qualified. Why? Because they are famous. The cynical part of this practice is that the media has no problem doing so. If their ratings increase, it causes advertisers to pay them more money. So, in their minds it's a win-win situation. The end justifies the means.

Here is another thing that is wrong with Hollywood! Whenever they get the chance, they will bring up racism or sexism or whatever -ism that is the flavor of the month. The whole story could be about an albino white guy walking alone across Antarctica in a blizzard, and someone in Hollywood will have the story re-written so that on this solo trek there is a black person involved. If they feel they could get away with it, they would re-write the story so that the African American is shown to be the white guy's savior. Seriously, given the chance, they would do everything they could to convince people that Charles Lindbergh's solo flight across the Atlantic was only successful because there was a black man hiding in the back of the plane doing the flying, or that Lindeburg was really an African American. The only reason he's portrayed as a white guy is due to racism.

Here are some recent examples.

For the past few years, Hollywood has been on the "Me Too!" kick. Suddenly, it was decided there are too few movies with female heroes. So, what did Hollywood do? Did they scour the history books and look for heroines? No! Did they commission a group of writers to write a blockbuster about everyday women? No!

To satiate the race and sex charlatans, the powers that be looked at blockbuster movies from years past and re-made them with all female casts. Total time spent from inception to box office, less than 18 months. They failed dramatically. I watched one of the remakes and was entertained the first time, but the movie didn't have legs, so to speak. A blatant example of them bowing to the victim-laden mob is the movie, The Aeronauts. A movie about two people setting a high-altitude record in the 1800's. The *movie* shows the feat being accomplished by a two-man team consisting of one man and one woman. The movie is based on a true story!

However, there is a major discrepancy.

In real life, the feat was accomplished by a two-man team which consisted of two men, James Glaisher and Henry Coxwell. Both nearly died in the attempt.

There are many examples of racism being brought up in a movie or television show, even though it isn't pertinent to the story. It shows how racist Hollywood can be. One example is the classic, and often ridiculed line, "Always bet on black," from the movie, Passenger 57. The writers just couldn't help themselves and ruined a perfectly good and entertaining movie by insinuating the race of the hero is the deciding factor in a battle between good and evil. A movie which could have been used to further showcase Wesley Snipes' acting ability, but now his role is only remembered for that line. Are there times in movies when racism should be depicted? Yes, absolutely. But it doesn't need to be depicted simply because one of the actors is African American.

Here is the most egregious example of Hollywood going out of its way to ruin a movie just so they can show their "street cred"- Crimson Tide.

The movie <u>Crimson Tide</u> with Denzel Washington and Gene Hackman was a great movie. The entire movie centered around a moral conflict between a submarine's Commanding Officer (CO) and its Executive Officer (XO). The conflict was that while this ballistic missile submarine was punching holes in the water, it received orders to launch nuclear missiles, but it was an incomplete message. Neither the CO, nor the XO, nor anyone in the sub's crew knew what was contained in the entire message. The reason the message was incomplete was that the submarine had been attacked by another submarine, damaging the radio. Following the attack, the submarine could neither send nor receive *any* messages. It couldn't receive weather reports. It could not receive orders cancelling the launch of nuclear weapons. It was in essence, deaf.

Gene Hackman's character, the CO, wanted to launch the missiles based on the partial message. Denzel Washington's character, the submarine's XO, wanted to delay the launch until the radio was fixed so they could get the entire message, and if the order still stood, then launch missiles. The drama of this movie is the back and forth between the sub's captain and its 2nd in command, as both wrestled with the morality of nuclear war and responsibility that is placed upon the shoulders of both men.

The dilemma was hammered home when the XO, believing he was doing right by mankind and with the help of some members of the crew, relieved the captain of command. It was a mutiny if one wishes to be technical. Later in the movie, the CO re-gained command but by this time the radioman was seconds away from having the radio fixed. Having regained command of the submarine, the CO ordered the submarine to launch missiles. As one would hope, with seconds to spare, the radio came to life with a new message, and the launch was postponed while the message was authenticated.

Follow me on this. At this point in the movie, one of two things would happen next. Either:

1. The CO would be correct, and missiles would soon be launched. When the submarine returned to port, the XO would have been brought up on charges of conspiracy and mutiny. Or scenario two,

2. The XO would be correct, essentially saving the world from nuclear annihilation. The XO would be the hero. And the captain would probably be forced into retirement for being a dinosaur.

It all hinged on the last dramatic scene where the two officers were waiting for the new message to be authenticated. They had to wait. While they were waiting, did the characters discuss what they should do after receiving the order? No! Did they discuss the points each person was making which could have possibly resulted in WW3? No! The only thing they talked about was horses. Specifically, Gene Hackman's character said that there is a breed of horse that is all white, not a speck of color. Denzel Washington's character brought up the fact that yes, the horses grow up to be white, but they are born all black.

People in Hollywood cannot help themselves. They _must_ bring race into everything. Even when there is no reason for it. I call it We-Are-More-Racist-Than-Everyone-Else-and-Are-Trying-to-Hide-It Syndrome.

In case you are curious, in the movie the breed of horse to which they were referring is the Lipizzaner breed. Further research will show that Denzel's character wasn't 100% correct. Most of the horses are born black, but many are born brown or grey in color. But let's not quibble about whether or not it was a purposeful racist insertion on the part of Hollywood.

Okay, let's stop talking about racism in Hollywood.

Let's talk about the new requirement in Hollywood that requires all shows and movies to have a gratuitous scene of homosexuality.

I'm talking about The Imitation Game in which Benedict Cumberbatch portrays the genius code breaker and known homosexual, Alan Turing. Turing and his heterosexual co-workers are tasked with breaking the Nazi's Enigma code during World War 2. At one point his gayness is brought up and is relevant to the story, but that scene is almost useless because by that time the audience is focused on the rest of the story. The entire scene could have been thrown out without affecting the movie. The notion of him being homosexual is one of two conflicts with other people. The first conflict is that he, Turing, jumped the chain of command and now his boss is looking for any reason to fire him. The second is that one of his co-workers is a Soviet spy, and if Turing informs on him, his co-worker will let people know that he, Turing, is gay.

The movie starts at a police station. Why is Alan Turing in a police station you may ask? Because he was arrested for soliciting sex from another man. The writers could not find another way to inform the audience that Alan Turing was gay. They could not think of another way to begin the story. The entire conversation that was being had between Turing and the police officer in the interrogation room, could have taken place in a park during a game of chess. But nope! The audience had to know that Turing was gay.

This movie is a war movie. But rather than depicting the exploits of soldiers on the battlefield, the entire movie is about the code breakers trying to break an unbreakable code. This is a story of the unsung heroes of WW2. At the end of this movie the audience could have walked away mesmerized by the exploits of the people who worked at Bletchley Park.

However, Hollywood couldn't help themselves this time either. Instead of letting the movie end and letting the audience go home knowing that a homosexual helped- _helped_- crack the Enigma Code, Hollywood became activists. You know how some movies end with a quick summation of what happened to the characters? Hollywood had to tell the audience how thousands of homosexuals have been persecuted under "Morality Laws" in Britain. The entire movie was about how a small group of people, men and women, at a place known as Bletchley Park broke the unbreakable German Enigma Code. The movie showed that at the end of the movie, having successfully broken the code, they were reading German messages before Hitler read those same messages. But for some reason Hollywood wants everyone to believe that World War 2 was about how homosexuals were underrepresented and how we'd all be speaking German or Japanese right now if it weren't for a gay man.

Here's another example. I refer to you the movie <u>Operation Mincemeat</u>, also a movie about World War 2. Operation Mincemeat is the code name given to the operation set in motion to convince Adolf Hitler that the Allies were about to invade Greece and not Sicily. The condensed version of the movie, if we are to believe the movie, is that the fate of the Allied landings in Sicily and the lives of thousands of soldiers, sailors, airmen and marines- including General George S. Patton, Jr.- were saved because a British spy gave a German double agent a hand job on a park bench in the middle of the night. I'm curious, did this actually happen, or was it "artistic license."

The homosexual community just like everyone else, should have to prove the merit of their story before they are allowed to erect (no pun intended) altars to their heroes. In the movie, they went so far as to show the British spy's arm moving up and down. The whole scene lasted less than 10 seconds. The British spy saw the German spy and sat down next to the guy. The British spy then placed his hand on the German guy's leg. The German guy put the British guy's hand inside his trousers. The next scene shows everyone at HQ getting the news that the Germans bought the deception hook line and sinker.

They couldn't have shown everyone at headquarters sitting around stressing about the situation. No! They had to show the homosexual thing. They couldn't simply have shown everyone at HQ worrying about whether or not their plan worked, with jump cuts to the soldiers storming the beach. Oh, wait! They did show everyone in HQ sitting around stressing out about the situation. But they didn't show soldiers storming the beach. Nope! They instead, jumped to a scene in a park where one man was sexually gratifying another man. They couldn't have had dialogue in HQ take place between two characters while they were waiting to receive a Top-Secret message informing them the landings were successful. Oh, wait! There was a scene like that. It was the scene that immediately followed the gratuitous homosexual sex scene.

They couldn't have given Benedict Cumberbatch a cameo to show Alan Turing and his co-workers at Bletchley Park intercepting a message confirming the Germans bought the ruse. Nope! Had to show a gratuitous sex scene. In this case, the truth isn't quite as exciting. By the way, did you see what I did there? I gave them another way they could have woven homosexuality into the story. But since they didn't use that one, it must mean they are perverts that wanted to show a sex act on screen.

All they had to do is have the one spy make a phone call saying he was successful in fulfilling his part of the deception, but no! They had to show the world that a huge military operation was successful because of a jerk-off session. The men and women worrying about whether they had successfully fooled the Nazis could not be told until after the climax. Co-incidentally, the climax of the movie was the insinuation of a climax. The subliminal message…everyone must now worship the homosexual community because without their ability to get *hetero*sexuals to sexually gratify them against their will on a park bench, we would be speaking German.

Everyone in the entertainment industry today needs to quit believing they are trailblazers for whatever social justice movement is currently consuming their brain cells. Why? Because they aren't trailblazers in the least. These people believe they are breaking new ground by claiming to be queer on television in the1990s, but they are at least two *decades* too late. I remember watching an episode of MASH where Frank Burns was trying to get a guy thrown out the army because he was gay. MASH also had a regular character who was a cross-dresser-Corporal Klinger. Corporal Klinger became a fan favorite. People loved to see Corporal Klinger. Would anyone like to tell me today's Hollywood elite, et al, are trailblazers 40 years after the final episode of MASH?

How are these people trailblazers when in the late 1970s and early 1980s there was another sitcom about three unmarried people- two women and one man- living in the same apartment. The premise is that the guy, Jack Tripper, needed a place to stay, but there were no other apartments available except for this one apartment currently being rented by two women. The conflict is that in the show, the landlord being a moral person, would not allow a man to shack up with two women unless they were relatives by blood or marriage. But it happened. Jack, Krissy, and Janet lived together in the same apartment for seven seasons. How did the creators of the show make it possible for Jack to live with Janet and Krissy? Jack told the landlord it was okay for him, a man, to live with two women because he gay and therefore there would be no hanky-panky. There would be no baby making in any of the apartments in the complex unless the people were married.

Every time the landlord came around, the male character would pretend to be gay. Did you get that? The only reason he was "allowed" to live with the women is because he was gay. Gay, gay, gay. He wasn't allowed to live with them because he was married to one of them. He was allowed to live with them because the landlord thought he was gay. If he weren't gay, he would have discriminated against him for being heterosexual. One of the funny parts of the show was the fact that the landlords were the only people who didn't realize it was a ruse. This show routinely took on stereotypes and made fun of the stereotypes. This show brought awareness to the gay community. This show gave the homosexual community a hero even though the character wasn't gay. This show made fun of the archaic and ignorant dogmas plaguing the public's perception of homosexuality.

Here's another example of how much today's homosexual activists *aren't* blazing trails for the LGBTQRSTUV community. In the 1980s there was a different sitcom that openly supported cross-dressing. In this show, the only apartment two guys could find was in a woman-only building. Guess what they did. They dressed up as women! They left for work dressed as women and changed into their guy clothes on the way to or at work. When it was time to go home, they would don their dresses, wigs, make-up, and go home.

The truth of the matter is the self-anointed leaders of the homosexual community are actually causing the gains made in prior decades to be lost. *No one hates the gay community. No one hates the black community. They just hate getting beat over the head with stories of repression, real or imagined, 24 hours a day.* It is this hatred that is going to cause people to be ignored and discriminated against.

73

Not because the person is gay, a woman, or black. It will be done because people will find the consequences of discrimination are less repugnant than having to sit through another 20-minute diatribe of how they need to bow down to the person doing the lecturing and the fault for the new decade of discrimination will be rightfully placed at the feet of the ignorant activist community. In case people are curious, the shows I used as examples are Three's Company and Bosom Buddies.

And in other news about Hollywood and their corruption...

Netflix airs a television show about Jeffery Dahmer. He was a convicted murderer, and a cannibal. Not only was he these, but he was also a homosexual. In order to classify the show in the same manner in which they classify all shows, Netflix classified this show, DAHMER — Monster: The Jeffrey Dahmer Story' as an LGBTQ show. This upset the gay community. The gay community wants everyone to believe that everyone who falls under the ever-expanding LGBTQ banner is pure of heart and totally without sin. So, the LGBTQ community, more specifically the self-anointed activists who claim to speak for the entire community, threatened- Extorted- Netflix until they removed the show from the list of LGBTQ shows.

If people believe that Hollywood is not having an adverse effect on society, consider this. When I was growing up, I was taught it wasn't nice to make fun of people. It didn't matter if they deserved it or if they started it. I was taught that it was wrong. Imagine how it made me feel when one day I turned on the television and saw a show whose sole purpose was to make fun of other people. That was the whole premise of the show. Get up in front of a camera and make fun of your opponent. I'm not talking about shows involving practical jokes. I am not talking about the Comedy Central Roasts. I am talking about the show Drop the Mic. I know, I know, they are rapping and rapping is art. Still, why is that a television show when at the same time- in the same society- there are people being called names so vile and so hurtful, people need a safe place to which they can go, and come to terms with the hurt?

Finally, and I may have already mentioned this, celebrities and their fans need to understand the type of relationship they have with each other. Many people are under the impression that they have an intellectual or physical connection, but they don't. The type of relationship celebrities have with their fans is an emotional relationship. It doesn't matter if a person is a rockstar, an actress or a professional athlete- It is an emotional relationship. Celebrities make the fans feel good about themselves, and the fans make the celebrity feel needed. That's the easiest way to explain it.

When a music icon writes a song that connects with people, most of the time it connects because the listener is experiencing or has experienced similar tribulations. It works in the other direction, as well. Couples have "their song" because the song was playing when they first made a connection to each other. When an actor plays a role that connects with people, it's because the audience members can see themselves in the character- Not the actor. When an athlete makes a game (championship) winning shot, the fans, even though they aren't a suited-up member of the team, feel just as happy as the players. Why? Because a sports moment like that might be the only upbeat part of a person's life at the time.

There are reasons doctors, especially those with degrees in psychology, are ethically and by law forbidden to have other-than-professional relationships with patients. Do doctors and nurses suffer from the Nightingale Effect? Yes! Ethically minded professionals end either the professional relationship, or they end the personal relationship. Any professional whose job results in or requires them to establish an emotional connection with another person should avoid politicians and political organizations at all costs. And I am not solely thinking of doctors. Celebrities need to treat politicians as if they are the black plague personified.

There are two reasons politicians socialize with celebrities of any magnitude or profession.

First, they want to be entertained.

Musicians need to count the number of times a politician calls them simply to talk and what they talk about when they do call. Dearest celebrities, if the politician wanting you to perform at their daughter's wedding (or whatever) truly thinks of you as an equal, you would have received an invitation, not a contract. To a politician, a celebrity is merely a court jester, and a tool to be used in their quest for power.!

Second, politicians want to be seen with celebrities to get access to their fans.

In recent years this has become more and more prevalent. A slime ball politician wants to be seen with a celebrity to exploit the emotional connection the celebrity has with their fans. When the fan cries at a concert, at a movie, or at the ballpark watching the game, the fan is emotionally compromised and is more susceptible to propaganda. This is how cults increase their membership. They prey on people who tend to be emotionally compromised.

It's the same reason celebrities have endorsement deals. Ad agencies, and their clients know that many people will buy a product simply because a celebrity is the spokesperson. The difference is when a celebrity endorses a product, they are saying an inanimate object is good. When a celebrity endorses a politician, they are endorsing a person who is seeking to have power over another human being; "Power over" in the most subjugating sense of the term.

If a celebrity-endorsed product turns out to be bad, no problem the item can be discarded. The consumer (the fan) may lose a couple of hundred dollars, but that's it, no big deal in the grand scheme of things. However, if the politician turns out to be a raging dirtbag psychopath, it may be difficult- if not impossible- to get the politician to relinquish power. The consumer (the fan) may lose their freedom, their home, their way of life, or their life trying to "dispose" of the politician.

So, all you celebrities out there, endorse politicians as you see fit. But understand that when you do, *you* are complicit in the exploitation of your fans and anything bad that happens subsequently.

Before I move on to the next section, I need to hammer this home. Quit acting as if the politicians who invite you to their $10,000 per plate parties think of you as their equals. They do not! To them you are the court jesters. Oh, they will wine and dine you, but while that happens, they are aching for you to perform for them. If you are truly equal to them on the socio-economic scale, you would be sitting in the audience with them watching another performer sing *their* latest hit song; They would have someone else recite Shakespeare. But they don't, they want you to give them a private performance.

All Presidents have thrown out the first pitch at baseball games. Some have attended the Superbowl. Do you really think there is no way for them to attend one of your concerts? It's not like you suddenly decided to have the concert that week. Your concert was scheduled a year ago. That is plenty of time for the Secret Service to do what they do. It's the same with politicians who don't have the Secret Service protecting them. They can have their people call your people and voila, *they* are at *your* concert in the arena, not in their house, giving a private show.

But you indulge them. Why? Because you know if you turn them down, they will never talk to you again. You will be banished to the children's table and never invited back. You will never have the opportunity to make amends. Remember, actors are a dime a dozen. This holds true for singers and musicians, as well. If you don't do it, they will find someone who is hoping to get noticed, and the people they find may end up more successful than you.

CHAPTER FOUR

SILICON VALLEY- THE INFORMATION MEDIA

Here's the difference between me and those who are my juniors. I look at a computer and see a tool that can make my life easier. Those who were born after me look at a computer and see a toy that can entertain them.

I haven't forgotten about Silicon Valley. Let's get one thing straight right off the bat. Having a degree in the computer sciences doesn't make a person a genius. I know there are these places called, "Genius Bars," but working at a "genius bar" in no way makes a person a genius. Most of the people who work at these places aren't geniuses, they simply have lots of experience with electronic equipment. Calling a place where people can go to get help operating electronics a Genius Bar is a bad PR move. Why? Because of the messages sent to the consumer. One message is that only a "genius" can truly know how to operate the device. Another is that, because only a "genius" can operate the device, everyone who goes to the "genius bar" for assistance is stupid. But, if that is the image or message a company wishes to convey, fine. Being able to program a computer is not unlike being able to write in a different language. In fact, computer programming is simply writing in a "foreign" language. That's it.

I said this earlier while talking about another profession. Having a college degree in any discipline does not mean a person has been anointed with all the knowledge of the universe. There are plenty of people in this world who don't know the difference between a laptop computer and a desktop computer, but they can field strip an internal combustion engine quicker than anything. Not only that, but they can also explain the purpose of every part and quote the good-bad specifications of each part. Believe me, high and mighty computer geniuses, when a person's computer goes bad, it only affects them for a short amount of time. Computers have become so inexpensive they are essentially disposable property like paper towels. The only reason a person's life will be dramatically altered following a computer crash is if they stupidly *put their eggs in one basket* and store everything on one device. Other than that, a broken computer will be a big deal for a day or two. *OMG, I can't access my bank account because my computer crashed. Now I have to go to the bank in person. The horror!*

If a person's car goes bad however, that is life altering. If a person cannot immediately replace their automobile- and most people cannot- it will dramatically change their life. They might not be able to get to work or go anywhere because public transportation only exists in major cities. Replacing a broken car may see a person going further into debt simply because cars are expensive. If a person is away from home when their car breaks down, they might be stuck in a city hundreds of miles from home, or on a road a hundred miles from anything. If this person is delivering food to the grocery store, the food might not make it to the market which *will* have downstream consequences.

I said all that to preface telling computer geniuses that most of their ideas they believe are brilliant really aren't all that brilliant. In fact, most of their bright ideas cause other people pain. If computer geniuses were to stop having bright ideas, there would be no need for customer and troubleshooting services. Why? Because eventually us idiots who know nothing about computers, would figure out not to download their ridiculous app. Don't get me wrong, I love computers for what they allow me to do, but it should be the consumer who decides what the computer does, not the computer programmer. If the consumer wants to use their computer to maintain household finances, gaming companies should not be allowed to monitor computer usage. No computer should be asking the question, "Do you want [enter the operating system] to remember this password?"

Every time programmers create an update to an operating system, especially the ones that run my phone or my computers, *they* screw up *my* property. Yet, they have no remorse! (Don't be coy! You know what you did.) Every time an automatic update happens on my phone, every application gets turned on. Sometimes after an update, there are new programs I never wanted on my phone or computer in the first place. In the end, updates require me to spend an hour finding the apps and then shutting them off. If I didn't do this, my phone would always be charging because for some reason *every* app needs to know where

I am, where I went, and where I am going next. And it is getting worse! Nowadays, I can't turn off the automatic updates.

My phone comes with fifty (50) different applications. Why? Because one day a computer guru hibernating a cubicle decided that I couldn't live without certain programs because *he* couldn't live without them. I'll let the computer companies in on a secret. Over the years, I have owned only a handful of computers and other electronic devices. I haven't owned as many devices as a professional gamer, but I have owned a fair amount. I would have owned more, but my experiences weren't always positive to say the least. Plus, a computer can't build a fence. I usually use the same device for 3 years before the thought of upgrading even crosses my mind. And when I do upgrade, it amazes me just how many pre-installed apps and programs I never used. This includes the games.

Speaking of games, I apologize for the digression upfront, why must I suddenly watch advertisements when I want to play a simple game of Solitaire or Free Cell? Why can't you people just let me relax and be ad-free while I play these games? I'm not playing these games because I am curious about what new item is about to hit the market. I am playing these games to relax. I am playing these games because they are simple and don't require much thought, if any. I am playing these games because I am constantly inundated with advertisements in every other aspect of my life. These games used to be places where I could go and not have my train of thought interrupted by an ad campaign. But Big Tech had to screw that up too. At one time, new computers came with simple games like Solitaire and Free Cell installed. In order to play these games now they have to be purchased *online* and after every game, before a person can start a new game, they must watch a commercial. And these are the games that used to come with computers.

You and I both know there is no need to update the games themselves. These games have been around for decades. The rules of these games have been in existence for centuries. The only reason Solitaire programs are updated is because in addition to selling hardware and software, computer companies now sell advertising space. In the past if an ad company wanted to change an advertisement, they had to send people out to change the signs along the interstate. In today's modern, totally on the grid environment, all an advertiser needs to do is send a million dollars and an email with the new ad to the computer company who will in turn perform an *automatic* "software update." Yes, I'm on to you. Most of your so-called updates are nothing more than your company being greedy.

In their twisted version of reality, every computer company has convinced themselves into believing that every computer, every phone, every electronic device which uses their software is an extension of- and therefore owned by their company- and *NOT* someone's private property.

It's even worse now because buying these games requires me to be online. I can't do it old school. That is to say, buy CDs of games and install them that way. I am now forced to purchase games online. When I play the games, I must be online. If the internet ever short-circuits, I will not be able to play these games. So, I either don't play games or, just so a computer company can make billions of dollars by sending me junk emails and advertisements, I buy the games online. It irritates me to know that unless I pay them $20 per game, I will never be allowed to opt out of or turn off the advertisements. In essence, computer companies are extorting consumers. There is no privacy.

Silicon Valley does not have a need to know where I am at any given moment, nor do they need to track my browsing history. Their having this information will never result in me having a better experience. Stop it! Stop it! Stop it!

On a side note, I don't need my phone to talk to my refrigerator, either. Why? Because I know the two of them are conspiring with the washer and dryer and are planning a coup. One day for no discernible reason, the four of them will stop working one after the other, causing me to lose my mind. (And no, Google, you don't need to know how often I do the dishes.)

Heed this warning.

It's not just that Big Tech is tracking people's usage, etc. I know for a fact that hospitals are either tracking how their employees use their own (not the company's) personal devices, or they are allowing Big Tech to do so via the hospital software. I once worked at a hospital where I didn't get reception inside the hospital because the hospital lacked an agreement with my chosen phone company. And because of this, I would turn off my phone, so my phone didn't spend the next ten hours constantly searching for a signal, thereby draining the battery. One day- the day I realized what was happening- my job required me to need stainless steel bolts, but our usual supply company didn't carry the type I needed. This in turn required me to use the hospital's computer to find what I needed elsewhere, and I did. I found exactly what I needed on the Home Depot website and submitted a parts request to my supervisor. I did all of this while my phone was turned off and safely stowed in my locker.

When I got home that night, I turned on my computer at home and was instantly barraged with Home Depot advertisements for stainless steel bolts and other fasteners. Not only was the hospital's computer system talking to my phone without my permission, but the hospital's software was also causing the information to be sent to my personal computer. *Yeah, healthcare sector CEOs, it's the employees that pose the greatest security threats to your precious computer system. I will just bet that you are still trying to figure out how hackers were able to the get viruses into your "secure" systems.*

Here's my favorite example of how utterly stupid computer programmers can be. Over the course of the past few decades, no matter what I do I have never, ever been able to get any of my computers nor any of my portable devices like my phones to sync up. Why? Because software updates, automatic or otherwise, fix one thing and break something else in the process. The first time I tried to sync up two electronic devices was after buying a new computer and a PDA within a month of each other. Here's the kicker, I bought them from the same company. No matter what I did, they would never sync up. If I wanted to schedule a meeting, I had to enter the information twice, once in the computer and once in the PDA. Needless to say, when the PDA stopped working, I didn't care all that much. I simply downloaded the information I wanted onto the minidisk and loaded it onto the computer. I then took the PDA to the driving range, and...

With that last paragraph in mind, if I want to check my Yahoo email with my phone, why *must* I log-in to a Google account I never wanted to open, but had to otherwise Google wouldn't let my phone work?

I mentioned earlier, about Big Tech screwing up _my_ property. I didn't stutter. I didn't misspeak! I didn't misunderstand the user agreement! It _is_ my property. I am the one who paid for it. I am *not* renting it from them. They have **_no_** right to monitor my computer usage. They have no right to track my location. These are facts! Allow me to use a car analogy...

Just as I can't run Microsoft Word on an Apple desktop, I can't start a Ford using a key for a Chevy. I can and have used a Ford vehicle to jump start a GM vehicle. I have driven vehicles made by different companies. This means I have taken my coffee cup from one car to another. And no matter which car I drive, the car company has no right to know what type of coffee I am drinking. They have no right to tell me to put a quarter cup of sugar in my coffee. They have no right to tell me I can't drive my car on the Interstate. Car companies can't dictate to me the uses of my car. If I want to haul two 80-pound bags of ready-made concrete with my Ferrari, it is none of Ferrari's business. Enzo Ferrari can haunt me all he wants, but it is still my car. Do you get the picture?

Here's a case in point. I mentioned it earlier. I suddenly lost the ability to check my Yahoo email using my phone one day. When I say suddenly, I mean *suddenly*. I hadn't just bought the phone. I had checked my email the day before with no problems. It was simple, I would tap the Yahoo! Mail icon and when the app opened, I swiped down to ensure I was looking at the most recent emails. The whole process took ten seconds. Being able to check my email quickly was and still is a huge benefit to me because most days checking my email is the *only* reason I sit in front of a computer. (Yes, some people can still go days without needing to sit drooling in front of a computer.) My phone's ability to quickly check my email, no matter my location, simplified a part of my life.

That all changed, however. One day just as I had the day before, I swiped down to update and nothing happened. I swiped left; I swiped right. I swiped up, I swiped down. My phone would go through the motions thereby giving me hope, but the only emails displayed were the emails from the last time I successfully checked my email. (No, it wasn't because no new emails were sent. Spam emails made short work of that troubleshooting step.) I tried everything. I went on the internet and asked the question, "Why can I no longer check my email on my phone?" I have been unable to check my email on my phone since July of 2018. Why? Because the Android operating system would not allow it. Sometime later, and after much angst, I discovered it was a purposeful change installed during an automatic update.

At some point in 2018, genius computer programmers decided they had the right to track and read my emails; even the ones sent through other companies. In order to fix the problem, I had to log into Google and give Google permission to track stuff. Did you get that, for me to use MY property, I *had* to give Google permission to invade MY privacy.

Food for thought… Lately, have you noticed this interesting tidbit? Many tech company CEOs are foreign born citizens of countries that don't exactly like the U.S.? They routinely- and adamantly- scream how they will never help the US government or US military but then whore themselves out to governments and militaries with adversarial relationships to the United States. And to add insult to injury, these same CEOs, whose US citizenship status is questionable, brazenly lecture US citizens about the meaning of the US Constitution.

Let's discuss the reasons which tech companies always put forth when confronted about their blatant violations of privacy and the US constitution. The argument made is that by tracking a person's location, the company can make a person's experience better. This is a bunch of horse crap.

Knowing my location will not make my on-line experience or phone call better. Why? Because like most people, if my location changes it's because I <u>must</u>

go somewhere. Most of the time, if not all the time, I only go to a different location because something needs to be done and I can't do it at home. Usually this is predicated on someone else requiring me to go to the new location. There are very few times when I will go to a new location out of sheer curiosity. This isn't 1915. I don't go on Sunday drives for a recreation. If I want a paycheck, I *must* go to work. If I want to eat, I *must* go to the grocery store. If I want the nagging to stop, I *must* realize that *I* wear the pants only because she allows me to say so.

This is why Amazon is such a juggernaut. If they don't have to, most people will not leave their homes. No matter how adventurous they claim to be on their Facebook page, they will stay home as much as possible. The advent of Amazon and on-line shopping in general, caused a new sport to be invented, Co-ed Naked On-Line Shopping. A person no longer needs to plan to go to the store. They don't need to create a shopping list. If they want, they can do their shopping as the need for something pops into their head. They don't need to have a plan to go clothes shopping at 10am, followed by grocery shopping at noon just to save gas. All a person needs to do is jump on the internet. They can shop for clothes and groceries at the same time. They don't even have to get dressed. They can buy it online, take a nap, and use the doorbell as an alarm clock. About the only sacrifice, one most people are apparently willing to accept is that the watermelon might not be as ripe as they were hoping. Yes, not only does the path of least resistance apply to flowing water, but it also applies to human beings as well. Whatever makes life easier determines what a person will do.

However, Amazon wasn't the first business to recognize the fact that humans are always looking to make their life easier. That distinction falls to the Sears and Roebuck Co. and their infamous catalog. In the 1800s, a person would walk into the town's general store to get needed raw materials like flour, and "surf" the Sears catalog. If they had enough money to buy something in the catalog, they ordered it through the general store. The customer paid for the item and then waited for the item to be delivered by stagecoach, train, wagon train, etc. One reason, if not the only reason that Amazon is such a monstrosity is because the logistics system in the United States has steadily improved over the centuries. If cars, trucks and go away, Amazon will also go the way of the dodo.

Ironic how the Sears and Roebuck Co. prospered by sending people catalogs for a century but failed to recognize how the internet could have revolutionized their catalog. Had the CEO and board of directors of Sears not been the consumer goods sector equivalent of "battleship admirals", the Sears and Roebuck Company might still be a shopping juggernaut. Not only that, had they understood simple marketing principles, Walmart wouldn't be as popular. Let's face it, Walmart is simply Kmart without the stigma that was allowed to fester by out of touch CEOs.

When tech companies claim they can make my life better by knowing where I am and what I'm doing 24/7, they are telling the mother of all lies! My routine only changes when I go on vacation. And with the advent of the "Staycation", it doesn't even change then. A person's daily routine never changes. Leave home and go to work; return home via a restaurant or store. That's it! That is why they are called "routines." There is nothing special or life altering hiding in a person's dreary life habits.

Computer companies are not going to solve world hunger or get a rocket into space by applying pattern recognition to people's daily habits. The only thing that will be accomplished is that vast amounts of data concerning people's routines will be collected and it will then be sold to other companies (Amazon/Google/Alphabet). A more sinister use of the data may be because computer programmers believe themselves to be a superior species of homo sapiens than are non-programmers, they will use the data extorted from their customers to determine if someone shares their philosophies on life and find crimes accordingly. And because no one wants to charge people or non-government institutions with violations of people's constitutional rights, the slimeball programmers will anonymously give the information to law enforcement and circumvent the need for a search warrant of any kind

The point of the previous few paragraphs is that people have a right to anonymity. They have the right to privacy. Even in public they have the right to privacy of their person- A person should be able to walk down the street and not wonder if a computer company is paying people to watch them solely to document them committing crimes. People value their privacy. Privacy is a basic need of human beings. They need something that is their own and no one else's. There was a prison complex in Cuba where all the cells face a central tower from which the guards watched the prisoners. But there was no way for the prisoners to know if someone was *actually watching* them. Many people in this prison went crazy because there was no privacy, they were always on display even when they weren't.

If someone still does not believe that most people only reluctantly venture more than a couple of miles from home, they should explain the phenomenon of people not wanting to return to in-person work after being forced to work from home for two years. I don't mean they don't want to work. I mean they don't want to leave their homes and drive to work. I worked from home for two weeks. I took a two-week vacation from my job to work on my thesis. That was my only focus. I woke up when I wanted. I went to bed when I wanted. If I was hungry, I ate. If I got tired of reading, I stopped reading. Sometimes I started my day at 2 am and crawled into bed at noon. I finished my thesis in less than two weeks because I wasn't saddled with a dogma which dictated the hours and location of where I could study. If I wanted to study on the roof while standing on my head at 2 a.m., then by God that is what I did. It was great. I loved it! Those were the days.

Weirdly, it was the technology companies- more specifically the companies' smug, superior leaders- who promoted and backed the campaign to keep people at home during a fake pandemic (in my opinion). For two years these companies fueled the pandemic hysteria by telling people if they go outside, they will catch COVID-19 and drop dead within five minutes. (During the pandemic, I went fishing and caught this manufactured virus. I know it was a manufactured virus because there was a tag on it that said, "Made in China.") Now, they want people back in the office or as they smugly say, "Back on campus." And because they have multiple college degrees in different disciplines, their smugness prevents them from understanding why no one wants to return to campus. There is absolutely no reason a technology company needs to know a person's location.

87

Here's another experiment that can be done. The purpose of this experiment is to provide scientific proof of hypocrisy. Get a bunch of your friends together. You are going to need to take off work to do this. Hang around outside the house of a tech company's CEO or COO or a member of its board of directors. Follow them everywhere. Don't get into high-speed pursuits. Don't tailgate them, just calmly follow them. Film everything! When they stop for coffee, inform the X-verse. Do this for a couple weeks. At some point they will call the cops. They will claim you are harassing them. They will try to have you arrested. If you are arrested, explain to the court that this person, through the software their company installs on electronic devices, at any given time, knows where you are located; they follow you digitally. Further explain that at any given time, for no reason whatsoever, this person can "break into" your phone and read personal stuff; that at any given time they can listen to your private phone calls; that this is the only way they will have any idea of how eerily creepy the company for which they work has become.

Just to warn the various consumers out there, turning off your phones will not keep your location a secret. Yes, the phone isn't actively tracking the location, but there is a back door. Somehow phone companies and technology companies have conspired to lull you into thinking this. You may turn off your phone before driving from one location to another, but as soon as you re-energize the phone it will download the history of the cell phone towers that came into range while it was off. Yes your phone is off, but it isn't truly off. You can never shut off your phone. It's not off the way a light bulb is off when you flip the switch or open the circuit breaker. It's more an off the way a computer is off when you put it in hibernate or sleep mode. There is no way to truly turn it off without breaking your phone. The only way to keep whichever company is tracking your location from knowing that you travelled from Illinois to Mississippi, is to leave your phone in Illinois or completely take out the battery which you cannot do on a majority of phones.

Explain this to me, Mr. Smarty Pants Computer Programmer. Why did Amazon recently admit they freely give to law enforcement officials the Ring Doorbell footage of people's homes without first obtaining permission from the homeowners or a search warrant from a court? Are they aiding and abetting law enforcement's denial of **_Constitutional_** rights of citizens as a political means to an end? There it is, that pesky document known as the U.S. Constitution and guess what one of the amendments says,

> *"The right of the people to be secure in their persons, houses, papers, and effects, against unreasonable searches and seizures, shall not be violated, and no Warrants shall issue, but upon probable cause, supported by Oath or affirmation, and particularly describing the place to be searched, and the persons or things to be seized."*
>
> *Fourth Amendment, United States Constitution*

Hey, wait a gosh darn minute. I mentioned this earlier. The Ring Doorbell videos are stored on the providing company's server, right?!?! This proves what I will talk about in a few pages. If they don't already believe it, or haven't already tried to claim ownership of it, tech companies will one day claim that because the information is stored on their "cloud", any person who uses their servers forfeits all claims of ownership of the information.

Honest to God, if other people did to a programmer's car what programmers do to people's personal electronic devices, the programmers would be livid. There are no words in any language past, present or future able to describe how angry a computer programmer would get if suddenly an auto mechanic swapped out their heated seats for non-heated seats for no perceptible reason. A person would easily be able to see them in a crowd of thousands of people. They would be the ones with an eerie iridescent glow. Even worse than them being angry is if someone did something to their property without their permission, they wouldn't shut up for a year. You know it's true! If one day I decided on my own to swap out the air-filled tires on their cars with solid tires, the geeks would have arrested me. They would jump up and down screaming words and phrases like, "Destruction of Property," "Trespassing," and "Grand Theft." They are such hypocrites. The sad part is they can't see it. They blindly go about their lives believing computer programmers are the smartest people on the planet. Just as the Robber Barons of the 19th century thought themselves the smartest people in the country, so do today's multi-gendered Robber Barons.

I'll say it again for the computer geniuses out there. My computer is *my* computer. My phone is *my* phone. You have absolutely no right to read or know the contents of either. You have no right to know where I take these devices. You don't pay my phone bill, nor do you pay for the paper I use to print out information. Your company is just like every other company in the world. It provides a product or a service to consumers. That's it. A furniture company has no right to come to my house and monitor how often I sit on the couch or what I do while I am on the couch. The same goes for computer companies as well. Computer companies are not special.

Talking to other people must be difficult for computer programmers. They don't speak English, so to speak! I'm not saying they should all know and speak English. They can speak any language they wish to speak. I'm saying they don't speak a version of their native language that non-computer programmers can understand. The sentences they speak can only be understood by other computer programmers. However, that too is in question. Throughout their lives, programmers may have taken honors classes in high school, and may have a college degree in English, but when they started programming computers, they stopped speaking any understandable form of any known language. In my case, the programmers speak English words, but the noise that comes out of their mouths is anything but. It's a veritable potluck of words. They go to a buffet and when they ask for pot roast, they expect their plate to be piled high with beets. Here's a case in point!

I once sought out an IT guy to help me with a Microsoft Excel problem. Based on my past experiences with Excel, I was certain the problem was me, not the program itself. Hindsight from past experiences led me to believe that I couldn't find a solution to my problem because I wasn't using the proper terminology. I was certain that I could fix the problem just as soon as I figured out what programmers considered me to be doing. In other words, I was asking for help on how to peel a banana so-to-speak, so I needed to know what a programmer calls the act of peeling a banana. To them, am I peeling a banana or am I changing the oil? I spent plenty of time asking myself, "What are some other terms a computer guy might call this function?" Every search I conducted yielded the same results. After a few weeks of trying to advance my project with no resolution in sight, I decided to seek help from a computer guy. I was hoping he could save me time. I couldn't have been more wrong.

I explained to the IT guy what I was trying to do and that I couldn't figure out how to make it work. He said he knew what I was asking and that he had done it in the past. He said he couldn't remember how he did it. He asked me if he could spend a couple weeks working on my problem. It wasn't life or death, so I said it was okay. The next time we met, he said he couldn't remember how he did what he did. He started showing me how to reinvent the wheel and we started working on my problem together. He opened a new workbook in Excel, and we got started.

He kept asking me, "What are the parameters for this column?" Me being the guy I am, when he said the word "parameters," I immediately started thinking of math formulae and the different parameters that are contained in problems. I started picturing in my head Einstein's theory of relativity. I started to think of the formula used to find the area of a circle, or maybe the circle's circumference. I started thinking of Boyle's Law and other laws of science. I kept telling him I wouldn't know the parameters until I entered the data I needed to enter. This only confused him. Now, both of us are confused.

Being the all-knowing, smarter-than-than-thou computer guy though, he kept asking me the same question over and over, never changing any of the words, never thinking that maybe *he* was asking the wrong question. So, I gave him the same answer repeatedly. Finally, I responded by telling him I didn't understand what he was asking. His response was typical for a member of the "smarter than everyone else" socio-economic class. He asked me the exact same question, using the exact same words, in the exact same order. Thank goodness I am smarter than the average bear because that could have gone on for a while. I engaged my brain and finally figured out what he was asking. I did this by consulting my "IT Guy to English" dictionary. Had he not thrown away his he would have been able to ask the question using the English language right off the bat. Had he been fluent in English, his first- and only question- would have been, "What do you want this column to be labeled?"

If computer companies continue to immediately implement the bright ideas of computer programmers, they need to forbid all programmers from writing instruction manuals. I don't mean it would be okay for a computer programmer in Milwaukee to write the instruction manual for the app created by a programmer in Miami. I mean no computer programmer should ever again be allowed to write any instruction manual. Ever! I don't care how many languages they speak. I don't care if they graduated from Yale University with 500 degrees in every language ever spoken since the dawn of human existence. They should never, ever, ever be allowed to write an instruction manual. The proof is in the instructions that come with all the products which require instructions. There are no words to describe these instructions.

I mean that literally! There are no words! It is all pictures.

The evolution of language has taken more than 10,000 years to get to this point. First, there was cave art where paleolithic man painted stick figures on cave walls. They were not Rembrandts.

Then the Sumerians came up with cuneiform which, although much simpler in appearance than hieroglyphs, probably took just as long to learn. What was its claim to fame? The ease at which mass amounts of information could be written down and easily understood when compared to pictographs.

Then came the hieroglyphs where multiple pictures or depictions were grouped together to form words. Very time-consuming, but apparently it got the point across. Because it was difficult and time consuming to write hieroglyphs fell out of favor when other societies came to conquer.

Finally, at long last, human civilization- the Phoenicians specifically- invented today's Western alphabet. It has remained relatively unchanged for almost four thousand years. Most of the letters in our modern alphabet can be recognized in the Phoenicians alphabet.

It is our (the Phoenician) alphabet which is being used around the world. When explorers visited faraway places, they brought it with them. These societies started adopting this alphabet. Even in the Americas! Fearing that their native tongue will soon be lost to the ravages of time, Native American tribes, which for ten thousand years had no *written* language and no way of converting their ancient Aural-Oral method of communicating into words, began using the Phoenician alphabet to codify their language.

And now- with the advent of the modern-day college graduate- the human language has evolved once again. We have a new method of communicating. This method is brought to you by the people who know everything. They have single-handedly advanced all human languages to their next evolutionary step- Pictographs and emoji's! Or in the case of today's youth, abbreviations Lol, smh, yolo, and others pepper text messages with the appropriate emoji of course.

Gone are the days of reading words and instantly understanding what is being asked. Gone are the days of learning to read and write starting in the first grade. Remember cursive? Gone are the days of the great authors. The great authors are dead. The great authors were racists anyway. Never again will you need (or be able) to read the works of William Shakespeare. Our intellectual superiors born out of the world's universities have evolved writing to the point where people only need to learn how to draw. And when our intellectual superiors deem it necessary, they will teach us how to interpret the meaning of these pictures. Pictographs! Today's pictographs they will tell us, are superior to ancient pictographs because our ancient ancestors weren't using true pictographs.

The historical timeline of human communications is now: 1) Pictographs 2) Cuneiform, 3) Hieroglyphs, 4) the Phoenician Alphabet, and 5) Pictographs. In their quest to advance the cause of mankind, our leaders have brought us roaring into the Age of Regression. *Is it okay if I don't move forward with you? If you don't mind I would prefer to wait for you to catch up again. The only thing I dread is your insufferable bragging about how your ideas have brought improvements in human life after you first destroyed all prior progress. When it comes time to pay the piper, you always forget that you took one step forward only after taking two steps backwards.*

Computer companies are not innocent technology companies making the lives of their customers better. They are identity theft cabals. If you wish to use their programs, you must first fill out a form that lists names, addresses, emails, and phone numbers just to name a few items. If you wish to use Google Maps, for instance, you *must* enable location tracking on your device. You are not allowed to look up a location without someone in Silicon Valley knowing about that too. Why? They claim it is to make my experience better, but everyone knows they are lying. If an honest investigation were ever carried out on these companies, it would probably show they are storing people's information for illicit reasons. Remember, the people who run these companies come from a superior species of Homo Sapiens and are therefore better than you. They need to monitor your actions because you don't know what you are doing, even though you have been doing it successfully for decades. If you don't believe they are actively doing this, you are as naïve as the computer programmers who believe America's *enemies* would never use their inventions to do evil.

The frightening thing is how the United States Congress actively protects them. An honest investigation would probably find members of Congress receiving kickbacks from these companies. Congress could end all the problems we are currently having with technology companies if they would simply quit protecting them. Think about what Congress did a couple decades ago when cell phones became cheap. Before cell phones became prolific, the only time a telemarketer could get someone on the phone was when they were home. The cell phone allows people to take their phones everywhere. Cell phones also gave telemarketers the ability to annoy people regardless of their physical location. And annoy them they do. To this day, they are doing that.

Even with the "Do Not Call List" telemarketers can still call people. Why? Because Congress put in a loophole. If you make a purchase, or fill out a questionnaire, make sure you read everything. The loophole is if you fail to check certain boxes on the website, you automatically authorize telemarketers to call you. This isn't an oversight on the part of Congress. There is a specific line in the legislation which allows this to happen. We won't talk about the fact that Congress put time limits on your wishes, too. Every now and then you need to put your phone number back on the list. Why did Congress do this? Because they have friends in the technology sector who benefit. And if those friends benefit, individual members of Congress benefit financially.

Why can't computer companies keep things simple? I have never been able to easily synchronize my phone with my computer. I had a new computer and a new PDA, from the same company no less, and I could never get them to talk to each other. Today, I have the same problem with my phone, my tablet, my desktop, and my laptop. They don't talk to each other. They can recognize each other, but they will not sync up.

During brainstorming sessions while writing this book, I would write some fairly long notes on my phone so I wouldn't forget them, but then I had to manually copy the notes into my computer. It was a huge waste of time. But that was the only way I could transfer the notes from my phone to my computer. Why? Because I could not get my phone to send files. It wouldn't even send a document via Bluetooth from my phone to my laptop. Why? Same reason I was unable to check my Yahoo email on my phone.

On the same subject, at the time I began writing this book, this laptop was less than 2 months old. I still had my old laptop, and it had files I wanted to transfer to my new desktop. It too was less than a year old. Yes, I finally broke down and replaced my electronic devices. Transferring the files from one computer to the other is a very time-consuming process. It's bad enough that a person needs to go through the device and find the files, but in order to transfer the files, a removable storage device is needed. Here is the process, although simple, it is time consuming.

1. Insert portable storage device.
2. Save the files to the portable storage device.
3. Remove portable storage device from the old computer and insert it into the destination computer.

4. Transfer the files from the storage device to the destination computer.
5. After confirming the transfer was made, delete the files from the USB drive to free up space
6. Repeat Steps 1 through 5 until finished. In my case, I went through the steps ten times.

I spent three hours doing that. I inevitably transferred a set of files multiple times because no matter how much I tried, I would lose track of what I truly transferred. Why? Because sometimes it takes almost half an hour to complete the transfer, and sometimes I couldn't remember if I transferred the files or if I walked away before clicking the send button, so to speak. Why can't it be simple?

Here's how simple the process should have been. This is how I originally planned on doing it, but nothing is ever simple.

1. Plug any type of computer cable into a corresponding outlet on the old computer.
2. Plug the other end of the cable into the same type of outlet on the destination computer.
3. Turn on both computers.
4. Have the two computers realize that I was creating an Ad Hoc network, and work with me instead of ignoring my desires.
5. Sit down and transfer files as if I were transferring them to a thumb drive.

I know what Silicon Valley is going to say next, "You could have saved yourself the frustration and time had you just transferred them to "the Cloud."

To which I query,

1. Are you people nuts?
2. Are you currently sitting there telling me that with a straight face?

96

3. Do you sincerely expect me to believe you don't have a program written that scans my personal files for key words and highlights files for review by your own Gestapo? Or do you call them the Stasi?

I would be willing to bet that computer companies are covertly and illegally monitoring what people save to the Cloud. I base this not on my experience with saving documents to the cloud, but on experiences I had while writing this book. It took me well over three years to write this book due to my laziness. Not to mention the fact that it is difficult for me to read something ten times and remain interested. This book is over four hundred pages long (pre-formatting) and takes up 0.96 kilobytes of memory. Did you get that? This book uses less than 1 megabyte of memory in a laptop having many gigabytes of memory. However, as I was working on some chapters there were times when the computer suddenly slowed. When I say slowed, I mean it would take five to ten seconds for a single sentence to show on the screen.

I went online to try to figure out what was happening, and the explanation (excuse) was that large files sometimes take more time to save, process, etc. Did you catch that? The physical size of the file was causing the computer to suddenly slow to a crawl. A one-megabyte file was using up so much RAM, etc. I could literally type a sentence and watch the letters slowly appear on the screen as if I was typing using the two-finger method of a second grader. The only way for me to fix the issue was to save the file, close the program, and then re-open the file again.

After a while I started noticing that it only happened when I was working on certain subjects or typing certain words. What was the word? Obama. Yes, if I typed the messiah's name multiple times the computer suddenly started slowing. It's as if something was scanning my laptop. The conspiracy being that Silicon Valley is tracking what people are writing about Obama. The fact of the matter is that I have been going through the different chapters editing them and have not had a slow down for a few months now. Of course, for the most part I have not used the emperor's name.

I'm neither a conspiracy theorist nor a naïve spring chicken. With that said, it is only a matter of time before someone working for/or independently of a tech company dreams up a new idea on intellectual property rights. More specifically, it will concern the ownership of intellectual property. Not being a spring chicken allows me to believe that somewhere, on behalf of their client, a sleaze ball attorney is attempting to steal intellectual property using the adage that possession is 9/10ths of the law. This will be readily apparent if someone writes a wildly successful book or scientific treatise; one in which the monetary rewards are significant.

The argument made by the company will be that because the works were stored on their "Cloud", the company, is either the full owner of the work or entitled to royalties generated by the work. Companies are already doing a version of this. Read your contract, or whatever employment agreement you have with your employer. Somewhere it will state that if a person comes up with an idea while at work, if they use company property to develop or write down the initial idea, the idea immediately becomes the intellectual and/or physical property of the company. Thomas Edison did this constantly. Most of Edisons patents are not based on *his* ideas. They were his *employees'* ideas. There are companies which believe that a machine dreamed up by an employee is the property of the company, regardless of the employee's location and actions when the employee invented the machine. Yes, some companies will try to claim they have a right to an employee's intellectual property even if the employee was halfway around the world on vacation when the epiphany struck.

In the case of personal property being stored on the "Cloud", one would think cases such as these would be thrown out of court shortly after a lawsuit is filed. But just as there are sleazeball attorneys, there are also dirtbag judges. The court- the judge- will support their ruling by citing the company's pesky user agreement. Even if the user has no other storage option available, the user agreement will be used to justify a company or an individual stealing another person's intellectual property. Somewhere in the agreement will be found a line which essentially signs over to the company all rights to property stored on the servers provided by the company. The line might not be in user agreements now, but they will be soon. Just as banks now charge fees for everything because they believe your money is their money, computer companies will begin charging the users of their products fees for everything as well. Essentially, courts of law will deem users to be renting their computers; that users will be seen as a company's uncompensated inactive reserve employees.

SECTION 2

THE WESTERN WORLD

CHAPTER FIVE

THE SYSTEMATIC DESTRUCTION OF WESTERN SOCIETIES

There is an active campaign in progress to discredit Western Civilization. All the people involved truly hate Western Civilization. They not only hate western civilization, but they believe it to be so bad it needs to be removed from the face of the earth. In their minds, western civilization is the only reason there is any type of angst in the world, and that if it is gotten rid of, it will be replaced by a utopia that is nothing short of heaven on earth. To achieve this end, they are purposely ignoring the facts of history. Not the trifling facts inflated by their counterparts in the media and academia to be bigger factors in human history than they truly are, but the facts as discovered by archaeologists and historians who have no desire to be ideologues; Who are able to keep their personal belief system out of their work; who don't have an overriding urge to contort the facts- as discovered- to support their own religious zealotry.

For those who wish to see western civilization wiped from the face of the earth to be successful, two things must happen.

First, they need you to believe their suddenly discovered version of world history is the correct version and that all previously accepted versions are lies. They use phrases like, "The victor writes history," so people are more apt to not believe what they have known. Case in point on this phrase. World War Two was won by the Allies. The Allies discovered the concentration camps and the horrors they contained. The Allies filmed these atrocities. Now what is happening on college campuses? Professors are either downplaying or flat out denying the

Holocaust happened. The end game is to make villains out of the Jewish faith whenever possible.

Over time, and hopefully before it is too difficult to correct the falsehoods, people will come to realize the very people they trusted to be impartial were nothing more than neo-religious zealots obedient to no one unless there is material gain for themselves. It will be discovered that these people not only knew the centuries-old facts they deemed to be wrong were correct. It will also be realized that when confronted on the issues, these hacks will ignore them because acknowledging them would disprove what they want people to believe. This is what religions do. Regardless of who is the Almighty. This is how one religion displaces another. Evolution is wrong! God created the Heavens and the Earth! Or vice versa.

Here is another example of how people who hold positional authority over others are trying to discredit accepted- and proven- historical facts to promote their religion. My older sister went to college. As all degrees require, she had to enroll in courses that had nothing to do with her major. She decided to take a course in world history. When the subject of World War Two came around, the professor convinced my sister and others that the United States deserved to be attacked by the Japanese on 7 December 1941. This fraudster's reasoning was simple. One day for no reason whatsoever the United States stopped selling oil to Japan. As if early one morning, President Roosevelt awakened and decided to halt all shipments of oil to the largest consumer of American oil simply because they ate raw fish. The dishonest professor made no mention of the fact that for the previous three years- since 1938 even before Germany invaded Poland- the United States and the League of Nations were trying to get Japan to halt its invasions of China and Indochina. The professor also made no mention of what was dubbed the Rape of Nanking where the Japanese Army took everything by force and killed over 100,000 Chinese men, women and children- Non-combatants all! But his diatribes didn't stop there, he extended his beliefs into contemporary happenings and told his class that Saddam Hussein's invasion of the Kuwait was justified, and that the Kuwaitis deserved it too.

Second, they need to change the anthropological history of humanity to reflect their "newly discovered" version of the human race's ancestry. They are attempting to do what Adolf Hitler and his Nazi thugs did for over a decade. Grasping at any piece of history and doing all they can to make it theirs. They grasp at any piece of history and do all they can to make it theirs. They claim religious relics and philosophical axioms were theirs first, and that the inventions of western civilization weren't invented in the west but were invented elsewhere. They want everyone to believe that western civilization stole the ideas and inventions from other civilizations that were subsequently destroyed by western civilization. Here is the most atrocious example that has been ongoing for the better part of thirty years.

The identity of the last Pharoah of Egypt has been known for two millennia, Cleopatra VII. There is archeological evidence proving her identity. There are two-thousand-year-old inscriptions etched in rock and stone annotating her family lineage. Yet her legend is so great, other people are trying to claim her as part of their heritage. She is known as a great ruler, a great diplomat and a great beauty. She is said to be one of the most powerful and consequential women in all of human history. Yet activists in the African American community are attempting to commandeer Cleopatra. They claim she was black. Even when all the evidence proves she was Greek. They claim she had really dark skin and all the other traits which distinguish sub-Saharan Africans from all others.

The reality is she was Greek. Her brother, and co-regent, was Ptolemy the Twelfth. Ptolemy the First- the dynastic founder- was Alexander the Great's right-hand man; one of his generals who was himself a Greek. Activists in the African American community are claiming she is one of them simply because she was born in Egypt, more generally Africa. These same activists believe that everyone from Africa looks like those from sub-Saharan Africa.

What these people are trying to do are not new concepts. Sorry Karl Marx and Saul Alinsky were not the first people to think of these methods. They are not the so-called trailblazers of political science theory we are supposed to believe them to be. They simply regurgitated and restated a failed societal method that

103

western civilization invented- then rejected- multiple times. What these people are trying to do is institute an unsustainable way of life. Be it known now, commandeering identities and destroying histories is not original to the socialist thinkers of the 19th and 20th centuries. It also happened 2,000 years before Cleopatra walked the earth.

It is how King Tutankhamun came to be the most famous Pharoah to ever reign over Upper and Lower Egypt. His contemporaries erased him from history because they wanted people to only remember the history of which they approved. Statues of him were toppled. Hieroglyphs with his likeness were modified. His face was obliterated from all wall carvings. After all of this was done, there were no memories of him having lived at all. Tomb robbers didn't rob his tomb because they didn't know to look for his tomb. It is for this reason, and only this reason, he became more famous than all his predecessors and successors combined. Rameses the Great may have been the greatest, but Tut is the most well-known. Ironically, by attempting to deny him his afterlife, by erasing him from their contemporary history, Tut's detractors ensured he would have the greatest of all afterlives. Not only that, but he also became the most loved!

The liberals who want to run the New Liberal Order which they wish to establish, need you to believe their version of history. If they deem something blasphemous to their religion, it will neither be taught nor talked about. Their heroes will be deified, yours will be vilified. If they think you are worshipping a false god- someone other than their deity- they will make sure your fate is known by people far and wide. The message will be, "Sinning against the liberal god will not be tolerated. The punishment will be fierce and swift." They will attempt to convince you of *their* superiority. They are the smart ones; you are the rubes. What is common knowledge today will require cited references to make it more difficult to counter and disprove their new-found enlightenment. If it cannot be changed and cannot be used to further their goal of total subjugation, it will be ignored and discussing it will be outlawed. At one point they will begin talking of, "The Enlightenment." The Enlightenment will consist solely of them renaming places and chiseling the faces off statues. The Fertile Crescent will no longer be called "The Fertile Crescent."

It is in progress as we speak. Slowly, all things good about Western civilization are being ascribed to other cultures. All things bad are being emphasized.

CHAPTER SIX

WHAT IS WESTERN CIVILIZATION?

Western civilization is all the cultures, from the ancient to the modern originating in all of Europe, North Africa, Lower and Upper Egypt, and the ancient orient. When I say all of Europe, I mean *all of Europe*. When I say North Africa, I mean the parts of Africa that are bordered by the Mediterranean Sea in the north and the Sahara Desert in the south. When I say Upper and Lower Egypt, I mean all parts of the Nile Valley that were conquered by the Pharaohs and settled by the ancient Egyptians. The ancient orient does not refer to China, Japan, or Korea. Those countries are in the modern orient. Scholars of ancient civilizations consider the ancient orient to basically be what we call the Holy Land and the lands to the east conquered by Alexander the Great. However, to consider the lands between the mouth of the Persian Gulf to the Indus River part of the ancient orient, might be stretching the term. The Persians originating from modern-day Iran are definitely part of western civilization, but after Alexander's return to Babylon in 326 BC, there was little to no contact with the cultures east of Persepolis until the establishment of trade via the Silk Road.

People may think that by virtue of their skin color that they are not part of western civilization. If they do, they would be wrong. By virtue of where they live and the country in which they matured as humans, they are part of western civilization. They may hate western civilization but hating one's culture- the only one they have truly known- is easier if they grew up in that culture. The people who hate western civilization *always* find other cultures to be exotic and more moral. Always! This is a function of them being clueless about the other culture and their own culture. Most cultures outside western civilization would love to be part of western civilization. It's a classic outside-looking-in situation and if left unchecked, it will be a classic didn't-know-what-we-had-until-we-lost-it situation.

The people who hate western civilization would do well to remember they are reaping the benefits of western civilizations. If they do not like western civilization, they are free to leave. There are many countries that do not subscribe to the ideals of western civilization. They do not have the morality, nor do they have the laws of fairness and equality found in western civilization. You can't miss these countries. Many are still mired in the Dark Ages. Some of these countries, even after having arisen from western civilization, have decided to renounce western civilization.

CHAPTER SEVEN

MAJOR HISTORICAL TIME PERIODS

It is very important that I present information about Western Civilization through the lens of the different anthropological ages assigned to human history. These ages are the basic anthropological divisions we use to document and logically format the human condition for a better analysis of civilizations and cultures throughout; their accomplishments and reasons why they did not progress through the Ages simultaneously. It can be difficult to determine when a particular civilization progressed to the next anthropologic age and the ages of invention within, however, for many reasons. One of the reasons for example is that a culture may have been strictly aural-oral based- they didn't or don't have a written language. Prior to the invention of standard writing systems, be they hieroglyphics and pictograms or Cuneiform A and Cuneiform B, or the modern alphabet, civilizations passed on information by rote memorization and word of mouth. The literary works of Homer; The Iliad and The Odyssey, were written down centuries after he died. Homer didn't wander about his known world reading from a scripture of sorts. He memorized the stories and from such memories, recited the stories to a gathered audience.

A modern example of this type of culture is the Navajo culture of North America. They still can only pass on information in the Navajo language by hearing the information and then repeating what they heard. They do not have a *written* language. Their language has no alphabet. Their history relies on people's memories. Any documentation of their history is in the form of another culture's alphabet. This is one of the reasons, if not the main reason, the Navajo code talkers of World War Two were so successful. No one, Japanese, Italian, or German, was able to learn the Navajo language by reading a book. A person could only learn the language through physical interactions with the Navajo. Thankfully, members of the Navajo Nation have banded together to remedy the situation so that their culture and knowledge can be read about in ages yet to come, in the Navajo language. However, the Navajo alphabet is *not* being invented. They are using our alphabet and Arabic numerals.

Human history is divided into five anthropological ages. Those ages being the Paleo and Neolithic Ages (Old and New Stone Ages), the Copper Age, the Bronze Age, and the Iron Age. Western Civilization has progressed to a modern anthropological age, but what is that Age? The Oil Age? The Computer Age? The Steel Age? Historians won't make that determination for a few more centuries. Some will say we are in the computer age, while others will say we are in the oil age. It is a debate to be had at another time. What can be said is that *all* the cultures within *western civilizations* reached these major milestones within a couple generations of each other.

To the contrary, cultures outside western civilization wouldn't attain these milestones for centuries after western civilization. No amount of hyperventilating by clueless fools is going to change this fact. Yes, it is true that individual inventions did originate outside of the western world, but they are rare. China may have given us gunpowder, but we passed on our knowledge to them as well. Want proof? Why are all the swords found with the Terra Cotta Army made of Bronze and not Iron? I'll tell you why. Because when this particular army was buried, China either had yet to enter the iron age, or they were in the embryonic stage of their Iron Age and could not afford to waste the iron. It is possible, and likely probable, that the emperor was economically minded and decided out of the goodness of his heart to entomb this army-in-effigy with bronze swords to not waste the iron. It can be safely uttered that western civilization is the catalyst which caused the world to civilize and for the human condition to improve.

The Paleolithic Age lasted for close to 2.5 million years. It is considered to have ended about 10,000 years ago, at the end of the last ice age. During this age, there were multiple species of humanoid beings, including Neanderthals, walking the earth. Civilizations were mainly hunter-gatherers. The tools and weapons used by mankind during the paleolithic age were very crude. Many tools were situational and at hand tools. That is to say, if a hunter needed to kill his prey, he simply picked up a rock and threw it at the animal. If he needed to pulverize a root to get at the soft meat inside, he picked up a stone he found on-site. When his need for the stone was sated, he dropped the stone on the ground and never picked it up again.

In the Paleolithic Age, humans were merely discovering how everyday objects could make tasks easier and their lives a little better. What differentiates the paleolithic from the neolithic is the quality of tools produced. Tools made by Paleolithic humans were crude. If these crude tools didn't shatter when used, the owner of the tool might fashion and affix a handle to the stone to make it a little easier to use the next time. Improvements to their tools were rough improvements at best. Maybe they chipped a hole through the stone so that it could more easily be carried.

The Neolithic Age ended in about 5,000 BC. It was in this age of invention that human thought really began to expand. The Neolithic Age sees the building of Stonehenge in Wales, and Gobekli Tepe in Turkey. The latter being the oldest. The Neolithic Age is characterized by stone constructions and polished tools. This is a very important designation. Had western civilization as we know it not existed or not come into contact with other civilizations; those civilizations would still be mired in the Neolithic Age.

In the Neolithic Age cities were becoming the norm. Animal husbandry is becoming abundant. Different family groups are settling together and job specialization is becoming common place. Tools are becoming more efficient. Humans have figured out which stones are harder. They have figured out which stones are best for the job. Humans are truly beginning to think scientifically. Life is becoming easier. Due to animal husbandry, humans are able to stay in a single location because they don't have to constantly search for food. Not having to hunt freed up time for thinking and experimenting.

When compared to the Stone Ages, the next anthropological ages in human history were achieved in rapid succession. Looking over the numbers, there appears an anthropological version of Moore's Law. The whole Neolithic age is a time span of five thousand years. However, once western civilization realized that copper wasn't just pretty as a jewelry, and could also be smelted into tools, the human condition began to advance exponentially. From the beginning of the Copper Age to a point where in the western world the Iron Age was in full swing is a mere 5,000 years. Yes, that is correct. In the span of 5,000 years, western civilization advanced through the Copper Age, the Bronze Age, and the Iron Age. It is the ancient equivalent of today's advancements in computer technology where the new computer model is obsolete within six months.

The Copper Age began around 5,000 BC and ended around 2500 BC. The pyramids of Giza, even though they were built from stone, because the tools used to work the stones were made of copper, the pyramids are Copper Age constructions. Not only were tools and jewelry being made of copper, but weapons of war were made from copper as well. It was easier to melt copper and shape it into arrow heads than to find rocks on the ground and shape them into arrow heads. The same with swords, axes, knives, and pikes. One advantage copper has over stone is it can be recycled. If a warrior's sword got bent or broken in battle, he could simply have it recast. There wasn't a need to first mine for more ore in the same quantity. Stone tools and weapons, by contrast, if they broke were useless and could not be repaired. A stone arrowhead, for example, could be reshaped if the cutting edges weren't excessively chipped, but if it broke into many pieces, it could not be put back together.

Whenever people are asked who or what they would visit if they could travel back in time, they usually want to visit a relative or a famous figure in history. Whenever they want to visit a certain era of time, they always want to visit the romanticized version of that era. No one ever thinks about what life was truly like during that time. Yes, ancient Rome had bath houses, etc., but they didn't have the internal combustion engine, sewage treatment facilities, or deodorant. No matter what people think, ancient Rome, with all its white marble columns and facades, stank to high heaven. The Tiber River, as dirty as one may find it today, was an open sewer in the time of Caesar Augustus.

The paved streets of Rome might have been mud-free, but they weren't free of animal dung. It wasn't until the mid-19th century that public sanitation became a priority anywhere. The high-heeled shoe wasn't invented to emphasis a woman's posterior. The high heeled shoe was invented so rich people could walk down the street without worrying that fecal matter and urine were seeping into their shoes and soaking their feet. Men didn't lay down their capes, cloaks, and waist coats so women didn't have to step in *water* puddles. They covered puddles so women didn't have to walk through the ever-present and numerous, small cesspools found on the streets in every major city.

If I could travel back in time, I would visit the boundary line between the neolithic age and the copper age; the copper age and the bronze age; the bronze age and the iron age. I want to bear witness to the epiphanies. I want to watch a clumsy smithy knock tin ore into molten copper thereby inventing bronze. I want to watch the cook tending to the hearth notice the pebbles he thought were coal or dark pieces wood are glowing orange and are now malleable. I want to see the smithy's mouth hang agape the first time he made something out of iron, and it didn't bend or break as it would if it were made cast in bronze. I want to watch a chef preparing a large meal sharpen his iron knife and a week later realize this is the first time he has resharpened it since, as opposed to sharpening it a couple times every day.

A civilization or culture is not considered to be in the next age of invention until its tools are widely made from that material. For instance, when Tutankhamun was walking the earth, Egypt was a couple thousand years into the bronze age and a couple hundred years from attaining the Iron Age. One of his most prized possessions was a dagger made of iron. At the time it was worth more than its weight in gold. It is believed to be the remains of an iron meteorite, and was the only iron known to the ancient Egyptians. If the moment Tutankhamun took possession of this small quantity of iron was considered Egypt's Iron Age D-Day, archaeologists would have to explain why the Egyptians spent the first half millennium of *their* Iron Age casting mass quantities of tools and weapons from bronze and not iron.

This next sentence or two will cause a lot of people consternation and constipation. Even though a few tribes were making jewelry out of copper, the Native Americans- in North, South, and Central America- never achieved the Copper Age. Yes, you interpreted that correctly, Christopher Columbus managed to stumble across two whole continents populated by Neolithic Age civilizations. The cheesy B-movies where someone travels through a mysterious portal and ends up in the year 10,000 BC...true stories to an extent. All the Native American artifacts predating the arrival of western civilization are neolithic artifacts. There were a few native American tribes blinging up with copper jewelry, but none had copper tools. When people discover native American arrowheads that pre-date the arrival of Columbus, they only find ones made of stone. None are made from copper, bronze, or iron.

The Native Americans and college activists that hate the arrival of the Nina, Pinta, and Santa Maria, should revere Columbus. The day Christopher Columbus landed in the New World, October 12th, 1492, should be celebrated by Native American tribes in the most rigorous of fashions. On that day, *all* Native American tribes- north, south and central- instantly became Iron Age civilizations. And not an embryonic Iron Age, they instantly became civilizations and cultures in a well-developed Iron Age. And *they* didn't have to spend five thousand years advancing through different ages by trial and error. It was dumped into their laps.

Except for the indigenous tribes of the Americas, the beginning and end dates of all the Ages are fuzzy. Depending on the historians writing the books, the beginning and end of a technological age can vary by half a millennium. It is entirely possible for one group of people in the western world to be in the Copper Age while another is in the Bronze Age. This explains the variation in start and stop dates. When do we consider all of western civilization to be in one age or another? Is it when all civilizations within the western world have achieved that technological age? Is it when one civilization of all the component civilizations becomes the first to enter that Age? Or is there a happy medium? What one historian believes and another historian believes, may result in an opinionated difference of 500 years.

The cause is simple, logistics. Trade routes were relatively archaic. Prior to the Bronze Age, trade flowed only as fast as a human or horse could walk, and usually only over land. As a result of these archaic trade routes, one culture would be rich in copper ore and poor in other metals, while another could be rich in tin and poor in copper. Trading between towns and cities didn't only spread materiel goods, it also allowed ideas to be traded. Only by improving the logistics involved in trading could this obstacle be overcome. This takes time.

It's not unlike driving to work. Every day there is an almost infinite number of routes a person can take to get to work. Over time people learn which is the best route for a particular day's drive. It may take a person a year to learn the best route. Trade routes for most of human history are little more than a couple of scout ants returning to the colony with a handful of food taken from an ant from a rival colony. Now their colony knows another source of food is available, they just don't know its location. Only further scouting can make that determination. Maybe on the next trip there will be a dozen scouts dispatched.

The pyramids of Giza, just as the pyramids built earlier, were built from stone by kings of the 3rd and 4th dynasties. This was the golden age of pyramid building in Egypt and it is entirely within the Copper Age. The first of the pyramids, the Step Pyramid, was constructed circa 2,630 BC. The last of the pyramids to be built during this age rose from the sand about 200 years later. Yes, pyramids were still being constructed following the 4th dynasty, but they were smaller, and the precision and care of construction suffered greatly. Many were built using mudbricks, not stone. Most third and fourth dynasty pyramids are large, well-built and are still recognizable as pyramids today. 5th dynasty pyramids are now almost indistinguishable from simple mounds of dirt.

The ancient Egyptians worked the pyramid stones using copper tools. The main reason for this is that while they had access to large quantities of copper, their access to tin was limited. As a matter of fact, Egypt would continue to be rich in copper and poor in tin until well after the death of Tutankhamun. Most of the tombs chiseled into the walls of the Valley of the Kings, were built using copper tools. Through archaic trading routes Egypt was finally informed of the existence of a stronger metal but was unable to secure it in the vast quantities it needed. This, however, would change as trade networks expanded.

The Egyptians were able to dive headfirst into the Bronze Age because of another ancient civilization in the Mediterranean- The Minoans. The Minoan trade networks are responsible for bringing western civilizations into the bronze age. While the Egyptians were building pyramids, the Minoans were mapping the Mediterranean. As the Minoans improved and increased trade with other Mediterranean cultures, ideas and inventions spread rapidly amongst them. In an instant, Egypt learned of Britian; and Gaul learned of Israel. Improvements in technology were addictive. Everyone wanted to turn their grandfather's copper sword into a newer state-of-the-art bronze sword. There was no turning back.

At some point before the Minoans disappeared from history, someone realized that the things on the ground that look like blueberries could be smelted as one would copper and tin. They then came to realize that unlike copper, tin, and other metals, these blueberries by themselves were a much stronger metal. Minoan trade routes set the western world on the fast track to the Iron Age. We can debate later which civilization within the west was the first to smelt iron. What is unmistakable though, is that the trade routes established by the Minoans are the impetus for Western Civilization being the first *in the world*- as we know it to be today- to fully enter the Iron Age. Yes haters, the western world- the hated and reviled western world- was making its swords and tools from iron almost a thousand years before China.

When comparing the Minoan trade routes to the ones which came previously, and continuing the ant analogy from earlier, it isn't even close. Trade logistics were so great under the Minoans, it was as if the entire colony of ants, not just the scouts, were dispatched to *multiple* sources of food whose locations were known. In itself, this is remarkable. In order for the Minoans to trade with anyone outside their own general area, they first needed to leave the island on which they lived- Crete.

Minoan ships were dispatched throughout the Mediterranean Sea. Being a seafaring nation, Minoan ships were able to reduce travel times from years to weeks and months. Minoan cargo vessels were built to carry more than one mule, or ox, or horse, or human could possibly carry. The Minoans brought so much material to the awareness of the western world, that once the western world experienced it, they wanted it. It was the Bronze Age equivalent of using a computer to type a document, after spending years using a typewriter and carbon paper. The western world needed these new materials in great quantities and set about getting as much as it could get. So, when the Greek island of Santorini exploded in 1250 BC or thereabouts, it did not matter. The western world would simply carry on without the Minoans. The Minoans may have been gone, but other civilizations had figured out how to build ocean going cargo ships, and they replaced the Minoan navy and merchant fleets with their own.

One of the other things the explosion in trade caused is that some cities outgrew their own ability to support its burgeoning population. Forced colonization became a common practice. This is when a city-state either asked for volunteers or forced a hundred or so people to move elsewhere. The Greeks did it. The Phoenicians did it. The Assyrians did it! The Persians did it! The Egyptians did it! There are ancient Greek ruins in Sicily and Sardinia that can be visited. I am going to burst some people's bubbles here too, but one of the greatest military leaders of all times- Hannibal Barca, is a descendent of colonizers sent out by a "mother" city. Because the current fad in academia is to attribute to non-western cultures all that is great and noble about western civilization, let me nip this in the bud right now. Hannibal, just like Cleopatra, was *not* of sub-Saharan African descent.

Hannibal is descended from the Phoenicians. The Phoenicians, in about 800 BC, around the time Rome was being founded as well, realized that their population had outgrown their logistics network. As a result, the Phoenicians sent forth colonizers to find a suitable place to live, thereby reducing the population of Phoenicia and the demands on its economy. This new city, as did colonies from other cities, remained loyal to the mother city. The name of this newly established city on the Tunisian shores of the Mediterranean Sea was Carthage. I'll say it again; Hannibal was a Carthaginian descended from Phoenicians. The nearest modern genetic match would be those people from Israel. Yes, Hannibal is more closely related to Jewish people of Israel than any other culture. Now people can more easily not miscast people in movies and television.

The Copper Age lasted from 5,000 BC to 2,500 BC. The Bronze Age lasted from 2,500 BC to 1,200 BC. The Iron Age began in 1,200 BC and is still ongoing but has morphed into the Steel Age; the Oil Age, the Computer Age. Think about all that has taken place in those years around the Mediterranean Sea. Empires have risen and fallen. Knowledge has progressed, regressed and progressed again. Religions have come and gone. Armies have conquered and been conquered. In 7,000 years, the plight of a human went from living in a tent made of animal skins, to multi-story buildings with air conditioning and running water. In case I have yet to say it, I'll say it now, an ancient Roman could live in our world, but we could not live in his. All this progress was brought to the world by western cultures. How else does one explain the fact that all other civilizations have been at least half a millennium behind western civilization?

CHAPTER EIGHT

INVENTIONS AND SOCIAL IMPROVEMENTS

Ninety percent, that's 90%, if not 99% of the inventions that improved the human condition and advanced civilization occurred in the west. You are welcome! It is dishonest for people to claim for instance, that the Chinese invented astronomy 300 years before the west and therefore they invented astronomy because there were no advancements made. The Chinese did not take their new knowledge of the orbit of planets and spread it around the world. It is not dishonest to say the Chinese invented spaghetti. Up until the voyages of Marco Polo, a westerner, no one in the west knew of spaghetti. When Marco Polo returned to Venice, he brought with him amongst other things, spaghetti. He also brought with him gun powder, but the Chinese did not invent the firearm. The Chinese' were using gunpowder as an elixir to extend life and later to make fireworks, rockets.

That brings us to another example. Did the Chinese invent rocketry? No, they did not. Did they make rockets, yes, but they had no intention of launching them into orbit or going to the moon. The contribution of the Chinese to rocketry is very minimal. The most advanced rocket the Chinese came up with is little more than a large bottle rocket. Rocketry was invented in the west. Everyone knows of the advances made by Werner Von Braun and the Nazis during World War 2, but they were not the inventors of rocketry either. That distinction falls to Robert Goddard- The namesake of the Goddard Space Flight Center. Robert Goddard studied rockets for years. He wrote papers on rockets. Von Braun used the research conducted by Goddard to advance his own pre-Nazi research on rockets.

The rockets used by the Chinese in the Middle Ages were not meant to kill. If they did kill, the person was hit by a falling rocket carcass. The purpose of these rockets was psychological. It was a new way of screaming at your enemy. It was a way to make your army seem more fearsome. That is it.

What are the contributions to western civilization from other civilizations? There are some, but they are few. If you google the question, "Inventions made in Africa?" The list is short, and the inventions are minimal. The biggest inventions listed are the invention of mathematics and the medical CT scanner. One is the oldest invention the other is one of the most recent. There are many listings of what was invented in Africa. The problem with the lists though is they claim big, all-encompassing concepts. One of the inventions listed in one list is art. According to the list, art was invented in Africa about 75,000 years ago. Okay, so define art. If someone is using a charred stick to mark on a cave wall the number of animals in the herds that pass the cave every day, is that art? Art is a broad concept as is mathematics. What makes the "artwork" found in a cave in Africa the invention and not the "artwork" found in a cave in France? Did this "artwork" lead to the advancement of civilization. Art is a concept that is in the eye of the beholder. What I consider art, another person may consider scribble.

I have no doubt of the existence of epic African inventions. Claiming mathematics as an invention is a stretch too. There are lots of civilizations that have contributed to modern mathematics. For instance, the concept of the number zero was an advancement made in the Middle East. Prior to that, no one had any concept of there being a zero sum. Roman numerals have no representation of the number zero. To the Romans the first number is one, annotated "I". There is factual proof of this too. The Colosseum in Rome has its entrance portals numbered. There isn't a portal number "zero". Inventories never showed a warehouse with no olive oil. They just showed a line labeled, "olive oil," but there was no zero drawn next to it. The invention of the number "zero" changed economics and mathematics forever even though its existence has yet to be proven. Weird, I know! How can the number zero not be a scientific law as is Newton's First Law of Motion? Here is the reason why mathematicians have yet to prove the number zero exists, "If you have nothing, how can you prove it exists?" The problem with claiming ancient inventions is the pedigree of the invention may not exist.

In modern law, if there is a dispute between who invented something the credit goes to the person whose claims are the oldest. It can be the invention of concrete by the Romans in the centuries before Christ and not the British in the mid-1800s. Or it could be the invention of the telephone by Alexander Graham Bell, where because his patent application was farther down in the stack of other applications for the same invention, he is considered the inventor of the telephone. These people show the pedigree of their invention. Finding a drawing in a cave does not prove an invention. Here's a more recent example of what I mean.

The potato chip. Who invented the potato chip? Popular culture says it was a chef in New York. As the story goes, Chef George Crum, was working at Moon's Lake House in Saratoga Springs, New York, and a demanding customer kept sending back the French fries because they were too thick. So, he sliced them as thin as he could and fried them to a crisp. He sprinkled some salt on them and viola, the potato chip was invented. This was in 1873. That is the pedigree of the potato chip as we know it. However, there is also this guy in Britain who *may* have invented the potato chip sixty years earlier.

The British call potato chips, "Crisps." (I know, who do they think they are? Next thing you know they will be claiming they invented the English language. Everyone knows the English language was invented by the French.) What could be used as proof of pedigree in this case is a recipe book. The book was written by Doctor William Kitchiner, and titled, ***The Cook's Oracle.*** In this book, there is a recipe for slicing potatoes thinly, not more than a quarter of an inch thick and frying them in oil. So, who invented the potato chip? It's a matter of common usage I would think. Just because someone wrote about it in a book, it doesn't mean it was invented by them. Leonardo di Vinci famously made a sketch of a helicopter, but did he invent the helicopter? In 1865, Jules Verne wrote a book where people travelled to the moon. Did Jules Verne invent rockets? By the way Britons, a potato sliced not more than a ¼ inch thick is a "chip" not a "crisp." (Read this next sentence with a British accent.) Besides, everyone knows that a proper crisp has ridges, and Kitchiner didn't say anything about ridges, did he?

Here's a better example of the "who invented what" dilemma, but from a different perspective with arguments for many sides. Even though it has nothing to do with inventing something per se, it will illustrate the dilemma.

The oldest human remains were found in Ethiopia in 1974. The remains were of a female nicknamed Lucy, which were dated to be about 3.2 million years old. Scientifically they are the remains of Australopithecus. That is until about 25 years ago when additional human remains were discovered in a cave in South Africa. These remains were dated to be 3.7 million years old. I need to tell you these aren't the remains of the oldest *human* ever found. They are the remains of the oldest human *ancestor* ever found. These remains could concurrently be the remains the oldest Neanderthal ancestor every found. I fully expect anthropologists to disagree with what I just said. I am only trying to explain the difference between human remains and human ancestor remains. I digress!

What do finding the remains of these 2 ancient humans prove? If you are a black supremacist and race hustler, apparently it proves that human civilization began in Africa and everyone is, therefore, forever indebted to African Americans; all non-Africans are engaging in cultural appropriation! To an anthropologist it may prove that humans evolved in Africa. To the anthropologist attempting to map a timeline of humanity, it could prove the "out of Africa" theory. To someone studying weather and climate, it may prove that parts of Africa have been hot and arid for millions of years enabling human remains to survive for millions of years while most would dissolve completely within a couple hundred years. So, what does finding the oldest human remains in Africa really mean? It means simply that the oldest known human ancestor was *buried* in Africa. That's it! End of story!

Finding the remains in Africa does not prove a civilization in Africa. Finding the remains in Africa does not prove having been born in Africa. Finding the remains in Africa does not prove having lived in Africa. Finding the remains in Africa isn't even proof of having died in Africa. It only proves that the remains were buried in Africa. For all anyone knows, Lucy could have been born in China, kidnapped by aliens, died while being probed, requiring her remains to be thrown out of the spaceship which was coincidentally over Africa and immediately covered by a sandstorm. It is possible that Lucy could have lived her entire life in Australia, but upon her death her kids decided to "bury" her at sea, but the boat never sank subsequently beaching itself in Africa and somehow making its way to the site of burial.

Try to fathom this with an unbiased brain. Doesn't the Out of Africa theory prove the existence of Adam and Eve? Does it not also make the Bible and Torah factual references? If the Out of Africa theory is to be believed, doesn't this mean that *all* species of life, flora and fauna, themselves originate from a single point on earth? Since trilobites can be found in the sandstone layers of the Grand Canyon, does this mean sea life began in Arizona? What the Out of Africa theory asks people to believe is that only humans sprang forth from one single spot on earth. While butterflies as an example, evolved into multiple versions in multiple places from multiple ancestors. For all we know the oldest humans lived in Antarctica, but we have been unable to discover them because they are safely entombed under a mile thick sheet of ice.

The same goes for inventions. Unless you can prove pedigree, you can't claim invention. Throughout the world, there are drawings of carts and chariots with wheels, but we do not know who invented the wheel. Seeing a cave painting on a cave wall showing a wheeled chariot doesn't prove that the wheel was invented by the people who drew the picture. The people who drew the picture could simply be drawing a graphic representation of something they saw while visiting Antarctica thereby making it easier to explain to others what they saw. So, be honest with yourself. Look at all the inventions that have ever been, obsolete or not and answer this question, *"Which of the things that improved the plight of human existence were not invented in western civilizations?"* Your list will be short and concise, I guarantee it.

The western world's greatest invention is the invention of dignity in *all* humans. It took a while, but the western world got there first. Even the abolition of slavery was first attained by the western world. All modern slavery is a result of a resurgent Marxist culture using slavery as a method of controlling the masses to prevent individualism. Oh yea, there's another of the greatest inventions to come out of western culture, Individualism. A concept lost on today's college graduates and Marxist thugs.

CHAPTER NINE

LIBERAL'S AND MARXIST'S HATRED OF WESTERN CIVILIZATION

These past few decades have resulted in the weakening of people. I'm not talking about being physically weakened. I am referring to the weakening of a person's determination and drive. Weakening their ability to overcome adversity. It is now considered chic for a guy to get in touch with his feminine side. Crying is no longer a sign of weakness, it is praised. Men who cry are said to be comfortable in their manhood which we are further told, makes them more attractive to women. These feminized men are the new heroes we must now worship and adore.

Today, no one knows how to deal with pain and emotional distress. We are unable to process adversity as our ancestors who lived through the Great Depression did. If there are no jobs available where we live, we jump up and down screaming, droning on and on that the government must provide us with a job. There exists quite a contrast between us and our recent ancestors. Despite racism and sexism- real or imagined— it was engrained in the minds and psyche of our noble ancestors that if the jobs left Biloxi and ended up in Detroit, then they should move to Detroit if they wanted a job. If they didn't wish to uproot their family they left the family behind, journeyed to where there was work, and sent home their earnings. Did everyone involved walk away with a fairytale ending? No! Were families split apart never to be reunited? Unfortunately, yes. Were parents separated from their children? Absolutely. That was the cost of surviving. Now people expect the jobs to follow them. Everyone wants the new factory to be built near them, but not in a place where it disturbs them.

We should not be calling ourselves, our generation, the "Gen Z'ers," or the "Millennials." We should be calling ourselves the "Cry Baby Generation". That is all we do. If we are not crowned Homecoming King, it's because people are racist. If we aren't given an obscene amount of money a short time after graduating from college with a useless degree, it's sexism. We label our parents losers, but in truth it is we who are the losers. We no longer know how to win, nor do we care to win. We are complacent! We will be the last generation before major changes are made to our way of life. It is our complacency causing low birth rates. We have become hardwired through millennia of human evolution to look for a mate that can survive. Give me a Viking warrior woman and I will personally re-populate the United States. Okay, I'll re-populate the United States after I explain to her about bathing and brushing her teeth.

If you don't think music affects popular culture and how people treat others, you have never read the love poems of a wannabe rapper. I have! Their idea of a love poem has nothing to do with love. It's about submission! Their poems are about how they want power over another person. I have watched reaction videos where a social media personality listens to songs from the early days of rock and roll. The reactions the women have are always the same. They end up crying or close to crying. The women explain their tears are because of the music or the singer has a beautiful voice. What they don't realize is in these cases it is the lyrics. These women have been raised on "love songs" that express how the man wants to exploit their bodies for sexual gratification.

The great Paul McCartney has said in the past and I am paraphrasing, when it comes to hit songs, the lyrics don't matter. It's all about the music. That's quite revealing. But is Paul McCartney qualified to say that? Do I really need to answer that question? I better because there are people in United States, living in major cities who have no idea of Paul McCartney's identity. No, the words don't matter most of the time. But one must take into account a person's needs. We all want to feel needed. We all need an ego boost occasionally. We all seek some form of validation. So, when a woman hears a 1950s love song, regardless of lyrical corniness, she cries because the lyrics are verbal representation of Prince Charming telling her how beautiful she is, how he wishes to care for her. Or how *she* could, by whispered breath, subdue a Viking warrior. And, unfortunately, no one has ever serenaded her with a song that supports her dreams.

125

Here's a question that will prove my point of our needs. It's a question whose answer is widely known by everyone even before the question is asked, the answer is known and the answer never changes. It's a trick question. It's a trick question in that those asking aren't asking the question because there is quantitative value in the answer. They are looking for the intrinsic value, the emotional value. They are asking the question not for the answer, but for the dopamine response they get when the proper answer is uttered. They are looking for validation from another human being. So, what then is the question?

"Do these pants make my butt look big?"

No man on earth, except maybe Sir Mix a Lot, would dare answer that question by saying, "Yes!" If they did, it's because they are either insane or they are purposely picking a fight. So, why do women cry and are rendered speechless when they hear songs like "Unchained Melody" by the Righteous Brothers, and not rap songs? It's the words the rapper wrote being in stark contrast to the words written by a poet years ago. In short, it's because women don't have anyone talking to them in the words of a poet from yesteryear.

Liberals allowed this to happen. In years past, if a poem was deemed raunchy or "X-rated", it was not published. Look at the poems written in Elizabethan England. Some of the poems are downright pornographic even by today's standards. However, at the time they were written they may not have been published and the only reason we know of those poems is through pure luck. People's morality played a key role in their lives, whereas today, liberals and Marxists claim everything is art or protected speech. That is unless its speech or art that shows their amoral ways. I'll say it again, liberalism is the embryonic stage of Marxism, Socialism and Communism.

CHAPTER TEN

THE WORLD WITHOUT WESTERN CIVILIZATION

What would the world look like today if Western Civilization had not made the advancements that it did? What would have become of Native American civilization had the "white man" not discovered the New World. Well, had the "white man" not discovered and conquered the New World, native Americans would still be walking everywhere. Horses are not indigenous to the New World. Yes, herds of bison millions of head strong would still be roaming the Great Plains of America—Food for many native American tribes. But these tribes would still be hunting on foot. Remember, no horses.

Communism would not have been invented, or maybe it would have been, but not thoroughly defeated and shunned afterwards. Patriarchal society would not have been tempered by a matriarchy. Tribalism and slavery would still be running rampant. No one would be able to travel abroad without the fear of being kidnapped and enslaved by another clan twenty miles away. The population of the world would be much less due to diseases. Human beings would not be at the top of the food chain.

Western civilization civilized the world, FACT! How do I know this? Because Marco Polo went to China; The great Kahn didn't come to Venice. Montezuma didn't land in Spain; Cortez landed in Mexico. The Shogun didn't send a samurai army to San Francisco to demand the United States accept Japanese wares; Commodore Perry and the US Navy anchored in Tokyo Bay and demanded Japan trade with the US. Western civilizations fanned out throughout the world while all others stagnated and went away.

SECTION 3

UM, SAY WHAT?

Chapter Eleven

Communicating

In today's fast-paced world where instant gratification is a must, being able to properly communicate with each other is a necessity. However, we are having problems in that area. The problem society has communicating with each other is caused by the social justice warriors coming out of colleges. They have paralyzed members of society into believing that all conversations must use *"the perfect words"* every time. Additionally, they have created a second requirement where we must not only use the perfect word every time, but of the multiple options we have, it must be the first word used- The perfect word! The words must be perfect right now, not when we think about it later. There is no leeway. The phrase, "For lack of a better word," shall never be used again.

There is a third and equally absurd requirement imposed by the idiot-morons with college degrees now infesting many corporate board rooms- You must take into account the feelings of *anyone* who may hear or read the message being conveyed. It does not matter if the person is part of the conversation either. If anyone can hear the conversation in passing, if they watch a video of the conversation three weeks later, if a conversation is being had by two people and a third person walking by hears a word which they deem to be offensive to themselves, then that unconcerned third party can file a complaint and have someone fired. It does not matter if they overheard the entire conversation or just that word, the newly offended lout can have a person fired.

In itself, that is frightening enough. This should scare the crap out of everyone. There is no way for the offending parties to defend themselves because HR departments themselves are populated with useless slugs who are never required to admit *their* mistakes. If a person in the HR department says you did it, then you did it. Even if you have high quality video evidence, with sound showing that it wasn't you who committed the offense, if HR says you did it, you are guilty and they are not wrong. They are HR!

Let's talk about the phrase "for lack of a better word" for a minute. In the past when a person said the phrase, it told the listener that the person speaking knows the word they are about to use isn't the correct word, but at the moment, for some reason they can't think of the correct word. Today when a person utters that phrase, it means they are about to offend someone. And no one must ever be offended ever again. Instead, we are taught in training sessions and retreats that we must never start a sentence until our entire thought has matured, and we have found the perfect words. All the perfect words. Yes, the listener must endure a period of uncomfortable silence while the correct words are all determined.

The phrase, "stream of consciousness" no longer exists. Holier-than-thou-do-gooders have now deemed that in the communication process the message itself no longer matters! What matters is that no one ever feels hurt or offended in any way. Remember that! If you use the wrong word someone may feel hurt causing them to focus on their feelings and ultimately miss the message. It means nothing to these people that some thoughts are fleeting never to return, or that the new extended deliberation process of message formulation may cause the reason for sending the message in the first place may be forgotten. These days what you are trying to say means nothing.

In my own experience, on many occasions, as I was climbing the ladder of success, multiple supervisors taught me to never be the guy with a secret. In other words, if I saw something was wrong, I was taught to tell someone about that something and not keep it a secret. I was also taught that no matter how much I dreaded calling someone in the middle of the night, in emergent times I should do just that. I might dread calling them because I wouldn't want to be called while I was sleeping, but that is one of the benefits of being a supervisor. Well, that and the much larger paycheck.

However, in the past couple years of employment I have personally experienced supervisors not caring about the message. Instead, they were more concerned that someone might get their feelings hurt. It is so bad in Corporate America, if a supervisor thinks you are about to call out a co-worker for something which may show that person in a bad light, they will lie to you to protect that co-worker and themselves. It is also a function of them not wanting to have a paper trail which would show the supervisor's incompetence.

Once in a pass down email, while trying to convey to my supervisor and my co-workers how much work still needed to be done before a major inspection on a major piece of equipment by the federal government, I named one of my co-worker's. My supervisor and his supervisor lost their collective minds. They weren't upset that six hours before the inspection there were still 5 hours of work that needed to be completed. It didn't even cross their arrogant minds that for the preceding 7 days I was the *only* person who did any of the work on the equipment being inspected. No! They were only concerned that someone *might* be offended.

Allow me to fill in a couple of gaps. They didn't care that for six straight days I was the only one working on the equipment. They didn't give a rat's ass that neither of my four co-workers did any work on the equipment whatsoever. Nope! They didn't realize that no one else had done any work until my email. An email- as were the five previous pass-down emails that week- lacking any sentence where I complained about being the only person working to get the equipment ready for the inspection. Emails in which I had every right to complain about my co-workers' lack of work, because it wasn't a one-off occurrence. It happens every year and every year it is the same. My co-workers did next to nothing, and my supervisor never realized it.

The most insulting part of all is that by the end of the whole evolution, I ended up being counselled. Why? Because even though I personally expended 20 honest-to-God man-hours each week doing 95% of the work, while my co-workers did the remaining 5% and claimed to have expended 100 man-hours of work *each*. To my supervisors it was business as usual. They were upset because in an email I mentioned one of my co-workers by name. In their minds, my use of a person's name in the email was so egregious, I was formally counselled with

HR as a witness against me to protect my supervisor. To them I had no cause to be upset.

The American people really are stupid

I am going to utter a phrase that would be political suicide for a politician to say, but deep down they know to it to be true.

The American people really are stupid.

How many times have politicians gone on television and explained how the American people are waking up to whatever is the cause du jour because they aren't stupid? How many times following elections have these supposedly not stupid people done the exact same thing they have been doing for 20 years, then ranted on and on about how nothing ever changes? Every day leading to an election everyone complains. Every day after the election everyone complains. Even on election day, these not stupid Americans can be heard complaining that nothing ever changes as they cast their vote for the same politicians who have been in office for thirty years!

How many television shows or YouTube videos showing people incorrectly answering simple questions about American history must we endure before the American people collectively have an epiphany. I hope it comes soon because I for one, am tired of hearing the supposedly smart electorate claim we fought against Great Britian during World War 2. I'm sure there are people out there who can answer the questions correctly. I know there are smart people out there. I have had conversations with them. But, when a reporter asks someone to comment on a political debate that never happened, and the person to whom they directed the question responds with something other than, "I didn't watch the debate," it's time to start flogging people in the street, figuratively speaking.

A better way for me to phrase my earlier statement, "The American people really are stupid," would be to say, "Collectively, the American people are stupid." It seems that every time people gather in groups to discuss things, the average IQ of the group plummets. There is a good reason for this. It's because the group doesn't necessarily take its cues from its members who are truly knowledgeable on the subject being discussed. In many cases, the group takes its cues from the person who speaks the loudest or the person who won't stop talking. In both cases, it is these people who become the de facto leaders of the discussion. Every one of us has had to endure this type of person. They are almost impossible to miss because they hate being ignored. They usually make their presence known a day or two after they hear a true subject matter expert explain something. They can be picked out of a crowd easily because they walk around with puffed out chests and suddenly using words and catch phrases they noticed a subject matter expert using when they were talking to people.

If you would like to see this happen in real time, watch a news program. You will bear witness to the anchorman or anchorwoman suddenly becoming experts on the subject at hand. This happens for every story. One story they will be discussing federal law, and the next story they will discuss how to properly make a velouté sauce. How did this happen? Because a few minutes before a camera was shoved in their face, they spoke with someone who is truly an expert on the matter, or because the expert was on their show the previous day.

Here's an example. Prior to September 11th, 2001, no one in the media ever cared about the US Marine base in Cuba. In fact, prior to 9/11, the only time members of the media had ever realized there was a Marine Corp base in Cuba was when they watched the movie <u>A Few Good Men</u>. In that movie Jack Nicolson's character was the Commanding Officer of the Marine Corps Base. Prior to September 11, 2001 members of the media couldn't even tell you the name of the base- Guantanamo Bay. After 9/11, more specifically when the US military started capturing terrorists and there became a need to house the terrorists, the high paid frauds behind the news desks suddenly knew everything there is to know about Guantanamo Bay. Once it was determined this was where the prisoners would be housed, the media stumbled all over themselves trying to sound like experts. They started calling the base, Gitmo.

For those of you who are unfamiliar with the concept, Gitmo is the unofficial abbreviation for Guantanamo Bay. It's what US Navy and Marine Corps personnel have been calling Guantanamo Bay for decades. These boots on the ground types call Guantanamo Bay "Gitmo" because if one is required to say Guantanamo Bay more than twice a day, there arises a need to use fewer syllables because saying Guantanamo Bay is a mouthful. After a while it does sort of roll off one's tongue poetically, but it's a bit of a tongue twister. So, those that were stationed there began calling the base, "Gitmo." It's the jargon of those who are intimately familiar with the base.

Journalists have their jargon too. Rubes on the street call the people who write a news story the story's author. Journalists say, "The story's by line."

The abbreviation evolved over time with the military personnel. The media had nothing to do with it. They began calling the base Gitmo from the start. The media skipped a couple steps in their use of the abbreviation, though. To this day they probably can't pronounce the proper name. I don't begrudge people using abbreviations if a name or word is difficult to pronounce. I'm upset that reporters sit at their broadcast desks, and with arrogance and puffed out chests, they use the abbreviation in a tone that would suggest expertise. The anchors need everyone to know that they aren't simply reading words off a teleprompter. They needed everyone to know that *they* are experts, and that *they* have a history with Guantanamo Bay. To this day, if you ask a news anchor what Gitmo stands for, most will look upon your inquisitive face with blank stare because they have no idea. To them it has always been, "Gitmo."

There's a better way, and it's probably the best way, for me to restate my earlier statement where I said, "The American people really are stupid." It would be better to say we are clueless. We walk around not knowing things which we should know. Seriously, how many of us know the name of our town's mayor? What about the names of the people sitting behind the raised dais' at city council meetings? Many of us don't even know the names of our federal senators and representatives. When we are confronted with our ignorance, we shrug our shoulders, giggle and make up an excuse about why it is okay for us to be under informed. Obviously, no one can know everything.

One of the reasons modern societies have become so successful is because past societies recognized that no one person can know and do everything. Society subsequently distributed its collective knowledge amongst the whole of society. No longer was one person, the village elder, the repository for all knowledge and wisdom. As society began to advance from the Stone Age to the Copper Age to the Bronze Age in rapid succession, society's knowledge became the dominion of artisans. The knowledge of the blacksmith was entrusted to the Smith family. The knowledge of sewing became the domain of the Taylor family. Other than maintaining this knowledge and advancing it through the technological ages, society's only other ask of its members was to not get a knowledge tunnel vision where the only knowledge a person deemed necessary was knowledge of their tradecraft. The American society has jumped headfirst into tradecraft tunnel vision in recent years.

Every trade, be it of doctors, nurses, lawyers, electricians, welders, now constantly delude themselves into believing that society will fail if their profession goes extinct. In this book, and I consider myself to be amongst them, history is replete with examples of tradesmen believing this. Think about the occupations which today are not needed, but 60 years ago were essential. Think about all the professions that were once prevalent but are now extinct except for those being kept alive by nostalgic organizations. Think about the door-to-door salesman, phone company switchboard operators, news anchors. Yes, news anchors, your pretty faces are slowly being replaced by independent journalists, computers, microphones, and the internet. The sad part is the news media knows it. If the nighttime news anchor wasn't in jeopardy, news outlets would have no need to turn every purported news show into an opinion show with 10 hysterical pundits. News anchors have become the babbling Betty's at a church social who are only in attendance for the drama.

How does this prove that Americans are clueless? Think about what happens when people get tunnel vision. They don't notice things they should. When a catastrophe occurs, investigations often show people getting tunnel vision during the emergency. This is due to the stress of the situation. *The pilot was so focused on getting #2 engine back online after it lost thrust, he forgot to keep track of his altitude and BLAM...into the ground at 600 mph.* It's sad to think about, but it happens. We want to believe that people with thousands of hours of experience are not susceptible to such things, but they are. In the end, they are human beings.

That is the cluelessness we have bestowed upon ourselves. We have convinced ourselves that because of our profession or because of our individual intelligence we will know instinctively if something is amiss, and we get tradecraft tunnel vision. We forget that while we are at work, we are thinking only of what we are doing in the moment. We aren't paying attention to what is happening in other aspects of society. When we go home after a hard day's work, we don't want to watch the news because we work in the real world and therefore we know what is happening. Just as we have through constant proclamations, taught young people that college graduates are "all knowing", we have bamboozled ourselves into thinking we know what is happening with our government and society as a whole with no inquiry whatsoever.

It's to the point where we don't know who to trust to tell us the facts of a certain matter. It's sad that I have to say this, but if it weren't true, I wouldn't have to say this. We blindly believe the people we elect to high office would never deceive us. Even with countless examples of corruption, some of us refuse to believe our leaders are corrupt and we continuously make excuses for them. It has become so bad that our elected officials have come to believe they don't need to tell us what they are doing in our name. *To see what's in the bill, we first have to pass the bill.*

So yes, Americans are stupid!

CHAPTER TWELVE

POLITICAL CORRECTNESS AND THE MECHANICS OF LANGUAGE

Use of Language

Throughout this section I will find the need to say something over and over. However, out of concern for the reader, I will only say this one time.

If you are an English teacher, you need to start speaking up.

You need to stop being offended. If you are one of the people perpetuating this fraud, you need to choke down your pride and admit you have been wrong. Let people communicate freely. It is beyond me why I have yet to turn on the news and see *any* high school English teacher scolding people about their improper use of the English. The people who routinely corrected my grammar and spelling have now become deaf and mute. Because of this I have lost all respect for you. I'm not talking about accents and regional dialects. I am talking about people using the wrong word because they are too lazy to look it up. I'm talking about people using phrases simply because they think it makes them sound knowledgeable and mature.

"You've got your work cut out for you," comes to mind. No, you are not saying it ironically. What happened, as it usually does, is someone heard someone they adored say it in one situation and when they found themselves in a similar situation, they repeated the phrase simply because the situations were similar. They did not think about the situation. They did not think about the context. They simply repeated a phrase they heard someone else say. It's not that they said the wrong phrase (in this case they did), rather, it's that they said the phrase incorrectly. Think about that phrase. When people say it, they are telling people all the work finished; There is nothing for them to do; Only the easy stuff

is left. But what they mean is there is much work to do; That they are going to spend hours and hours doing the work; That all the work will be strenuous. Saying phrases in an ironic sense is no way to convey a thought. Saying phrases in an ironic sense requires sarcasm for it to be properly interpreted. I am a big fan of sarcasm, but only when used in a proper context.

Here is the biggest problem I have with how the English language is being used. For some reason hysterical people who should be sent to an insane asylum for a couple days merely for observation are claiming words are offensive. But they only do it for the English language. When was the last time there was a news report explaining that when addressing a group of people of both sexes, deferring to the masculine form of a Spanish word is insulting to women. Or that the feminine form of a French word is insulting because it insinuates the subjugation of women. All languages, after thousands of years of evolution, have assigned masculine and feminine properties to their words. Some words have only one form. Some languages assign feminine attributes to an object, while in another language that same object is considered masculine.

The best example of this is when referring to a ship or boat. In the United States, we assign female attributes to ship. Therefore, we address ships as, "She," and "Her." *She is the best ship to ever sail upon the seas.* Or *I have never seen a ship plow through the waves like her.* Whereas in Russia they use the masculine pronouns. However, there are women in this world ready to scream bloody murder if we dare to call a ship, "Her." To them it is sexist. They will never be happy. Their lives are so perfect they are inventing problems just so they can be offended. These women need to be ignored.

This has been going on for decades. Suddenly, one day in the 1980s calling a woman a secretary became sexist. Even though for years, decades, centuries even, men were doing the job and had no problem being called a secretary. In fact, using the word secretary to describe the job is a situation not unlike the chicken and the egg debate. Did the job title come from the type of desk, or was the desk named after the title of the person sitting at the desk. Yes, there is a desk called a secretary. Being called a secretary is only offensive to women when

138

the job title "secretary" is not followed by the word, "of." Not once, during all their theatrics, do people ever claim offense when women are burdened with the title, "Secretary of State."

Another example of the feigned offense is the use of the word stewardess. We are required to call them flight attendants. However, what would they be called if these newly minted flight attendants were working on a ship. We can't call them flight attendants because they aren't flying. The masculine form of stewardess is steward. All male stewardesses are therefore called stewards. Even on early passenger flights when flights from San Francisco to Guam took 3 days, the men who attended to the needs of the passengers were called stewards. The men who attended to the needs of passengers on the RMS Titanic were call stewards. Once again, no man was ever offended by the word. It was only when the feminists of the 1960s and 1970s attained positional power that the offense was noted. No stewardess ever complained about how the job title offended them. The same goes for the word host. Why is no woman offended by the word hostess?

It is imperative that we stop listening to hysterical activists. Their hysteria is only for the English language, not all languages.

To the idiots in the US Congress, the correct word is, "lady." The correct word is not "gentlelady!" Also, the phrase is, "Ladies and gentlemen," not, "Gentleladies and gentlemen." I bring this up because once again our leaders have shown us their utter stupidity. It is infuriating. When Hillary Clinton was running for president, people began wondering how Bill Clinton would be addressed should Hillary be elected. When Bill Clinton was president, Hillary was called the First Lady, not the First Gentlelady.

When you say, "The gentlelady from…" you are being redundant. A lady is the female equivalent of a gentlemen. Women who embody poise and grace are called and have always been called, "Ladies." If you find it insulting to be called a lady, you need to go have your head examined. You should not be a member of Congress because you are creating a conflict where no conflict exists. The conflict is in your head because you have an inferiority complex.

We need to stop using foreign words when there are perfectly good English words that can be used. It used to be funny when people first started doing it, now it's insulting. By constantly using foreign words over English words we are saying the English language is inadequate. When it really means that we are too lazy and dumb to use a thesaurus. Don't say something is *uber* exciting, say it is *very* exciting, or extremely exciting.

Twenty years ago, if we used the term "tidal wave" we were referring to a very, very big wave. That's it! No one had a problem with it. It was the freaks in academia, the ones always needing to show people how intelligent they are who cried. Through alligator tears they decided that they needed to teach us the *true* definition of the words. The media is culpable in this too! The media morons are great at pointing out that some words have multiple meanings when they get caught lying, but not this time. The media never question academia. Academia contains smart people. Smart people to whom they bow down and worship but who are incapable of getting a job anywhere else because people might realize they are truly retarded. But the media trots them out and elevates them above the little folk every day. It baffles the media how people with varying degrees of intelligence can hear a sentence containing a word that has five definitions, and how many people can inexplicably manage to always interpret the sentence as intended.

It is insulting how our superiors in the media try to make themselves sound smart by using foreign words instead of using the perfectly fine words we have in English. Let's use the words tidal wave now being called a "tsunami" as an example. Why? What is the definition of a tidal wave? A really big wave. The word tidal has long been used as another way of saying something is "very large" without actually saying "very large". *It is colossal, it is giant, it is tidal.* Up until the 1990s in the United States we did just that, we called a huge wave, an abnormally large wave, a tidal wave. But then, as I mentioned earlier the smart people in academia got their panties in a bunch. They began arguing that the only true tidal waves are the twice daily ocean tides. When the tide is high, the crest of the tidal wave has arrived. When the trough of the tidal wave has arrived, it's low tide. They are taking the word tidal and defining it literally instead of metaphorically, figuratively, or whatever the word would be.

Oceanographers want us to believe that the twice daily tides are properly called "tidal waves" simply because "tide" is the root word of "tidal." They argue that because tidal waves are created when water is displaced as a result of the seismic actions of the earth's crust and not by the gravitational pull of celestial bodies, it is incorrect to call a tidal wave a tidal wave. Instead of going with the fact that different languages have different words for the same object oceanographers opt to proclaim that "tsunami" is the proper term and they will not hesitate to correct people.

But why? Why is "tidal wave" incorrect and "tsunami" correct? Because they tell us, the label must reflect the source or cause. However, in Japanese, "Tsunami" means "harbor wave" not "really big wave." I am curious to know what the Japanese call a tidal wave. Surely, the most seismically active country in the world has a word for that type of wave. Maybe "tsunami" is the word the Japanese use for that type of wave, but it doesn't mean using the term tidal wave to describe a really big wave is incorrect. Tidal wave is the term used when speaking English and when speaking Japanese, it's tsunami. Both can be correct. Just as in English the words are man and men whereas, in Italian the words are uomo and uomini. Ironically, the scientists who chastise everyone for incorrectly using the term "tidal wave" are themselves, using the term tidal wave incorrectly in their reasoning.

If people are going to insist that we name things after their source or cause as is the case of the tidal wave, then saying that the twice daily tides are true tidal waves is incorrect as well. Based on the metrics used by the all-knowing academics, the proper name for the twice daily tides would not be to call the tides a tidal wave, it would be to call them gravity waves. Why? Because the twice daily tides are created by sun's gravity and the moon's gravity tugging on the earth's surface. The ocean tides don't just happen. Named for the source, right? *But, but, but…gravity waves occur in outer space when large objects like stars and galaxies explode.* Well, rat spit, here's the solution to that childish retort. Us little guys should continue using the term "tidal wave" while the oceanographers and the

141

physicists of the world argue over whose use of the term "gravity wave" is the most correct.

We could just as easily start calling a tidal wave a "titanic" wave. Over time the word titanic has come to be mean large, also. A person could argue that the ship was named Titanic because it was meant to signify to people that the ship was really big. Which it was. At the time the RMS Titanic was one of the largest steam ships built. She was one of three ships in a new class of ocean steamer. Her two sisters, the RMS Britannic and the RMS Olympic, were equal to her in size. The Olympic was launched first and was at sea steaming when the Titanic struck an iceberg and sank. It was the number of deaths which cemented the name Titanic in our lexicon. Had there not been such a great loss of life when the Titanic sank, we may very well have adopted the name Britannic or Olympic to convey something as being larger than anything known to man. Olympic (as in the Greek Gods, Mount Olympus) is used to describe objects as being excessively large, but not in the same vein as saying something is Titanic in size.

Here's another example of people using foreign words for no reason. If a person were to watch a documentary or a news report from today where World War 2 in the Pacific is the subject, inevitably the subject of the Japanese suicide pilots arises. The Japanese called them kamikazes. We called them suicide pilots. No one has ever had an issue with us calling them suicide pilots. In fact, every time the subject is brought up in the documentaries what is usually said is, "…Japanese kamikaze, or suicide pilots…" the word Kamikaze is *always* defined as if people, after 80 years, still don't know what it means in this context. Sometime the narrators only say suicide pilots and omit calling them kamikazes. Why the double standard? I don't know.

Here is another example.

On 6 August 2022, there was a ticker tape headline scrolling across the bottom of the screen talking about an island off the coast of Maryland having off its coast a "tornadic waterspout." What the hell is that? Do fools in the media do this on purpose? What the hell is a "tornadic waterspout?" You say it's a tornado-like waterspout. Okay, so what is a non-tornado like waterspout? The point I am trying to make is that calling it a "tornadic waterspout" is redundant. A waterspout is a vortex on water, whereas a tornado is a vortex on land. A waterspout sucks up water whereas a tornado sucks up land. They are the same thing. You watch, here in couple years when reports of waterspouts become more frequent- caused by climate change as will be reasoned- news anchors, news reporters, and know-it-alls in general will stop calling them waterspouts and start using a term used by the Portuguese or by Iranians. *Such hatred for the English language.*

To combat the crisis of the people who should know better constantly misusing words either ignorantly or on purpose, I propose the following for the reader's consideration. It is time to require that an annual vocabulary certification be placed upon those person's working in certain professions, and to make the renewal of their licenses contingent upon their passing the test. I am thinking we should mandate this for *all* media personalities (journalists, actors, news anchors, et al.), as well as lawyers. Why lawyers? Because if it weren't for lawyers, we would have no need for lawyers. (Think about it!)

They will be tested on spelling and definitions. They should be required to prove that they can use words properly. For extra credit, they can take the list of words on which they are being tested and make another list containing different words with the same meaning (synonyms) and the words which have the opposite meaning (antonyms). This test can be an open book test, but they can only bring one book. I'd be willing to bet that no one will think about bringing a dictionary.

Here are a few examples of why certain professions need annual vocabulary tests. It happens multiple times a day. The proper word is:
- Preventive, not preventative.
- Regardless, not irregardless.
- Set foot, not step foot. A person sets foot upon, and they step into…
- This isn't a word- Inc. It's the abbreviation for a word. When you are reading a sentence and come upon the abbreviation Inc. you read out the word as if it weren't abbreviated.
- The name of the movie is, "Monsters Incorporated." Not "Monsters, Ink"

- Acronyms and abbreviations are not the same thing. Acronyms are words made up of abbreviations of other words, such as, "RADAR," "SONAR," and "AWOL." Acronyms are read as if they are words. CIA is not an acronym, it's an abbreviation. LOL is not an acronym it, too, is an abbreviation. They are not being pronounced as if they are words. We say, "C, I, A." We don't say, "Chi uh," "Key uh," or "Cee eee uh."
- When spelling out the Star Wars droid's name R2-D2, the number "2" is spelled Two, not "Too." By the way, R2D2 is a model number not a name. Think about this, in many Star Wars movies other droids are known as R4s. No one is going spell it out, "Are For."

Speaking of Star Wars, allow me to digress for a bit. These few paragraphs are for any person born after 1995. These people should never be allowed to provide commentary on the Star Wars franchise. I wish to God they were never allowed to write the scripts for the Episode 7 through 9, but alas it has been broken. I don't care if it is Episode 1 or Episode 1,000,000, people born after 1995 should never be allowed to opine on these movies. They should resist the urge to voice their opinion and keep them to themselves. I have watched multiple documentaries that discuss these movies and how they have mesmerized audiences for over half a century. And whenever anyone born after 1995 voices their opinion, it becomes readily apparent that these people have been taught-trained- to always look for a reason to be offended. They never seem to grasp why the movies were and still are so successful.

To the people born after 1995, when you experience these movies, much of your experience is based on you innately comparing the Star Wars movies to films that were made years and decades after the original Star Wars trilogy. When you complain that the special effects look cheesy, your baseline for how the special effects look in the Star Wars movies is based on how specials effects look in contemporary movies. To properly understand the effect Star Wars had on people you need to compare the Star Wars movies to the other movies at the time. You also need to take into account what was happening in the world at the time. Why? Because the special effects in modern movies are the grandchildren of the Star Wars special effects. Star Wars invented modern special effects. If you want to appreciate the special effects in Star Wars (not <u>Star Wars, A New Hope</u>, Or <u>Star Wars Episode 4</u>) you need to spend a couple weeks watching other movies from the 1970s. These other movies will show you not only how special effects looked prior to and for some time following the release of <u>Star Wars</u>, but they will also show you what was considered to be a good movie at the time. Try not to laugh at the costumes.

Further, and this goes for *all* movies. If you find yourself sitting in a theater unable to enjoy the movie because you can't get over the subliminal messaging, you need to keep your mouth shut. The other people in attendance of that movie don't care about your purported dog whistles. They are there to escape reality for a couple hours. Only a brainwashed college student or college graduate at any degree level can look at the wide variety of alien life depicted in <u>Star Wars</u> and emphatically claim that one alien depiction is representing the African American race, and it is therefore offensive. Or that it is somehow a subliminal message of white supremacy. Why can't you let people find enjoyment in movies? I can guarantee this to you, in 1977 when <u>Star Wars</u> was released for the first time, no one who watched it left the theater complaining that the movie was racist. No one! Neither the person who watched the movie fifty times in one year nor the person who only saw it once left the movie feeling offended. People who find a need to analyze things ruin those things for everyone else. Why can't a poem just be a poem? Why can't a movie simply tell a story?

Back to the subject at hand…

Using the incorrect word, or adding syllables in the above respects, has become so common place that spell check does not recognize "preventative" as an incorrect spelling. This is the fault of all the people who know better not correcting the person making an error. It could also be the fault of those who make the mistakes not being able to take criticism because they are immature. It's one thing to spell "harbor" using "our" because one form of the word is the Americanized spelling, and the other is the King's English. It's the same as one person saying, "Do not go in there," while another person says, "Don't go in there." Saying "preventative," is either someone being too lazy to find out the correct pronunciation, or someone thinking that adding syllables to a word somehow proves or adds to their credibility.

Calling a group of buildings a "campus" does not make it a school. It's in the same vein of people thinking that wearing a colorful shirt miraculously makes their muffin top a cupcake. Don't fret though, I know what you are doing. By calling an office complex a campus, people are insinuating that the place where they work deals with children, or that it is a place of higher learning; that the company's process does not matter; that the company does what it does for the greater good. Those involved are trying to get immediate immunity for all social, and most legal infractions. Law enforcement is more apt to look the other way if the company is considered "school-like."

Tell me I am wrong! Tell me that when a company gets caught doing unspeakable things that the CEO is not hoping people will give the company the benefit of the doubt simply because he called the company's building(s) a campus and not a complex. Everyone knows this is what is hoped. CEOs do this because when people hear the word "campus," they automatically without thought, think of a school. When they think of school they think of children. Cynically, when people think about schools and kids, they think of elementary, junior high and high schools. Rarely do they think of colleges and universities where there are fully grown men and women roaming freely. If they do think places of higher learning, they think of "smart" people…but that isn't always the case. The word you are looking for is either complex or compound- NOT CAMPUS!

I heard someone on the news today refer to The White House and its collection of buildings as a campus. The White House has been called a complex or a compound since before most people were born. That person needs to quit acting like they are still in school and grow up. If they wish to act like they are still in school, they should go back to school and stay there. They should go back to school and continue to live in their Marxist bubble while concurrently leaving everyone else alone. They could wallow there in the knowledge that they are unable to cope with conflict unlike 90% of the world. To them the only way they can deal with a difficult situation is to change the language in an effort to make people think they are smarter than their actions would suggest.

They won't say compound because of the conditioning they endured as they progressed from one level of education to the next. This conditioning borders on brainwashing and thus won't allow them to use the word compound to describe a place *they* frequent. To them a compound is a place where religious cults reside. When they hear the word "compound," this conditioning causes them to instantly picture in their heads a bunch of disheveled red necks running around in woodland green camouflage while calling themselves a militia. They have also been conditioned to immediately believe that all compounds are safe havens for white supremacists.

The people who can't hear a word, any word, without being offended need to act like adults who take responsibility for their actions. Right now, they are adults that make mistakes but then blame other people. That makes them children. When they go on television blaming other people for their mistakes, they become CRY BABIES! This makes the guys- the men- who act like this CRY BABY SISSY PANTS! Oh no, did I hurt someone's tender feelings, again?!?! If I did, here is the remedy which will allow them to survive the danger filled next several days of their lives. To make it easy, I will give it to them by the numbers:

Step 1: Stop what you are doing.
Step 2: Go home.
Step 3: Get in the shower.
Step 4: Turn on the water.
Step 5: Curl up on the floor in the fetal position
Step 6: Stick your thumb in your mouth.
Step 7: Commence sucking.
Step 8: After 10 minutes of thumb sucking:

If you feel like you can safely rejoin a world where 99.999999999999% of its inhabitants neither know you nor care about your feelings, you may return to your previously scheduled activity.

If after 10 minutes you can't think of what I just told you without bursting into tears again, continue sucking your thumb until someone comes to check on you. (Hint: No one is going to check on you for a very long time so get comfortable. They have better things to do than to wipe your runny nose, call you precious, and tell you other people are simply big meanies.)

The whole point of this section is to get people to realize they are either using the wrong words or are using words incorrectly. It is also to get people to stop thumbing their nose at proper grammar. Being unable to properly speak is not cool, and it does not show that a person is protesting. Nor does it give a person "street cred." It shows laziness and it is one of the reasons people don't do well in job interviews. It's not because the company doesn't like to hire minorities.

Joseph Pulitzer, yes, that guy again, did not speak English when he arrived in the United States in the middle of the Civil War. And,

> "He was admitted to the bar, apparently in 1868, but his youth, his imperfect English and odd appearance kept important clients at a distance."
> <u>Pulitzer,</u> W.A. Swanberg, page 9

Bad grammar can reflect negatively on a company causing potential customers to go to the company's competitors. For this next example, I cannot believe the fictional character from the TV show The <u>Big Bang Theory</u> Dr. Sheldon Cooper never raised this point. "Dr. Cooper" was able to correct the most obscure grammar and vocabulary mistakes but was unable to correct the other characters' chronic misuse of these two words. It's chronically misused by most people in real life too.

These two words *are not* synonyms. A certain online dictionary listing them as synonyms of each other is wrong. They don't mean the same thing. You cannot use these two words interchangeably.

Jealous

Envious

I cannot count the number of times in the past week, and every week prior, and every week yet to come, I have heard someone use these words incorrectly. It is absolutely infuriating. Not simply because they are using the words incorrectly but because they are trying once again, to elicit a reaction. They are not trying to convey a thought. People use words and phrases to communicate. Almost every time, 99% of the time I'd surmise, when people say they are jealous, they really mean that they are envious. Only once have I heard someone use either of these words correctly. Allow me to define these two words for the chronically illiterate members of media.

Jealousy is the feeling a person gets when they are afraid of losing something.

Whereas,

Envy is the feeling a person gets when they crave something had by someone else.

Envy is a cardinal sin. Envy is forbidden by the Ten Commandments. (Thou shalt not covet thy neighbor's wife, nor his ass.) If someone wishes to do some deep thinking on the Ten Commandments ponder this, does this particular commandment outlaw being alive? That is to say, when we are hungry is hunger not a form of envy? And if so, is this commandment telling the faithful to starve themselves to death?

When a person is informed that a co-worker is going to Barbados on vacation, they are beset with feelings of envy, not jealousy. The proper response is to say, "I am envious," or "I envy you!? The *incorrect* response is, "I am jealous."

Time to really irk some activists. All activists, including their media enablers, need to go back to school and spend the next few years repeating all grades starting at 3rd grade. With a focus on vocabulary and definitions.

Let's now take a look at the word phobia, as in "transphobia," "homophobia," xenophobia," etc. I have yet to see a person in the media use these words properly. Here is how the need to use these words transpires. Someone in a "protected" class is caught doing something wrong, and in order to protect that person from criticism, the idiots in the media claim that any criticism of that person is an example of ____phobia. This is yet another example of people using a big word to sound smart. What's worse is there is another reason for them to use these phobia derivatives. They are trying to scare people and to shut down speech. The idiots in the media, news anchors et al., are so lazy they don't realize they are using the wrong word. Hey, members of the elite it's time for school.

A phobia is an irrational fear of something. It is not hatred of something. When you claim someone is being homophobic, you are saying they have an irrational fear of homosexuals. You are not saying they hate homosexuals. That is what you hope people will believe. It's the same with practitioners of Islam. You in the media want people to believe that by talking or not talking about something that *you* are courageously stopping hate. However, once again the only thing you are doing is showing the world that you truly are morons.

Here is something that is an example of neither a phobia, nor a hatred of something. I bring it up because it keeps rearing its ugly head in the news, and the media always classifies it as one of the two. It's called the knockout game. More specifically, they call some people's reaction to the knockout game either a phobia, or hatred of a specific group of people or proof positive of racism towards those playing the knockout game.

For those who don't know what the knockout game is, it's a game played by urban youths where they sneak up behind an unsuspecting person and attempt to knock them unconscious with one punch for no reason whatsoever.

If there is a rash of incidences of young black youths playing the knockout game, it is not racism causing people to cross to the other side of the street. It also isn't an irrational fear or a hatred of black people that is causing them to cross to the other side of the street either. People are crossing the street because their fight or flight instinct kicking in. When people are faced with this type of situation, they have only two choices. They can either continue to walk down the street and *hope* they won't get assaulted, or they can cross to the other side of the street and *hopefully* diffuse the situation by running away. That's it!

The same holds true for other things as well. If there is a string of terror incidences where the perpetrators are found to be Arab, being wary of other Arabs is not an irrational situation. It too, is the fight or flight instinct. It would be a phobia, if the person with the phobia has known the Arab their entire life and the only reason they fear that person is because of the incidences. It is time for the media to exhume their heads from the dark holes in which they store their heads and use the correct words and better grammar to describe things.

To recap:

> Triskaidekaphobia is not a hatred of the number thirteen. It's a fear of the number thirteen.
> Arachnophobia is not a hatred of spiders. It's a fear of spiders.
> Acrophobia is not a hatred of heights. It's a fear of heights.
> A germophobe does not hate germs. They have a fear of germs.

I know, I know! You've heard it both ways, right? That may be so, but it doesn't mean they are both correct. You can't use the phrase "I've heard it both ways," to coverup the fact that you are wrong. It doesn't make you any less wrong or any more correct.

It's not just single words that people are using incorrectly. They are also using wrong phrases. Earlier I mentioned people using the phrase, "you've got your work cut out for you," to signify that the person has a lot of work ahead of them. Here are a couple more phrases that people have been using incorrectly lately.

- Full steam ahead
- Full stop

Full steam ahead is an amalgamation of two separate phrases. Those phrases are full speed ahead, and full head of steam. These two phrases put together don't make any sense. Ahead full (full speed ahead) is a nautical term coined when navies around the world went from sailing ships to steam ships. Full speed is a speed level. The ahead part simply tells the person controlling the ship's speed that the captain wants the ship's propeller to spin in the direction that will make the ship move pointy end first. Other speed levels are: Ahead 1/3, Ahead Standard, Back 2/3, Back Emergency. They are based on the known fastest speed of a ship. If the order comes down from on-high, the Bridge, to bring the ship to Ahead 2/3, it means the captain wants the ship to travel at 2/3 the ship's fastest speed going pointy end first. Ahead Flank is the speed delineation where the ship will be traveling at 110% the ship's fastest speed again pointy end first.

The phrase, "full head of steam," is an engineering term used when operating machinery that is driven by steam, not just ships or their engines. Simply put, when a full head of steam is developed, it means as much potential energy as possible has been amassed somewhere in order to operate a piece of machinery. Developing a full head of steam, in terms of a ship's propulsion does not necessarily indicate the ship's speed. A ship's engine can have a full head of steam built up, but it is only moving at 1/3 speed.

The term, "Full Stop," is an amalgamation of two phrases also, "All Stop," and either, "Back full," or "Ahead full." Saying full stop is incorrect because different degrees of stopping don't exist. You are either stopped, or you are not. If a ship is stopped, it can't stop even more. This doesn't apply only to ships. It applies to everything that is in motion. The All Stop phrase, again is a nautical term. It also refers to ships with engines. Specifically, it refers to ships having more than one propeller. When the captain gives the command, "All stop," he wants the people controlling the ship's speed to stop the propellers- All propellers. I emphasize, "All propellers," because it is possible to have a two-shaft ship with the portside propeller spinning in the ahead direction, while the starboard propeller is not spinning. Or one propeller is spinning in the ahead direction while the other is spinning in the astern direction.

Another phrase that is used incorrectly is people saying something is a "bald face lie."

The correct phrase is "bold face lie." Bold face is a typesetter's term. It means the type face is extra dark- bold. If a person is writing a letter using a pen, a regular face typeset would be a regular, no-frills pen. A bold face typeset would be the person writing the letter in magic marker. When people write in bold face typeset, they are trying to emphasize something. Another way of saying something is a bold face lie, it to say, "that's a very large lie," as opposed to something being a regular lie or a little white lie.

But now let's talk about something the lawyers in the media are promoting incorrectly.

The correct way to say the title shared by two or more people is to say, "There are 3 Attorney *Generals* in the room." It is incorrect to say, "There are 3 *Attorneys* General in the room."

Why is *Attorneys* General incorrect? Because the title is Attorney General, not General Attorney. In this particular title, the word general is a noun (the person, place, thing or idea) and the word attorney is an adjective. Attorney is describing general. We don't plural the adjective, we plural the noun. If there are two red houses on the hill we say, "There are two red houses," not "There are two reds house on the hill." An Attorney General is a general, as is a Surgeon General, a Major General, and a General of the Army. If there are five, count them, one, two, three, four, five, 2-star generals in a tank, we say there are five Major Generals in a tank. Again, the rank is General, major is the level of general.

So, let's talk about why we say multiple presidents are "Presidents of the U.S.," and not "President of the United Stateses." (Yes, I misspelled it. I misspelled it on purpose.) It's the same reason. The word president is the noun, and "of the United States" is the descriptor phrase (adjective). It's the same for Secretary of State, Secretary of Labor, and General of the Army,

And it happens on the business networks of the news media. Constantly scrolling across the bottom of the screen are the latest stock prices. When the markets close the closing results for the different world currencies begin their endless procession. Apparently, no one working for the business channels of their respective networks knows what this means:

JPY/USD

It means Japanese yen per US dollar. It means if I take one US dollar I can get that amount of Japanese yen. However, there are mysterious mathematical formulae at work when it comes to various currency conversion rates. The Japanese yen is just one of the many with this same problem, as seen when the number of yen a person can purchase with one US dollar is a fraction of a yen- 0.6804 JPY/USD.

The problem is there is no such thing as a fractional yen. One yen is equivalent to one US cent. What should be seen scrolling across the bottom of the screen is a whole number such as 114 JPY/USD. Believe me! It's true! I have been to Japan. If we could only get 0.6804 yen per dollar, then the dollar is in really bad shape. Today when I checked the actual rate, it was 141 yen per dollar.

CHAPTER THIRTEEN

MORE WORD PLAY

How can "Hispanics" be a race of people wholly separate from another race of people even though they have the same origin story? Shouldn't we consider the two groups to be the same race? Are African Americans a race of people different from African Canadians? Why are Jamaicans not called African Jamaicans? A thousand years from now, providing their bones have not completely dissolved, any study and DNA analysis of their bones by anthropologists and geneticists will show them to be of African descent regardless of where they lived. So are we to believe that somehow (magically) Africans are not African because their ancestors were kidnapped and brought to the New World. Same too, with Hispanics.

All Hispanics are of European descent and are therefore WHITE. They are WHITE by birth. They are WHITE by DNA. They are WHITE in all aspects except one, their ancestral line made a pitstop in Central or South America before coming to the United States. On a racism scale, it's mighty convenient how the two groups of people that were the first to colonize the New World and the first to bring Africans to the New World have been absolved of all the sins of slavery. (They were absolved by a Royal Liberal Decree of the Highest Order. Somewhere there may be a scroll once read by a town crier.)

The first two groups to colonize the Americas were the Spanish and the Portuguese. They were running amok in the Americas, North, South, and Central, for a hundred and twenty years prior to the first successful English settlement of Jamestown was founded. In fact, in 1494, only two years after Columbus sailed ocean blue, the Spanish and the Portuguese signed the Treaty of Tordesillas dividing the New World between them. However, contemporary scholars and societal elites have decided the descendants of *these* two peoples are a new race of people, called Hispanics. We are therefore, not allowed to think of them as we think all the other, non-Asian, non-indigenous people- As Europeans. As the first batch of Europeans who immigrated to the Americas.

Apparently, because their ancestors settled in the Mexico before their more recent ancestors or themselves migrated to the United States, they miraculously are no longer of European decent. They have magically been transformed into a quasi-native American race. By the way, Hispanics didn't want to migrate to the United States until after World War One when the US became a world power of the first order. As for the argument- which will be made- that mixing Hispanic DNA and Native American DNA is what makes them a new race of people- the same should also hold true for "whites" and Native Americans. I inquire again, how can one group of people whose ancestors came from Europe and settled in the New World be considered a race of people wholly different from another race of people whose ancestors also came from Europe and settled in the New World only 100 years later?

When people of Spanish or Portuguese descent are called Hispanic, they are being mislabeled. Hispanic men and women, just as the descendants of the English, are European. They are European by DNA, by birth and by family lineage. Because the Spanish and Portuguese were meticulous recordkeepers, the family tree of each so-called Hispanic "minority" can be traced back to Spain. This makes them legally European. The point here is we need to quit calling them Hispanics and stop considering them a minority group. Don't get me started on calling them Latino or Latina, which are also incorrect terms. We need to start calling them what they are. They are part of the White Majority. Being able to speak a language other than English does not miraculously transform a person into a different race either. If I suddenly start speaking Mandarin, no one is going to consider me to be of Asian descent.

SECTION 4

RACE AND THE LIKE

INTRODUCTION

You are about to be told things you may not want to hear. However, it is stuff you need to hear. This is the stuff no one is allowed to speak of unless they, the speakers, meet certain arbitrary conditions; conditions that can change without notice. I can't help you if you don't want to hear it. If you don't want to hear it, don't read this section. These next few sections are going to anger a lot of people. For clarification when I say, "A lot of people," I don't mean hundreds of people or thousands of people. I mean millions of people. Initially, these people will displace their anger on to me. However, over time their anger will slowly dissipate, until they ultimately accept the facts for themselves if they are honest with themselves. Unfortunately, their road to acceptance may be a long, winding road. Generally, no one reacts well after realizing they have been betrayed by the people upon whom they have showered respect and admiration for years. Their initial response will be to displace their anger onto the messenger. Ultimately however, their anger will turn into acceptance, but first they must grieve.

Just as people to this day continue to grieve the results of the 2016 and 2020 elections, people will be grieving over this section for years to come. Why? Because what I am about to say are facts. Facts, not truth! Truth is subjective. When people say something is "my truth," what they mean is it is their opinion. However, in recent years a fallacy has been invented which dictates that the opinions of some people are unassailable simply because they use the phrase, "my truth." Insultingly to most people, once these "truths" are spat out, the response everyone is supposed to have is that upon threat of losing their jobs, their friends, etc., they are to treat these faux truths as if they are recently discovered holy words of God in a lost Gospel.

When a person forms an opinion, they take into account their lived experiences. For instance, if at a young age a person is bullied, they may form an opinion that their tormentor's brother is also a bully. Worse still, that everyone who looks like their tormentor is a bully. Truths are what people have been fed in

158

mass quantities by liars and scoundrels. To that I inquire, *if a liar tells you "A truth," is it really the truth?* I take solace knowing that after reading this section millions of people *will* immediately become angry. I don't take pleasure in their anger. These people are not skipping the first and second stages of the grieving process. They have been stuck in the denial and shock stages for decades. I take solace in their anger because their anger is proof that they know what I am saying is factual, and they have been denying these facts for decades. Decades, not months and not years.

These people are in agony. Not because they are in physical pain, but because it is hard to believe one's heroes are anything but noble, and their fallen angels refuse to let them grieve. Instead, so they can continue to wield power over them, the fallen heroes conjure a reality based on the lie that nothing has changed. Hopefully, by the end of this chapter many people will realize their anger is not for me. That it is for those who for decades have fraudulently claimed to have their best interests at heart. There will be no bargaining. I will not apologize, nor will I retract. Doing so would cause those in the process of grieving to regress to an earlier stage of the process and render themselves unable to believe what they have witnessed.

Chapter Fourteen

RACISM

We need to get two things straight right off the bat.

The first thing is simple:

There is no such thing as "reverse racism.' It's all racism. If a black man refuses to give a white man a ride to the airport simply because he is white, that is racism, not reverse racism. Reverse racism is concept invented by the members of society who consider themselves the "elite" and who can't handle the facts about racism. What does one call racism in Mexico if a Mexican denies a white guy something based on skin color? It can't be reverse racism, because the Mexican is part of the majority. What the self-proclaimed elite can't handle specifically is the fact that *all* races of people can be racist. Racism isn't the sole domain of white people, nor is its origin found in the United States. Yes, Affirmative Action is racism. Just because it *benefits* as opposed to *punishes* a specific race, doesn't make it *not* racism. If the sole reason for me giving a black person a million dollars is because they are black, that too is racism.

Second:

As a member of society who wants our society to thrive and prosper so that it can become a better society, I am neither duty bound to chastise other people when they show their prejudices and biases, nor is it my job to offer penance for other people's misdeeds. No matter how atrocious they may be, I cannot be held accountable for the actions of others. My sole duty to our society is to recognize my biases and to **not** pass them on to the next generation. Over time I have come to realize that the most effective means of combating racism is through the conservative application of formal education and a healthy dose of time. When I say education, I do not mean through corporate retreats and semi-annual seminars. I mean through the self-education people experience as they grow and mature together. It is unfortunate that this is the best, the most effective, and the most long-lasting way to eliminate racism because it is a multi-

160

generational quest. Any other means will only breed more racism. It will first manifest itself in the form of resentment, then hatred and finally racism.

Yes, in the United States pockets of racism exist. Racism exists in *all* countries, not just the United States. Anyone who believes otherwise is either woefully uneducated or is a member of the current iteration of Lenin's Corps of Useful Idiots. Thankfully, the pockets of racism in the United States are largely unorganized and for the most part have been relegated to the fringes of society with little to no impact on society. These pockets of racism, which charlatans claim are holding secret, nocturnal ceremonies, are scattered around the country and their memberships are in the low thousands, if not low hundreds. It is interesting, in a country whose ethnic makeup consists of cultures from the entire world- a country in which *every* language in the world is spoken daily- we are browbeaten into believing that the only source of racism comes from White Supremacists.

On national television, pastors and other leaders of faith whose ethnic background is "other than white" are regularly shown espousing the supremacy of their ethnicity to crowds of thousands. However, we are told White Supremacy is the problem. We do not broadcast on national television the meetings of the KKK or other white supremist organization, but the media will attend, interview, and outwardly sympathize with organizations that believe in the superiority of the Black or Hispanic races over all others. When the existence of white supremacy needs proof, the same news clips are shown. They always consist of footage showing a small group of people which gathered in an opposing protest. No matter how long ago the footage was really captured, the media goes out of their way to convince people that it is brand new footage. By the way, when I say a small number of people, I mean 10 to 20 people, maybe 50 if the annual national convention is in town.

No one ever mentions the pockets of racism which many of us deal with every day. Pockets of racism that haven't been relegated to the back woods where people actively teach their children to not trust one group of people or to openly hate. Ones known by the words, "Da hood", or "The barrio." Will you continue to

161

tell me that no one in these places ever says anything bad about other races? Yes, you will because you don't want to deal with the racism that exists within your own American subculture. Yes black people, you can be racists too. As can Mexicans. As can the Chinese and the Muslims. If you are a media figure, the next time you go on television attempting to show the saintliness of your race, look straight into the camera and swear to the viewers that only white people can be racist. I dare you!

Here is another fact which proves blatant media corruption and complicity. Whenever something happens and the media can blather on about racism, there is always one pundit who utters, "No one is born a racist," or "Racism is taught." However, no one ever pushes back. For if they did, the media would be required to ask whether those clichés apply to *all* people or just white people. I for one, would love to know how a black parent telling their children, "You can't trust white people...," or that "White people are keeping you down." is not an example of teaching children to be racist. How is that different than a white parent telling their children, "All black people evolved from apes."

If people still don't believe that their subculture can be racist, they should explain how saying mathematics is the "white man's math" is not racism. They can't! Yes, racism does exist. Yes, racists do walk among us. But forcing people to endure days upon days of regurgitated rhetoric, whether it is factual or not, every time something bad befalls someone who is not white, is not helping to expel racism from our society. In fact, it will, and probably is, causing racism to become more prevalent. Not because people are racist, but because they are beginning to resent other races. If a person is never hired for a job because preference is always given to an oppressed group- of real or imagined oppression- eventually they will begin to resent that group of people. If it continues, they will start to hate that group. Is this what people want? Is this the road people want our society to travel down?

I know, I know, I know! In the past, blacks were denied jobs based on the color of their skin. Mexicans were not allowed to work in the fields of California because they were Mexican. The key word there is, "past." This was in the past. If

162

it does happen, it happens at greatly reduced levels, and there are now laws in place to combat these situations. There is even a division within the US Department of Justice that apparently has the ability to parachute investigators into an incident where there exists even the slightest possibility that a hate crime may have been committed- But only if the crime is against someone whose skin is darker than a snowball made of virginal snow. It happens in an unsolicited manner. I swear there is someone in Washington, D.C. watching television right now hoping for a news report that states that someone who is not white may have been attacked by someone who is white. Facts and confirmation are not required to deploy these people to the scene.

When people stroll down the street, they see no signs in the windows claiming they are hiring, but blacks or Mexicans need not apply. Were there in the past? Yes, I do not deny that. However, no one can convince me that their fresh-out-of-college efforts to make everything more "equitable" has made things better. Why? Because they have not! In order to have *equity* among the races, society must first segregate. African Americans spent decades desegregating the country, but now the grand children of those noble apostles of race *equality* are in the process of undoing what was hard won. They are bringing us back to the days they ironically claim to be trying to eliminate.

Racism is primarily being spread by minority groups and most of this racism is directed at other minority groups. (Many street gangs originate in this manner. Their unofficial mission statement being, "Protecting the barrio from Da Hood.") Even now there are places in the country where only non-white people can go. Twenty years ago, these places would have been tourist areas where anyone could go and experience a culture from far away. Places like Chinatown in San Francisco. This is another reason why colleges and universities need to be purged of Marxists.

The Marxists are abusing their positions, using their positional authority over naïve, newly independent adults to teach them the best way to stamp out racism is to implement the Marxist method and to segregate by race. Look at what is happening, the only people calling for segregation to be reimplemented are the newly minted Marxists on college campuses. These true idiots believe they are

163

doing good. Not only that, but the Marxist professors have gotten African Americans to demand they be segregated- Resegregated! They call for safe spaces. The epidemic of racism that is about to become rampant in the United States is going to be worse than the previous epidemic of racism. And it will all be based on lies!

Nathan Bedford Forrest, the founder and first Grand Wizard of the Klu Klux Klan, and all his minions must be in their graves laughing their asses off. Yes their direct descendants, political and familial, are now destroying statues of their ancestors to show their moral superiority, but they have inexplicably managed to get the descendants of slaves to agree to being re-segregated and not an early 20th century form of segregation. They are begging for a more intense version of segregation to be implemented.

Think back to the struggles of the Civil Rights era. Think about what has transpired since the Civil Rights Acts passed. The Democrat party somehow managed to convince *all* minority groups that it was they who freed the slaves, and that they are the ones responsible for passing civil rights legislation. Somehow the Democrats have managed to re-write history. The facts of the matter are that the Democrat party has been anything but responsible for race equality etc. Here are the numbers for the 13th, 14th and 15th Amendments. Of the Democrats in the US Congress- both the House and the Senate- the percentages that voted for those amendments are abysmal. 20.9%, 5.9%, and 0.00% respectively. Look it up.

The numbers improved for the Civil Rights Acts a century later as democrats began to be more accepting. However, if we believe the falsehood that the Civil Rights Acts were democrat bills, in order to pass the Civil Rights Acts with a simple majority, the Democrats needed over a hundred Republicans to vote with them. In the case of the 1964 Civil Rights Act, it required close to 200 Republicans to vote in support of the bill for the bill to pass. And these bills required a *simple* majority to pass, not a 2/3 majority. We won't talk about the fact that in both Houses of Congress at the time, the Democrat party had almost supermajority numbers. Their numbers were so great, if they were truly supportive of Civil Rights, they would only have needed a handful of Republican to pass these bills. The percentage of the Democrats that voted for the 1957, 1964 and 1965 Civil Rights Acts respectively are: 52%, 62%, and 74%.

Don't be fooled, even though those numbers are above the 50% margin required to pass an Act, they are not the numbers needed. For that you need 50% of the total members, not just 50% of one party. In each of these cases, Republicans need to vote for the Acts in large numbers for these them to pass with a *simple* majority. If the goal was to make these Acts amendments, the entire Congress would have barely passed them. In fact, the 1957 Civil Rights Act would *not* have passed the House of Representatives if it were meant to be an amendment. Interestingly, had if either Presidents Johnson or Eisenhower vetoed the bills, the veto override vote could have failed if a *handful* more had voted to not override the veto.

Here's a thought exercise. How much different would the lives of African Americans be today if one day in 1858 all the slave owners gathered up all their slaves and said to them, "You are free."

"You can go anywhere you wish to go, and you can have any job you wish to have. You can continue living here or you can go live elsewhere. The world is your oyster! But be advised, the Republicans who have been trying to free you through legislation will not let you. It is best for you to stay here where I can take care of you. I will give you a wage. I will give you a home in which to live. The wage won't be much. It would be more, but California has been admitted to the Union, and the Mexicans in California are undercutting my ability to pay you more. It's the Mexicans who are making sure you can't get paid a decent wage. Especially Don Antonio. He is so rich he can pay to have Mexicans brought from Mexico to work his fields. By the way, this is Juan, and this is Carlos. Show them and their families the ropes."

Following that up a week later with,

"I have just come from town, and I have good news. Starting next year, because you are black, because we feel bad about enslaving you, and because our intentions are noble, any time you need to send a message, you can use the town's telegraph for free. The newly formed Cotton Pickers Conglomerate will pay for the use of the telegraph. By the way, that whole education thing, that's the white man's education. It's designed to keep you subservient. But don't you worry about having to learn to read and write. I'll tell you everything you need to know to survive. Right now, the only thing you need to know is that I am going to take care of you, and if I fail it's the fault of white people who live hundreds of miles to the North, or the Mexicans in California, thousands of miles to the West. Pay no attention to my five new Clydesdales and that I am going to the south of France this summer. Don't you worry, that money wasn't earmarked for your wages."

I hypothesize the fate of African Americans would be much the same as it is now.

If after a quick show-and-tell, I could ask the founding members of the KKK what they think of today's African American community, I'm certain they would have an *If-I-had-known-then what I know now* moment. I'd bet they would have spent less money on pillowcases and more money on bourbon. Seriously, if there is an afterlife, regardless of where they are in it, they must be both proud and amazed at what their descendants have accomplished. To witness the great, great, great grandchildren of their former slaves begging to be segregated, begging to live in cheap housing, and *not* wanting to be educated would be positively orgasmic for them.

Think about it, the founding members of the KKK had open disdain, hatred and contempt for the black race. They didn't want their slaves educated. They spent vast sums of money trying to recapture "fugitive" slaves. Yet, the great, great, great grandchildren of their former slaves are refusing to be educated because it's "the white man's math," and are proudly marching into segregation. If they knew the easiest way to keep their slaves enslaved was to set them free and then promise to give them small tokens of assistance in perpetuity…Wow!

We are also being told on a daily basis by Hispanics that their ancestors too, were victims of racism. The Hispanic activist groups constantly compare their plights to those of African Americans. African Americans should be truly offended every time this happens. The only group of people that have had it worse than African Americans are the Native Americans. In the late 1800s there were no people putting pillowcase over their heads and riding through the streets of Laredo looking for Mexicans to hang. The KKK was not burning crosses in the Arizona Territory. Were Mexicans lynched? Yes, but not because they were Mexican. It was because vigilantes were taking the law into their own hands. But you know who was also lynched in the western states? Whites! Not because they were white, but because law enforcement officers were either unable to stop "the posse" from hanging the person, or because there were no law enforcement officers in the area to bring the offending party to justice.

This is how racist the United States was towards Mexicans in the early 1900s. When the State of New Mexico became the 47th State, they like every other state, first had to draft a state constitution. To this day, New Mexico's state constitution is the only state constitution written in both English *and* Spanish. It wasn't translated from English to Spanish; it was written in English *and* Spanish. Also, when New Mexico became a state those residing in the territory were given a choice, stay and become a U.S. citizen, or move to Mexico. Contrary to what people may be teaching, the good citizens of the New Mexico Territory found the United States to be so racist towards Spanish speakers, 98% of them opted to stay in the United States. Only 2% left for Mexico! If the United States of America were the racist country race hustlers claim it to be, the numbers should be reversed.

Here is the bottom line! We haven't had an honest conversation about race since the civil rights movement. What really and truly existed prior to the civil rights legislation of the 1960s, is what today's civil rights leaders claim currently exists. In other words, if you take today's leaders at their word, nothing has changed. If a person believes this, it means the leaders of the 1960s civil rights movements were failures. It also means that since they have taken the reigns of the civil rights movement, today's civil rights leaders are failures too. But the civil rights leaders of the 1960s did not fail. What has happened is the current generation of civil rights leaders have become the problem. Yes, the problem isn't racism, the problem is the self-anointed leaders of the neo-civil rights movement.

During the *real* civil rights movement, today's leaders (yesterday's followers no matter what they say) found themselves in a situation they had never experienced. People began to revere them. They would go from town-to-town building support for their cause. They would tell people to march on the Capitol and people would march on the Capitol. To be clear they did not actually mean, "march on the Capitol." They meant, "March to the Capitol." Some of them would give a speech that was televised, and they would bask in the cheers of the crowd. The cheers were intoxicating, and they began to amass power.

However, when their hard-fought dreams were realized, they noticed their power was beginning to dwindle. People, though thankful for what had been accomplished, began to live their lives without them. Shortly after the legislation was passed, these leaders realized that the only thing they could look forward to was reminiscing about and pompously spouting that they marched with Dr. King. That was it! It was over! Their glory days were behind them. Metaphor: they were popular in high school, but since graduation no one pays any attention to them.

In an instant, their life's work went from being one of attaining civil rights, to being one of self-glorification. They needed to have their egos stroked and they needed to know that when they are laid to rest that it would be to the same sound many gladiators heard in the arena as they took their last breath- To the roar of the crowd. Their biggest fear was not a return to segregation. Their biggest fear was that people would stop talking about them. Their quest for immortality, however, would require them to either invent a new civil rights issue, or claim nothing had changed. They could not simply ride into the sunset knowing they had accomplished something truly breathtaking.

Thanks to both the current generation of civil rights leaders, and the ones still reminiscing and unable to relinquish power, our society is in retrograde. This is what made George Washington arguably the greatest leader ever- not just the greatest president- the greatest leader of all time. The GOAT! George Washington did something the self-proclaimed leaders of the new civil rights movement would never do and will never do. He gave up power- Twice! To members of minority communities everywhere, it is your leaders who keep success out of your reach. They know that if you succeed, they will lose all power.

For those people who claim the United States of America is the most racist country in the world, answer these questions. If the United States of America is so racist:

1. Why are you not at every international airport and every port of entry on the US borders telling the people who are crossing to go back?

2. Why have you not created organizations similar to the Doctors without Borders to travel the world convincing people not to come to the United States because it is such a racist place?

3. Why is there no organization called, "Teachers without Borders." Why must we bring into the country every child from every third world country just to give them a "proper education?"

4. Why are you actively inviting more people into the country, claiming you will take care of them?

I hate to be the bearer of bad news for the various minority communities in this country, but when *you* go on television and claim to be oppressed, the racism increases. Your oppression is not because you were or are being oppressed, it is because you have been groomed to think of yourselves as victims. Think about what you are telling people when you constantly claim victimhood. You are telling people that you are weak. You are telling people that you are too stupid to do anything by yourself. You have been taught that your lack of success in business is because you're black; college is beyond your capabilities because you are Mexican. On and on it goes, and no one ever tells you to quit feeling sorry for yourself and get back to work. Why? They are afraid.

If they were to tell you to quit feeling sorry for yourself and to get back to work, they are afraid that you will call them a racist and attempt to have them fired. The companies for whom they and you work are afraid that you will look for a shyster lawyer and that you will try to milk money from the company. Need I point out, that if you are wanting people to give you special treatment simply due to the color of your skin, you are ordering them- forcing them- to be racist

169

towards you. But they have no choice. It's a damned if you do, damned if you don't situation for all involved. If they don't give you what you want, you will say it is racism. But if they do give you what you want, it is still racism. Racism is racism! There aren't different degrees of racism. It is either racism, or it isn't racism. Rewarding someone because they are a minority is equally as racist as denying them that same reward for the same reason. You can't have it both ways! <u>Affirmative Action is legalized racism!</u>

After a while it becomes exhausting watching people allow Hispanics-faux Native Americans- to act as if they have no fault in the settling of the Americas. Before I go any further, people of Hispanic descent are only a minority population group in the United States, Canada, and a handful of islands in the Caribbean. They are the majority population everywhere else in the western hemisphere. Yes, these faux-Natives are walking throughout society day-in and day-out, believing they bear absolutely no responsibility for what became of the indigenous peoples of the Americas- North, Central, and South America. This is readily apparent when two issues rear their heads, and they receive no push back on *any* of their prognostications.

The first issue is the one of slavery in the New World. Notice I said, "…in the New World," not, "…in the United States." Slavery was a hemisphere-wide scourge. It is not the original sin of the United States, solely. There is a separate section delving into the evil that is slavery, so we'll have no further discussions of the matter at this time.

The second issue which causes the faux natives to absolutely lose their minds and in the process, incriminate themselves for *all* the evils perpetuated upon the heads of others, is the issue of what should be the official language of the United States. Boy that was a leap, wasn't it? Be patient, dutiful reader, I'll explain and show you that my logic isn't quite as eccentric as you may be thinking. So, how can designating English to be the official language of the United States prove a group of people's culpability in the extermination and humiliation of another group of people? Let's embark on this magical journey together.

Many believe having an official language is a minor issue, but that is an illusion. The subject is of great importance economically, diplomatically, and culturally. Here is proof of that statement. If we were to tell the Spanish-speaking members of our society that they can no longer be allowed to speak Spanish, the responses would be swift and numerous. The first and by far the most prevalent response will be that forbidding them to speak Spanish is a violation of the First Amendment. The second argument they will make is that somehow if they were to stop speaking Spanish, their culture and heritage would be lost to the ravages of time. They will say their culture and heritage is inextricably linked to being able to speak Spanish. That their second language represents their culture and ironically, that the language they must speak when conducting business in the United States- English- has neither cultural relevance nor cultural significance.

By that response alone, persons opposed to English being made the official language of the United States inadvertently make the case for English being designated its official language. If denying them the right to speak Spanish is denying them their heritage, then denying English speakers the right to speak English is denying them their heritage too. If we fail to make English the official language, then the part of our culture which founded this country dies away. Just as Hispanics believe their culture is preserved by them speaking Spanish, we should believe the same about the United States and make English its official language.

There is a third and an even more absurd argument. When the subject of the country's official language is brought up, and after completely losing their minds, many Hispanic activist groups argue the official language of the United States should be Spanish because "...everything west of the Mississippi was once owned by Mexico." To which I would rebut, if Spanish should be the official language of the US based on prior ownership of the land, then Spanish cannot be the official language of any country in the New World. Every country south of the US-Mexico border would need to change their official language from Spanish to either Nahuatl or Quechua- the languages of the Aztecs and the Incas respectively. But rather than understanding all their arguments against English are futile when the script is flipped, the activists bring forth yet another debate. When their

171

argument of land ownership is beaten, their rebuttal is to jump up and down screaming *they* were here first.

For some reason, no one ever refutes that claim no matter how blatantly obvious the response would be if an Englishman said the same thing in support of the argument for making English the official language. No one ever tells them- the faux-natives- that *they* weren't here first either. That poignant fact is only reserved for "white people." Everyday someone is reminding "white people" that there were people here long before their ancestors arrived. Hispanics, or faux-Natives as we should call them, are allowed to continue believing they bear no guilt for the tribulations and trials of Native and African Americans. They are allowed to believe that the suffrage brought down on the heads of the Native Americans is their suffrage too. Prominent persons of Hispanic descent have gone on television and have exclaimed that to be Hispanic is to be Native American. To them it isn't about genetics. It's about not being white. Read that last sentence again, I did not say, "It's not about being white." I said, "It's about _not_ being white."

It's about not letting anyone associate them or their ancestors with the people whose ancestors came directly to the United States from Europe. It's about ensuring that when all is said and done, they will never be forced to atone for their ancestor's original sins of massacring one group of people and the follow-on enslavement of another. Penance for those crimes against humanity, as they will soon call them, must come only from white people. It is something only Europeans must do!

I hate to break the news to the "Hispanics" of the New World, you, too, are white. Your ancestors *are* from Europe, and like it or not, that makes you European! Your ancestors, therefore, must also bear the burden of and responsibility for the slaughter of the Native Americans and the enslavement of Africans. If your ancestors were judged through the same prism through which you judge the ancestors of others, the burden of guilt upon the shoulders of your ancestors would be *much greater*. It is only your *more recent* ancestors who left Mexico, Guatemala, Venezuela, et al; Your more distant ancestors left Spain and

Portugal. And as you are so fond of reminding others when you believe it will prove your argument, your European ancestors were here first!

The ancestors of today's Hispanics were the first in many things. They were the first Europeans to see and set foot in the Americas since the Vikings; The first Europeans to see the bountiful forests of the New World. They were the first Europeans to see plentiful fish stocks in the rivers, and the first Europeans to experience Native American culture. They were the first Europeans to realize the value of New World crops like potatoes, tomatoes, corn, and tobacco. They were the first to realize that sugarcane, a crop only grown in southeast Asia at the time, could also be grown on Caribbean islands. They were first to see, but not recognize, the intellect of the native peoples and the first to see the legacy of the New World was the promise of a better life in all manners of speaking. Yes, these people had many firsts. However, to all good there are bad, and credit must also be given to the ancestors of today's Hispanics for bringing to the New World bad things as well.

The ancestors of all Hispanics- the Spanish, and the Portuguese- were the *first* to massacre the natives of the New World. They were the *first* to call them savages. They were the *first* to slaughter whole civilizations and *forcibly* convert them to Christianity. These people, the noblest of all the European colonizers as we are also told to believe, were the *first* to rape, pillage and plunder the New World. They were also the *first* to bring European diseases and pestilence to the New World, which by themselves is estimated to have killed upwards of 75% of the Native American population even before Virginia Dare was born in the Lost Colony of Roanoke. But because they were from Spain and Portugal, because their ancestors didn't speak English, we are expected to explicitly ignore these facts.

The thirst for gold, silver, and gemstones by the Spanish and Portuguese was so great that by the time the English founded Jamestown in 1609, 75% of the Native Americans had been killed off. They were killed not just through war and disease, but also by being worked to death as slaves. You read that right; the ancestors of *all* Hispanics enslaved the Native Americans. It was because the Native American population was being killed off faster than it could replenish itself that the ancestors of *all* Hispanics also brought to the New World the first African slaves. I hate to be the bearer of bad news, but they weren't brought to Jamestown as the race hustlers would have us all believe. Again, you read that right! The first Africans brought to the New World arrived prior to 1619 and their masters were Hispanic, not English. These African slaves mined so much gold, Spain was able to use tons of it in the construction of multiple churches. If you don't believe me, vacation in Spain some day and visit some of their oldest cathedrals. There are medieval cathedrals with gold plating on entire walls.

What was happening to the Native Americans was happening throughout the Americas, not just the eastern seaboard of North America. As the Spanish explored the islands in the Caribbean Sea- The Caribbean Sea being known as the Spanish Main- they discovered some Asian crops could also be grown on these islands too. Not only could they be grown on islands like Jamaica but growing them in the New World drastically reduced the amount of time it took to ship them to market- from months to weeks.

Yes, the first slaves in the *English* colonies of North America were brought here in 1619. There is no denying that. However, equally undeniable is the fact that those particular human beings were not originally destined for Jamestown, Virginia. They only set foot in Jamestown because an English privateer captured the Portuguese slave ship- San Juan Batista- into which they were herded like cattle. The privateers who captured this ship sailed it to Jamestown because that was the ONLY place in the New World they could safely take it. Had the privateers taken the ship anywhere else in the New World, the sailors would have been considered pirates and hanged. Remember, in 1619 Jamestown was the *only* English settlement in the Americas. The Pilgrims wouldn't land at Plymouth Rock for another year and a half.

The privateers weren't trying to capture a slave ship. They were trying to capture ships laden with Spanish gold and other treasure. It was a shock to the sailors who boarded the San Juan Batista, to enter the ship's hold, and see a mass of humanity chained up and suffering. So, what could the sailors have done? They could have sailed the ship back to Africa after restocking the ship with water and other provisions. They could have sailed the ship to Jamestown, as they did. Or they could have risked being hanged as pirates and sailed the ship to its intended destination- Veracruz, Mexico. They couldn't sail to Jamestown, restock the ship and then sail back to Africa because Jamestown could barely stock itself.

Yes, Mexico had a thriving slave market long before 1619. Not only that, but it is a fallacy- a crime against education- to claim the first slaves brought to what would become the United States were brought to Virginia. The first slaves brought to what would become the United States were brought Florida- A *colony* of Spain, not England. As usual the race hustlers are wrong about the year the first slaves were brought to a colony that would eventually become part of the United States. The race hustlers claim the first slaves were brought in 1619. In reality, the first slaves were brought sometime around 1526. At this time, Henry the VIII was the King of England and he was still married to his first wife, Catherine of Aragon. Not only that, but England had a second-rate navy at best. The rulers of the waves in 1526 were the Spanish, and the defeat of the Spanish Armada was still 60 years in the future.

Yet, for some unknown but known reason, no one ever tells the Hispanics of the blame they *must* shoulder regarding slavery and of the plight of true Native Americans, and of the settling of the New World. In fact, they should shoulder *most* of the blame because their ancestors were here first, as they are always quick to remind everyone. But that is not what happens. They are allowed to walk around with a false sense of *purity*. That is probably the best way to describe their attitude. They have been raised with this belief in their purity, and the false belief that they are somehow native to the Americas when they are not. If you want to watch something truly funny, watch how a faux Native American reacts when they are informed that their revered "ancient" ancestor, who settled in Mexico in 1508, was a slave owner. And not just African slaves, but Native American slaves as well. The look on their face is, in a word, PRICELESS! I saw this happen twice in one day. You could tell they couldn't comprehend the revelation and were trying to think of an excuse.

Since I have brought them into the discussion on numerous times, I'll briefly mention the Native Americans, too. Is it sad what happened to your ancestors? Yes! However, if you are going to condemn "white people" for stealing your land, you need to blame each other too. Prior to Europeans arriving in the New World, your ancestors had been "stealing" land from each other for 1000s of years. When you say that white people should return all the land they "stole" from you, that's all well and good so long as your tribe/nation returns the land it stole from other Native American tribes/Nation prior to the arrival of the Europeans. The truth of the matter is not only were you stealing land from each other, but the Chinese stole land from the Mongols. The numerous tribes of Africa stole land from each other, as did the various civilizations in the Mediterranean and the Middle East. Having land "stolen" from one civilization by another group of people is not the sole domain of *your* history.

When the English finally began arriving en masse in the New World, most of the land was sparsely populated if not unpopulated all together. This was the result of disease, not genocide. Also, when they arrived, many of the Native Americans welcomed the English with open arms. Why? Because the English had firearms. Firearms, even the most rudimentary flintlock musket, were the great equalizer. We commonly associate that phrase with the difference between men and women today. But it is true of the Native Americans as well. When the Pilgrims arrived, the tribes of New England were constantly being attacked (and enslaved) by the Huron Nation. Introducing the firearm to these Native American tribes meant they could defend themselves from the more militarily superior Huron. Activists within the Native American communities want people to believe life would have been easier had Europeans not come to the New World but this is a fallacy too. If Europeans had not come in 1492, maybe a hundred years later, the Chinese or Japanese would have.

Here are three words Native Americans need to learn. Get over it! You are not the only civilization that had its collective ass handed to it. It has happened throughout history and in the future it *will* happen again. The Spartans got their asses kicked by the Sacred Band of Thebes. The Romans got their asses handed to them by Hannibal and Spartacus. Every battle fought in history has a victor and a loser. This is what happens when wars and lesser conflicts are fought, someone wins, someone loses. By the way, the talking point of you being a poor, innocent person is contradicted by the Battle of the Little Bighorn. Not only did your ancestors outnumber the US Army more than 3 to 1 (and that is just the warriors,) but your ancestors had better weapons than the US Army. Fighting a war to a stalemate or having a cease fire to allow one's enemy to rearm and resupply under the guise of humanitarian aid is a modern invention of the idiot liberals who have graduated from Ivy League schools over the past century.

One other thing, every Native American should bow down and absolutely worship Christopher Columbus. Not worship him as an explorer, they should worship him as a living God. They should absolutely and adamantly refuse to take part in the newly invented liberal holiday of Native American Awareness Day, or whatever liberals are trying to call Columbus Day. Why? Because of what Columbus did for the indigenous populations. Of all the civilizations in the history of the world, only Native American civilizations can pinpoint accurately when they advanced to the next technological age. They are the only civilizations throughout world history that did not have to spend thousands of years doing research and experiments in order to do so. If Columbus' original first voyage logs, or its official copy- Barcelona Log- are ever found, we could know the exact time the New World entered the Age of Discovery.

What am I trying to say? On October 12th, 1492, at high noon I'll speculate, every single Native American civilization in North, South, and Central America attained the Age of Discovery. Not only did they enter the Age of Discovery, but they simultaneously skipped over the Copper Age, the Bronze Age, Iron Age, and the Middle Ages. They instantaneously- they literally- went from being Stone Age societies to modern societies. Had Columbus not brought with him all the developments of the western world, or not sailed at all, most if not all Native American societies would only now be entering the Copper Age, and it would be another 1,000 years before they attained the Bronze Age. That is how far down the technological ladder were the Americas when Columbus arrived.

Thanks to Columbus implements would be brought to the New World that vastly improved the condition of the people living in the New World. Had Columbus not discovered the New World, the people living on the plains of North

177

America would still be walking everywhere and would still be having to carry everything they owned as they followed the great roaming herds of bison. Why? Because horses, draft animals in general, are *not* native to the Western Hemisphere. More importantly, before Columbus Native Americans had still not invented the wheel for themselves.

Every culture, every civilization has marginalized people they deem to be inferior to themselves. The only reason we speak of "white racism" is because that is the history we are taught in school. If we were to teach about African history, not African American history, we would discover that most of the tribes of Sub-Saharan Africa view their tribe as the superior tribe and all others are populated by inferior savages. Yes, Americans in the 19th century thought the Native Americans were savages, but the Japanese taught their civilian population the same thing about Americans. In the case of the Japanese, it was so engrained in the minds of the civilian population on the island of Okinawa, as the American military approached many civilians committed suicide by throwing themselves, and their children off cliffs. This has been documented not just by journalists writing stories, there is video footage of it taking place. The modern liberal theory of war fighting has not stopped the practice of marginalizing other people. The Russians are doing it to the Ukrainians; the Ukrainians are doing it to the Russians. The Arabs in the Middle East have been doing it to the Jews. The Chinese do it to the Mongols.

The point is that racism exists everywhere. Racism is *not* an invention of the western world. It happens everywhere and is happening contemporaneously. The Chinese believe in the superiority of their own race. The French believe in the superiority of their country. If people don't believe me, here is a homework assignment. Spend six hours watching all of Bruce Lee's movies most of which were Chinese (Hong Kong) movies, not Hollywood.

If people would just get over their "blackness" or their "Hispanicness" they will succeed. If people truly want racism to stop, they need education and time. These are the only things that will stop racism. Nothing else will stop racism. Forcing of one group of people to make amends for the sins of their ancestors does not, will not and will never solve racism. It won't even reduce the amount of racism. When one group of people is forced to capitulate to the demands of another, the people on their knees will resent the other. Especially if they believe their capitulation is unjust. If you don't believe me, ask yourself, why was Germany the only country punished and blamed for starting World War One even though it was Franz Ferdinand who was shot, and Germany was an ally of his?

Black people need to accept the fact it was their distant ancestors who were slaves, and that they have no claim to reparations. Hispanics need to accept the fact that the country they hold dear, the country whose flag can be seen hanging from the mirror in their car is truly a 3rd world shit hole. They also need to accept the fact that their ancestors had no role, none, in the founding of the United States. Their ancestors were in Mexico laying the groundwork for Mexico never being able to become more than a 3rd world country. Their distant relatives in Mexico, and other countries south of the US border, are currently directly involved in drug trafficking and the trafficking of human beings. The countries they revere so much, are currently reviving the slave trade in the western hemisphere.

Another thing that must stop if we are to ever eliminate racism. We need to stop celebrating *one* of our contemporaries simply because they were the first black this or the first Hispanic that. Who cares! They may be the first black US Secretary of State, but they are not the first black person to hold that position around the world. Every country has a Secretary of State, they just might not call them the Secretary of State. Yes, it shows the progress that the US has made in the field of race relations, but it is unsustainable in a country striving for equality. It creates a dilemma. Let's take the space race of the 1960s as an example.

If the space race between the United States and the Soviet Union were to take place right now, how would we celebrate accomplishments? If the first American in space were an African American, what would we celebrate? Would we celebrate the first American being launched into space? Or would we be celebrating his or her blackness? What if the first two Americans to walk on the moon were Asian and Hispanic, would we celebrate that America won the space race, or would we celebrate that the first two human beings to ever walk on the moon were *not* white. That is what we are doing when we celebrate "firsts" these days. We are not using them as proof that our country is becoming more tolerant of others. We are celebrating a person for not being white and in doing, so we minimize their accomplishment. We used to give trophies to people who won races to recognize the effort they put into their sport.

Why does NASA not celebrate the first Chinese astronaut? Why does the Chinese Space Agency not recognize Astronaut Taylor Wang as the first Chinese person in space? Now that the Chinese Space Agency has placed one of their people in space, does it render Astronaut Taylor Wangs achievements moot simply because he is a Chinese *American*?

CHAPTER FIFTEEN

CULTURES

Here is a point of culture that Hispanics don't think about. How utterly racist one part of their culture is towards other races of people. Yes, this is part of their culture! It is widely done; therefore, it is part of the culture. I see people of other races do the same thing, but it is the Hispanics amongst us that primarily do it to be racist. To what do I refer? The fact that people who speak Spanish will purposely speak Spanish in front of non-Hispanics. What is worse, and this is the most frustrating part, is if you ask them a question, they will pretend not to understand. I know this for a fact. I was once a delivery driver making deliveries to all manner of places including places where Spanish speakers were employed. On more than one occasion I would have a question, and when I asked one of the Hispanics, they would respond by looking at me with a big, toothy grin, continuously nodding, but never answering my question. Occasionally, if I asked a Hispanic person a question, the response was in question form, "Que?" More often than not I had to ask someone else.

One time when this happened the very next day- *The very next day*- I was making a delivery to the same place and found myself standing behind the person to whom I had directed a question the day before. I somehow managed to get behind him without his knowledge. I was standing so close to him I could clearly hear him speaking almost perfect English. So Spanish speakers, cut the crap! English speakers understand this, most of the people speaking Spanish in front of you can speak English just as well as you. Don't let them fool you. If you are at work and you happen to walk by a conversation where the participants are speaking Spanish, go to HR and write them up too. Tell them they offended you because they are speaking Spanish and that make you feel uncomfortable. It does not matter that you were not part of the conversation from the start. *Many* companies have an "English Only" policy. Why? So that its employees can communicate effectively.

In the mid-1990s the US Navy closed its base in Subic Bay, the Philippines. For decades following the US taking control of the Philippines from the Spanish in 1898, the U.S. Navy maintained a presence in Subic Bay. The only time there wasn't a U.S. presence in the Philippines was during World War 2 when the Philippines was invaded by the Japanese. Because the Philippines was considered a U.S. Territory, citizens of the Philippines were allowed to enlist in the U.S. military. Many opted to join the Navy because of its constant presence in Subic Bay. There was no requirement for the new enlistees to speak English fluently.

The Navy had to make an *official policy* that English will be spoken at every command, in all workspaces. They did this because after a while, the Filipino sailors stopped speaking English altogether. It was also discovered that the Filipino sailors were conspiring to keep non-Filipino sailors out of their work centers if the work center was considered a "cushy" assignment. If a white person walked into *their* workspace, if English was being spoken in the first place, it would cease to be spoken in favor of their native tongue, Tagalog.

On many ships the term the "Filipino Mafia" was often used. This was the group of Filipino sailors who always kept to their group, associating with the rest of their shipmates only if it was absolutely necessary. If one of "their kind" got in trouble, they would rally around the person to get him out of trouble. Then they would find out who reported their friend and do everything they could to get that person in trouble or reassigned. They were able to do this because they could speak to each other in the presence of everyone else and no one knew what they were saying. This is another argument for making English the official language of the U.S.

It is for this reason that I am writing the next paragraphs.

One day when you are arrogantly belittling someone in Spanish because you think being able to speak Spanish makes you their better, I hope the person towards whom you are directing your Spanish obscenities puts your foot in your mouth. I hope that after few minutes of ignoring you and your group of *not*

European and therefore not white, Spanish is my native tongue friends, the person confronts you. I honest to God hope the person you are belittling is from Spain, and I hope they correct your "Mexican," "Puerto Rican," or "Guatemalan."

I pray to the Gods and to the Winds that he turns to you and your arrogant friends and makes it known that he has understood all the vile, nauseating filth you have called him. I hope that person looks down their nose at you and explains to you that he is a true Spaniard. That he is not a Hispanic. I further hope they being from Spain, proceed to explain to you that they have spoken Spanish their whole lives too and that your Spanish sucks. Would you like to know what would make this dream of mine better? It would be better if it were a girl that did this to you.

I hope it is a girl because your so-called superior culture, after 500 years of being in New World, still holds women to be second class citizens. You belittle European Americans for the American culture, but no one has ever held you to account for your sexist culture. Yes, the culture you hold up to be superior to all *other* European cultures is a sexist culture. Your culture still believes in the Coming Out Party. Take away all the costumes, take away all the dancing, and all the drinking you are left with nothing more than human trafficking. The Coming Out Party is simply a legal way for a family to let the lecherous perverts of your culture know that your daughter is now available for marriage having attained breeding age; That the patriarch is now entertaining offers.

I said all that because of what I have experienced throughout my life. In the past I found myself many times entering a room with two or more people of Hispanic descent having a conversation. And because I have trained myself not to be oafish in my mannerisms, I don't make a lot of noise when I enter a room. When I need to open a door to enter a room, I don't manhandle the doorknob, while kicking and shaking the door in the process. Then, because it takes a couple seconds for the gossipers to realize that someone not of their crew has entered the room, I hear them speaking English. But as soon as they realize I don't "belong," they immediately start speaking Spanish. If one of these people were to walk into a room where the language being spoken instantly shifted from English to a language they don't understand, they would be screaming racism. If it happened at work, they would be running to HR claiming it creates an uncomfortable work environment.

My critics will claim I don't know what it is like to not speak the language of the country in which I find myself living. If they assume this, they would be wrong. I know exactly what it is like. I also know how difficult it is to learn to speak the language when no one will speak to you in the language of the host country- Even the indigenous people. I also know what it feels like to spend days, nay months speaking the language of the host country- albeit badly- then to suddenly have the opportunity to have a conversation in my native tongue. It can be positively bliss. Yes, I do know what it is like not being able to communicate. What I don't know is how it feels to smugly look down at my nose at someone simply because they don't speak a language which I believe represents a superior culture. I have never done that. Yes, I have complained about people not speaking English, but I stopped that practice when I found myself in a situation where the shoe was on the other foot.

Speaking of "culture"...

Culture! What is a culture? You can look that up for yourself. Here is what made the Roman Empire such a great and powerful empire. Their culture! I can hear the critics. They are saying, "Blah blah blah, slavery. Blah blah blah women's liberation. Blah blah blah, racism. Blah blah blah savages."

The part of Roman culture that made the Roman Empire so successful is the part that recognized every civilization has aspects that were better than the ones practiced by the Romans. When the Romans conquered a civilization, they didn't forcibly assimilate the people over whom they now claimed dominion. They allowed them to continue practicing their religion, and other traditions. Many military advancements made by the Romans were simply the Romans adopting a superior weapon or a superior tactic of the people they had just conquered. That is what made the Romans great. This is what makes America great.

The United States is collection of cultures. We actively welcome other cultures into our culture. That makes the culture of the United States a culture of togetherness. When a person from another country brings with them their culture, we allow the good parts of that culture to become part of our communal culture. It is for good reason that we don't allow into our culture the parts of other cultures that we deem to be bad. Yes, we have banned parts of other cultures irrationally, but as time passed we discovered our errors and we now celebrate those parts. The only thing we ask is that people assimilate and be loyal to the United States, not to "the old country."

However, that isn't what is happening now. People are now coming to the United States and instead of adapting to our laws, customs and traditions, they are expecting the United States to cater to them. Instead of them stopping the practice of child marriages, they are claiming racism, etc. Here is a thought for all the people who want the culture of their "old country" to be the culture of the United States. Why? If the ways of your old country are so superior, why did you leave the old country? Why not go back and save people the headache of having to listen to you drone on and on? It would be much easier for you to return to your country of origin than for you to change the culture of the United States. I pose the same question to the children, grandchildren and great grandchildren of people who immigrated to the United States. Why aren't you trying to return to the sacred land of your ancestors?

The main reason I have a specific section discussing culture is the recent and putrid practice of people claiming cultural appropriation. No one ever counters these lunatics. Their hypocrisy is on par with the climate change hypocrites. In recent years, we have seen white people being condemned for hairstyles one group decided was part of their heritage. We see people trying to get people fired from work because they work at a Mexican restaurant, and they are not Mexican themselves. I caution these people to stop this ignorant practice unless they are willing to stop appropriating other cultures themselves. Here are a few things these people will have to give up in the name of not appropriating other cultures. And since these ignoramuses only direct their ire toward "white people," here is a list of things non-white people will have to give up. This is just a partial list. It does not include everything. Again, this is what non-whites would have to give up just to satisfy the ignorant "culture appropriation" wretches.

Automobiles. If you are not white, you cannot own, ride in, or drive any automobile. This includes buses. If you want me to be specific, unless you are of German descent, you cannot own an automobile. Karl Friedrich Michael Vaillant invented the automobile in 1885. The version of his name we are most familiar with is Carl Benz. Yes, the person who invented the automobile was white. I heard a rumor that not only was he white, but he was also Jewish. If that is the case, at the very least, all the Jew haters in the Middle East and other places must stop driving their expensive Mercedes' lest they support a Jewish company.

Airplanes. If you are not white, you cannot fly anywhere. You must either ride in an automobile, oh wait, you can't do that either, or you must take the train. The airplane was invented by white people, too. No one with less than 50% white ancestry can fly in an airplane. You can ride in a balloon, but you can't fly in an airplane. But I am not too sure about the whole lighter than air flight. You may very well not be allowed in dirigibles either. (For the morons out there, the Hindenburg was a dirigible.)

Trains. Not only can people who are not white ride in passenger trains-light rail or other- they cannot ship anything by train. Nor can they own anything which was shipped by train. So let's recap, under the rules- the very rules adopted by hysterical liberals and other leftists- non-white people can't own, ride in or drive a car. They can't fly anywhere, nor can they take the train. And since the horse is indigenous to neither the Americas, nor Africa, no one claiming Native American or African ancestry (no matter how slight) can ride a horse. It's a good thing that many of these people love their Air Jordans because they are going to need them, and not just as a conversation starter. Why? Because in order to get from Point A to Point B, most non-white people are going to be walking everywhere. Again, these are the rules established by leftists, liberals, and others who scream about cultural appropriation.

Here's one for the women. A person who is neither white, nor female can be an automobile mechanic. Yep! That's right, regardless of the repairs being made to an automobile, all work being done in automotive repair shops must immediately cease until the entire workforce consists entirely of white women. Why? Because not only was the first automobile mechanic white, but she was also a woman. And not a newfangled woman sporting a wiener bigger than her husband's. This woman was old fashioned as they come. She was born with a womb. Her name, Bertha Ringer Benz. Also known as: Mrs. Karl Friedrich Michael Vaillant, or Mrs. Carl Benz. If you don't believe me, look it up!

In support of the next Women's History Month, unless a person is a white woman, they can neither use nor can they own a dishwashing machine. Dishpan hands are the new fashion fad for non-white, non-female people.

Also, invented by a white person is the clothes washing machine. I hope the "people of color" needing to wash their clothes not only have a decent rock upon which they can wash their clothes, but that they can free up 8 hours in their busy schedule every other day to wash their clothes in the same manner as *their* venerated ancestors. They can have a community *Suds and Scrub* to celebrate their non-whiteness.

This particular item has a bit of irony attached. One of the most common instances of cultural appropriation screamed about by clueless African American college students is the hairstyle known as "Dreadlocks." For those of you who don't know what dreadlocks are, it is a hair style where the hair is braided in big, oversized braids, and then not washed. Many times, it looks frizzy. The ironic part is if a person can only use or wear stuff from their culture, then the Africa American students who cried hysterically about a white guy walking around sporting dreadlocks must now walk around in unwashed clothes to match their unwashed hair.

I could go on with more examples until they number in the thousands, but I won't. If you would like to see people's hypocrisy on full display, begin enforcing the cultural appropriation rules liberal are trying to foist upon everyone. I guarantee to you that just as everyone is Irish on Saint Patrick's Day, overnight 99% of the people peacocking about how they are *not* white, will suddenly be embracing their inner Caucasian just so they can own a car. There will be a mass influx of DNA testing to find out the extent of their whiteness. The absolution, which they have denied others for the original sin of slavery, will suddenly be what they demand most.

As cautionary note, if our society continues down this road everyone who supports western civilization will need to stand up for history. They will need to stubbornly refuse the many one-for-one agreements where the results are lopsided in favor of one side or the other. Don't let people claim that the value of one item from their culture is greater than it truly is. For instance, if someone who isn't Caucasian wants to drive a car, don't let that person claim that the intrinsic value of the tomato is on par with the intrinsic value of an automobile. Make them regret their sickening arrogance. Make them regret it bigly.

Here's an example of homo-racial cultural appropriation. This example is apt for the next section of the book, slavery. Specifically on the subject of reparations for the ancestors of those slaves. I need to caution people, there is a considerable amount of contradictory evidence in the early life of Kamala Harris, specifically in the years she claims she was bussed to school. All the citations appear to be from recent works. There appears to be no source material used which was published prior to her being nominated to be and subsequently ascending to the Office of Vice President. My information was gathered from sources *prior* to her being named the Democrat party's pick for Vice President, and those sources have subsequently been removed from the internet or never show up in a search.

African Americans need to realize that our illustrious Vice President, Kamala Harris, isn't African American in the same vein that they are African America. When our society thinks of African Americans, we ascribe to them a history which includes slavery and civil rights issues. Kamala Harris is not entitled to that embedded respect. NONE! She is a liar. She is not a descendant of slaves. She is the descendant of slave owners. Her own father said as much prior to the 2020 election. She did not experience discrimination the same many African Americans experienced because she grew up in Canada. In fact, many of her stories about a childhood filled with instances of racism being directed at her are the fabrications a washed-up politician would create when they are desperately trying to reinvigorate a career marred with failure. Yes, she was born in the United States, but for much of her life she lived in Canada.

The most reprehensible way she actively appropriated African American culture- not being a true African American herself- is when she stood on the debate stage and lied about being bussed to school as a little girl. She was trying to get people to believe that she was a victim of segregation in the same manner as other blacks were in the deep south. She knew that if she said what she said, she could garner a sympathy vote, *Oh the poor black girl. I'll vote for her because her family suffered through slavery*. The sad part is that it worked. Almost everyone believes that she is a victim of the Jim Crowe Laws governing the actions of African Americans in the *deep blue, heavily controlled by Democrats,* southern states. If you were to ask people whether or not Kamala Harris was bussed to school like her black counterparts in Alabama, they will reply in the affirmative.

Here is the truth behind *her* family history. Again, this information is based on sources readily available on the internet. Had I known at the time I would need them as a reference for a book, I would have done more to safeguard them. Remember, no references being cited on the internet which support her story are dated prior to her being named the Democrat Vice Presidential pick in the 2020 election. To be fair, some of my recollections of her early life differ greatly from what is written currently, but there are discrepancies. However, here is what I discovered *before* she was anointed the next Vice President by a pandering, bootlicking media.

Before her mother moved to Canada and took pre-teen Kamala with her, Kamala Harris lived in Berkeley, California. Kamala Harris wants us all to believe in the late 1960s and early 1970s- during the free speech demonstrations- Berkeley, California was so racist towards blacks, its schools needed to be *forcibly* desegregated. This is what the bussing in the deep south was, forced *Desegregation*. If this is the case, Berkeley, California needs to explain why it took almost 20 years for Berkeley to desegregate its schools. But that is not what was happening to Kamala Harris, contrary to what is currently written as part of her biography. Yes, she was "bussed" to school, but the reason she was bussed to school is the same reason children are bussed to school today. There was one caveat, though. Had this caveat not been a factor in her schooling, she would have attended a school in *her* neighborhood with her peers.

Our illustrious VP wants us to believe that her ethnicity was the *only* reason she had to ride a bus to school, but that is contrary to the truth. If race had anything to do with her having to be "bussed" to school, it was not *her* race that required it. It was the race of her parents. Her father is an Afro Jamaican. Her mother is an Indian.

But the race of her parents wasn't the primary reason she was bussed to school either. If anything, her race, and her parent's races were secondary, or maybe tertiary reasons. The primary reason Kamala rode the bus is because her parents were secondarily not white, and that afforded them- not her- a special privilege. This is the caveat I mentioned earlier. Without *this* caveat, Kamala Harris would have been walking to school in all her Afro Jamaican Indian American glory.

Prior to Berkeley, California being known as the childhood home of a Vice President of the United States, Berkeley, California was better known as the location of the University of California at Berkeley, UC Berkeley colloquially. At about the same time Kamala Harris lived in Berkeley, California, UC Berkeley was the center of the free speech and anti-war movements. This is what was happening in the world when Kamala Harris was "bussed" to school. I purposely bring up UC Berkeley because UC Berkeley is the real reason Kamala Harris was "bussed" to school. Without UC Berkeley, Kamala Harris would have learned what it is like to walk to school. UC Berkeley created the caveat.

In the 1960s both of Kamala's parents were attending UC Berkeley as Graduate students. Because her parents were minorities, more importantly because they were minority *graduate* students, Kamala's parents qualified for a special program sponsored by, if not outright under the control of the University of California at Berkeley. This is contradictory to what is written today, which states that both her mother and her father attained doctorates in their fields of study in 1964 and 1966 respectively. I have no reason to doubt this. However, in 1966 her family began a nomadic lifestyle in the U.S. Midwest as her parents were hired by various schools until her mother, sister and herself moved back to California in 1970 where they took up residence in Berkeley, California. There is no mention of when her father moved back to California, but when he did, he lived in Palo Alto, not Berkeley.

Before I continue, in my effort to at least get the dates correct, I ran into a dilemma. That dilemma being what if I am wrong in all things? What if I am correct in some things? And, what if my original reference material was correct being purposely deleted so no one would find out the facts? Should I continue to write this section? I decided that I will continue to write this section because with such a litany of contradictions, only a discussion by the masses can sort out what is fact and what is fable. Which is the correct biography, the one prior to her being Vice President, or the one now being proffered?

Here is the real reason Kamala Harris was "bussed" to school. Earlier I mentioned a caveat about Kamala's childhood education. The caveat was that since her parents were graduate students at UC Berkeley and because they were not white, they qualified for a special program offered by UC Berkeley. In a nutshell the program was this, I apologize for the redundancy, if a graduate student is enrolled at UC Berkeley and they are a minority, their children could attend a school sponsored by the University along with the children of other UC Berkeley graduate students who were also not white. This means Kamala Harris went to a private school. While riding the bus to school if she looked around, yes, it was only minority children riding the bus, but they too were going to this private school.

Again, I have no way of knowing how much of this is correct because my reference material has been removed from the internet or algorithms are preventing it from being searchable. If all this is false, explain to me what Kamala's mother's profession was in the six years they lived in Berkeley, California prior to them moving to Canada. With only a few convenient exceptions where she talks about all the racial discrimination she experienced, there is no mention of her mother's nor her father's situation following their divorce in 1971. It's as if Kamala Harris was supporting herself from the age of six to twelve.

191

If what I am positing is true, then Kamala Harris needs to apologize to the African American community for attempting to appropriate a history that is not hers. If I am incorrect, the city of Berkeley needs to explain why it took them 20 years to desegregate *their* schools following the Supreme Court's decision in the landmark case, Brown versus the Board of Education.

CHAPTER SIXTEEN

SLAVERY

These next paragraphs need to be prefaced with the phrase,
"Ignorance of the law is not an excuse."

Ignoring the media's blatant lies surrounding criminal activities involving multiple ethnic groups, we are well on our way to *returning* to being a country where racism is the norm. The most egregious example of normalizing racism is done by the very people who swear to uphold our laws, the U.S. Congress. In 2021, Congress, more specifically the racist Democrat party, under the guise of recognizing racial disparity or whatever is the current nauseating platitude du jour, created the new federal holiday of Juneteenth. Why? The official reason is to celebrate the end of slavery by recognizing the date the last groups of slaves were notified that the 13th amendment had passed Congress.

This is BS, because slavery didn't end on 19 June 1865, the day now called "Juneteenth." It didn't end on January 31st when the amendment passed the House of Representatives. Nor did it end when the amendment passed in the US Senate almost a year earlier. Slavery ended when the 13th Amendment was "…ratified by the Legislatures of three fourths of the several States…" and that date was 8 December 1865. Almost 6 months *after* the date we now are to call, "Juneteenth," and a full 10-plus months after it passed in the House of Representatives. If we are to celebrate the date the *last* person was notified, we must celebrate Juneteenth sometime after 18 December, the date of the first notification that the 13th amendment had been ratified by the required number of states- 27 of 36.

Juneteenth is not a holiday that celebrates what pundits claim it celebrates. It's a holiday that celebrates the antebellum south and its archaic system of communication. The reason it took 6 months for the last of the slaves in Texas to be notified of the passage of the 13th amendment is because the southern states had an antiquated communication infrastructure. Not to mention the fact that a war was being fought and much of the existing communications network had been destroyed by the United States Army while it prosecuted the war. If we are to continue celebrating this faux holiday- one whose importance to the African American community was so great it went uncelebrated and unknown for 155 years- then we should at least use the proper date. If the Emancipation Proclamation freed the slaves, as many people are quick to believe, then we should celebrate Juneteenth on the date the last slaves in Texas were told about the Emancipation.

In an effort to dispel myths about slavery, let's discover when slavery truly ended.

It ended on the date the 13th Amendment was *ratified*. There's a good reason for this. Legal scholars will be debating this for centuries upon reading what I am about to say. Had the States failed to ratify the 13th Amendment, it would have been a dead Act- Not dead law. If a proposed amendment fails state ratification- even if it passed both houses of Congress unanimously- it does not become a run-of-the-mill law because it was intended to be an amendment. In order for it to become a law, congress would need to begin the process anew. Only this time to pass it as a law. Why should we celebrate 18 December? Because ignorance of the law is no excuse. It does not matter if the last slaves were notified of the ratification in 1903. The courts would still recognize the enacted date as December 18th, 1865, unless there is a time delay within the amendment such as, "Will be in effect the first Monday of July following ratification." Therefore, any slave owner who did not immediately free their slaves could and would be charged for kidnapping, holding people against their will, etc. beginning on that date. Otherwise, someone who is breaking the law could claim they weren't breaking the law simply because no one told them face to face that the law had been passed.

Quick example using a different subject, on 2 September 1945, Japan signed the Instrument of Surrender formally ending World War 2. However, no one in his chain of command personally told Hiroo Onoda, a Japanese soldier stationed in the Philippines that the war was over. He continued to fight the war until he surrendered in March 1974. If we continue to celebrate Juneteenth as the official end date of slavery because that is when the last slaves were notified, then we must also acknowledge that World War 2 ended much later- thirty years later- than we celebrate it ending now. There was a second Japanese soldier that continued to fight World War 2 longer than Onoda. Teruo Nakamura didn't surrender until December of 1974. So, when did World War 2 end?

Contrary to popular belief, President Lincoln's Emancipation Proclamation did not end slavery. The Emancipation Proclamation was a Standing Order issued by the Commander in Chief of the US Armed Forces to his subordinates. It simply says that when the US military takes control of a territory, any slave residing within that territory is immediately deemed to be free. The Geneva Convention of 1949 has a similar "order." It states that the occupying force is responsible for the welfare of civilians in the occupied areas.

President Lincoln knew this about his Emancipation Proclamation. As did the Democrats who did not want the slaves to be freed. It is why they were so adamant about ending the war prior to the passage of the 13th Amendment. Once the war ended, be it by a peace treaty or surrender, the US Armed Forces would no longer be an occupying force in the eyes of the law. This in turn would make *all* Standing Orders null and void thereby returning all people freed by the Emancipation to a life of involuntary servitude until the ratification of the 13th Amendment. And if democrats could end the war before the passage of the 13th Amendment, they could guarantee that the 13th amendment would not pass.

CHAPTER SEVENTEEN

GET OVER IT

Yes, I said it! Get over it. When I say that, I am not speaking solely to the black community. I am speaking to all races, including the white race. Quit being crybabies about something you cannot change and move on with your lives. No one denies that slavery is bad. However, no amount of hysterical caterwauling is going to change history. No amount of bawling one's eyes out is going to change the fact that, for a *brief* moment in the nation's history, slavery existed. Here's a fact the race baiters don't want anyone to know because it will shatter the façade of moral righteousness in which they have cloaked themselves. It will reveal them to be nothing more than a group of charlatans preying on people's emotions, emotional extortionists! Slavery has existed throughout the world throughout human history. It existed everywhere. It existed everywhere all at once. Slavery isn't just a scourge on the United States. It is a blight on all of human history. So, yes, get over it!

Keep this in mind too, slavery is bad, but only by *today's* standards. I know, it's reprehensible that I said that, but it's true. Long before the country was founded, and well after the US Civil War, a good portion of the rest of the world considered slavery normal and not immoral. It's sad that I am one who needs to tell everyone this because it shows that our revered teachers and professors are failures. Slavery WAS NOT invented in the United States, nor was it invented by the United States. What was invented by the United States are the concepts, "…all men are created equal," and "…Life, liberty, and the pursuit of happiness…"

Not even the ancient Greeks- the Athenians specifically- had those concepts. Yes, in Athens you could improve your lot in life and you could attain greatness in your own right but even following the reforms of Cleisthenes you weren't an equal *until* you succeeded. If you were born into poverty, you could not vote until you achieved a certain level of economic success. If you were born rich on the other hand, you could vote and attend the Areopagus as soon as you attained the proper age. The truly groundbreaking idea to come from Athens at this time was that one's participation in the Athenian government could be taken away if you squandered your inheritance.

Yes, both American concepts are contradicted by having a portion of the US economy dependent on the use of slave labor, but the founding fathers were aware of this contradiction. How else does one explain the 3/5 compromise?

For the purposes of representation in the US House of Representatives, the Constitution states, "…other Persons…" shall be counted as 3/5 of a human being. It does not say, "_Slaves will be counted as 3/5 of a person._" Neither slavery nor its root word are used in the Constitution until the years 1865 and 1867 respectively. Therefore, when the ignorant activists, to whom the black community has apparently tethered themselves claim slavery is enshrined in the Constitution, they are wrong. Literally wrong! But that too is wrong. The correct way to say that is to say, "They are literally, literally wrong." Yes, one must use the word literally twice. As result of this, all that was needed to free the slaves was a lawsuit, honest judges and honest Justices.

Had the Founding Fathers shared the same view about slavery, the compromise itself would not have been necessary. Obviously if everyone were against slavery, it would have been outlawed at the Country's inception and therefore there would not have been a need for the 3/5 compromise. Had everyone been okay with slavery, the wording in the Constitution would have been a variation of, "The number of slaves a person owns _will not_ be taken into consideration for purposes of representation," or "The number of slaves a person owns _will_ be taken into consideration for the purposes of representation." There may or may not be anything that stipulates whether they should be counted as a whole person or as a fractional person.

However, and contrary to popular belief, it was foreign _and_ domestic politics, not economics, which made the 3/5 compromise necessary. On the world stage, had the 3/5 compromise not existed, the slave states would have become a separate country unto themselves. This would have guaranteed two things:

First, that slavery would exist in the United State in perpetuity.

Second, that every foreign power able to project power abroad *would* view the splintering of the young United States into two separate countries as a sign of weakness. This, in turn, would lead to an invasion by a foreign power.

For everyone's information, the US Navy would not have been able to prevent an invasion because there was effectively no U.S. Navy to intercept other navies. Following the Revolutionary War, Congress sold off most of the ships to pay debts incurred during the Revolutionary War. The first ships built in the United States, by the United States, and for the United States would not be laid down until 1795.

Maybe Spain would launch an invasion from Florida. Spain could have gathered troops from all its New World colonies and massed them in Cuba or Mexico. Once they were gathered, they could have landed in Florida and marched north and attacked Georgia. Maybe Great Britian would mass troops and invade from Canada. This is what they did in the War of 1812. Or maybe our first ally, France, would have invaded from New Orleans under the leadership of Napolean Bonaparte. It was entirely probable one of them would have invaded. The first country to invade may have gotten its butt kicked by the battle-hardened US Army, but because the US Army would have been even more exhausted afterwards, the next country to attack would conquer us.

This is how the Chinese Communist Party came to power in China. During World War 2, while Chiang Kai-Shek and the Nationalists were actively fighting the Japanese, the cowardly Communists under Mao were cowering in caves. After the war, after 10 straight years of intense fighting, the forces under Chiang were exhausted. Mao only needed make empty promises of equity for all peasants and he walked into the presidential palace virtually unopposed. To be sure there was some resistance to Mao, but for the most part the Nationalists gave up because they were exhausted, and their enemy was well rested.

By the way, World War 2 started in 1937 with the Japanese invasion of China, not with the 1939 German invasion of Poland. It was the Japanese invasion of China which caused the U.S. to cut off the supply of oil to Japan. President Roosevelt didn't wake up one morning and suddenly decide to stop selling oil to Japan for no reason as the dishonest Marxist professors in academia would have everyone to believe. (Yes, professors in colleges and university are actively teaching students that the United States, for no reason whatsoever, stopped the flow of oil to Japan and therefore the United States deserved to be attacked on 7 December 1941.)

Since I brought up China, I would be remiss if I didn't bring up the Soviet Union. Lenin, Stalin, and Trotsky didn't overthrow the Czar by brute force or a populist uprising. The civilian population was starving because most of the food was being sent to the army fighting on the frontlines of World War 1. The army was exhausted, and the soldiers began to desert en masse. Not only that, but the interim government established following the Czar's abdication was in disarray. Lenin, Stalin, and Trotsky, as Mao would do thirty years later, essentially walked into power. There was no revolution in the street as Soviet propaganda at the time shows, that was all staged or were motion pictures of other incidents. That appears to be the modus operandi of communist dictators. When the going gets tough, hide in a cave or go into exile until the opposition has killed each other off, then when the people can least defend themselves, murder a few thousand and take over.

Back to the U.S....

On the home front when the country was founded, had the 3/5 compromise not existed and slaves counted as whole persons in accordance with the desires of the southern states, the Representative headcount in the U.S. House of Representatives would have permanently favored the slave owners. Yes, permanently! The only way for the Republic, *sans* the southern states, to counter the "extra" population would be through childbirth and immigration. In 1787, America increasing the population through breeding at the speed needed to overcome the instant legislative advantage slaveholding states would have exercised was unlikely since child mortality was much higher than it is today.

Immigration was equally unlikely because the United States was not a destination of choice. In fact, the developed countries of the world viewed the United States as a third world backwater. Some might have called it a third world shithole. Further, even if immigration and childbirth were able to counter the slaves being counted as whole persons, the southern states could nullify that population increase by importing more Africans. The 3/5 Compromise tempered the southern states unabated ability to instantly flood the country with more people. Any person brought into the United States may only have been counted as 3/5 of a human being, but ships could carry 400 people. After a while, it adds up.

If every day for a year straight at least one ship was to offload 400 people, the population would increase by 150,000 people due solely through forced immigration. For prospective, a 400-person slave ship is a medium to medium-large ship. Some ships that were designed from the keel up to transport humans as cargo could hold twice that much, if not more. If larger ships were used, the population could have increased by half a million people. Further, since there were no laws on the books outlawing slavery or the infrastructure supporting it, this would have been an annual increase. Five years would elapse between the ratification of the US Constitution and the first laws going into effect whose purpose was to stop slavery. That's five years, not fifty years as the race hustlers would have everyone believe.

Five years of importing 150,000 people annually would increase the population of the US by three quarters of a million people. By today's standards, this increase in population would result in only ONE additional representative being seated in the US House of Representatives. Increasing the number of representatives by one person would not have a great effect on the legislation being passed. But that is by today's calculus of one Representative for every 750,000 people.

In 1787 the rubric was one Representative for every 30,000 people. Without the 3/5 Compromise, five years of unabated and uncontrolled importation of additional Africans would have increased the Representative headcount by twenty-five. That's a two and a five jammed together! 25! By comparison, initial headcount of the U.S. House of Representative, as codified in the Constitution, was 65 Representatives. This number would not change until the next census in 1790. An increase of 25 people would be almost a 50% change.

Of these 65 initial Representatives, thirty would be the Representatives from states we traditionally think of as slave states. However, at the time of ratification New York was a slave state. New York would not outlaw slavery in its entirety until 1799. If New York were counted as a slave state, the representative count would be 36 in favor of slavery. That's more than half. Add twenty-five people to thirty-six, and the slave-holding states could pass an amendment. If you don't believe me, do the math. If the 1790 census found no increase in the population other than an increase in the African American population, it would have resulted in a House of Representatives having a total of 90 persons. Of which, 61 (including New York) would represent slave states.

Continuing, it takes two-thirds of the House to pass an Amendment, even to this day. Two-thirds of 90 is 60. An amendment forever legalizing slavery could have passed the House by one vote. With the 3/5 Compromise in place the number of additional Representatives would have been 15, not 25. It would take nine representatives from the non-slave states to pass an amendment. Before anyone starts in with their righteous anger let me finish with this, I can guarantee that none of these additional Representatives would be African American.

The practice of importing people to change the makeup of a country is not a fluke. It is happening before our very eyes. It is happening in real time in Ukraine. It is happening with mass uncontrolled immigration from predominantly Muslim countries into Europe. It is also happening to the United States with Marxist Joe Biden's mass influx of people from Latin American countries. The illegal aliens coming from Latin American aren't solely people who originated from Latin American countries. It is a free-for-all. If a person can make their way to any country in the western hemisphere- including Canada, President Joe Biden, the Marxist in Chief, is turning a blind eye when they illegally enter the United States. This isn't a new strategy.

The Soviets were able to keep control of the Baltic States because they forcibly emigrated to the Baltic countries large numbers of citizens who were more loyal to the Communist Party in Moscow than they were to their own mothers. And, in the split second it took those people to cross the border into those countries, not only did they become citizens of their new country, they were also given the right to vote in all elections. Who do you reckon they elected into office when elections took place? People whose loyalties lie with their new country, or people loyal to Moscow?

The Russians are currently reprising this tried-and-true tactic in Ukraine. Not only that, but they have added an additional twist. First, they are moving Russian citizens who would never vote against Vladimir Putin into the parts of Ukraine under the control of the Russian Army. Second, they are rounding up Ukrainians and deporting them to Russia. They are doing this concurrently. Here is *a known* but never talked about fact. The number of Ukrainians starved to death by Stalin *prior to* World War Two is greater than the number of Jews killed by Hitler during the war by a two to one ratio. For some reason, even with this knowledge, Joseph Stalin was named Time Magazine's Man of the Year in 1939 and 1942; Adolf Hitler 1938. This mass starvation was ordered so that Stalin could gain and maintain control of Ukrainian farmland. If you control the food supply, you control the people.

Here's a rhetorical exercise.

Are foreign countries and multi-billionaires- the global "elites"- buying US farmland because they believe farming is the next big economic boom? Think about that.

The first law passed under the Constitution designed to stop the spread of slavery and to hamper if not eliminate the international slave trade to the

United States, was enacted in 1794 - Seven years after the Constitution was ratified. For seven years, Africans continued to be imported throughout the Americas to every country, and territory in the western hemisphere, not just to the United States. In 1794, President George Washington signed into law the Slave Trade Act of 1794. While this law did not outlaw slavery, it did make it illegal for any person, regardless of citizenship status, living within the boundaries of the United States or its territories to provide material support to the international slave trade. It may not have abolished slavery, but it did make it more difficult, a lot more difficult, for new slaves to be imported. With passage of this law, all *new* Africans brought to the United States had to be sold on the black market. And any ship found to have been transporting slaves after 1794, could be confiscated and the crew imprisoned.

We do the same thing for modern problems. We make it illegal for US citizens to provide material support to terrorist organizations, for instance. The importing of slaves would not become illegal until the Act Prohibiting the Importation of Slaves of 1807 became law. Had the 3/5 compromise not been worded into the Constitution as it was thereby resulting in all slaves being counted as whole persons, what are the chances that either Act would have been signed into law?

The 3/5 compromise *ensured* the demise of slavery in the United States. Believe it or not, it made it possible to outlaw slavery through the interpretation of law. As I said earlier, all it would have taken to ban slavery outright prior to the US Civil War was a lawsuit, honest judges and honest justices. Amongst other arguments, a slave making the argument for emancipation could have stated that he or she is a free person since they or their ancestor was not born a slave in Africa. That they were kidnapped. That kidnapping only superficially makes a person un-free. That a person cannot absolve themself of one crime by committing another crime, kidnapping being the first crime. That being born to a kidnapped person does not give another person dominion over new life since a person cannot be property. That the Constitution itself considers slaves "...other Persons..." not property.

I said it once, and I'll say it here too. Slavery was not invented in the United States, nor was it invented by the United States. Slavery has existed *throughout the world* for the breadth of human civilization. If prostitution was the first profession, slavery was the second. If one wishes to determine the origins of slavery, there is one possible origin story the Race Hustling Industrial Complex (RHIC) will seek to discredit with all due haste. It is based on the hypothesis that because the oldest human remains were found in Africa, it was Africans who invented human civilization. If one subscribes to this hypothesis, then Africans invented slavery as well - Which would make the first slavers African, not European. Not Czechoslovakian

There is another origin story more in keeping with the approved RHIC narrative that white people invented slavery. Here is the rationale. The oldest known written reference to slavery was uncovered in the area of the world known as the Balkans. This is the area to the north of Greece. Evidence supporting this hypothesis is the use of the word "Slav," as in Yugo-SLAV-ia. Etymologists believe eventually the spelling of "slav" morphed into "slave." Further because getting people to run as a group was the fastest form of mass transportation in use when the first documentation of slavery was made, the use of slavery itself was localized to that region. And for that same reason, the first slaves were from that region too; not from sub-Saharan Africa, an unknown land 2000 miles away.

I hate to break the news to the RHIC, but Africans were the *last* group of people to be enslaved by a group of people not like themselves. They were not the first, and they were certainly not the only group of people to be enslaved. In fact, because Africans were being enslaved by their brethren, slavery was thriving business in sub-Saharan Africa long before the Europeans set foot upon the African shoreline of the Atlantic Ocean. Yes, tribes of Africans in Sub-Saharan Africa were enslaving each other. The mass enslavement of Africans by another race of people other than Africans didn't occur until the 14th century. Why? Because for most of western history no one knew the African race existed.

During the days of the Roman Empire there were token Africans who dared to trek challenge the Sahara Desert, but for the most part the African race remained south of the Sahara Desert. The first mass migration of Africans out of sub-Saharan Africa occurred along the Nile River with the period known as the time of the Black Pharaohs. This period began around 750 BC and ended a hundred years later. Prior to this period yes the ancient Egyptians did have contact with sub-Saharan Africans- the Nubians- but it was a relatively rare occurrence due to the great distances between the two civilizations, and because the ancient Egyptians had other worries. The greatest threat to their way of life came from the north, not the south- The Assyrians, Phoenicians, Babylonians, to name a few. It was only when the Pharaohs decided to extend their empire southward that they encountered the Nubians. The main reason for the two peoples' coming into contact with each other was war. Each side believed the Nile River was their domain; That they had to conquer and defend this land. The Egyptians did conquer. They were the superpower of their day.

If you would like documentation of people other than Africans being enslaved, there are countless sources. One of the oldest sources is the Bible. The Exodus! Moses leading the Israelites out of Egypt only after Pharoah freed the Jews. Pray tell, from what were the Jews freed? Oh, that's right, slavery. Historians believe the Pharoah who set the Israelites free, at the behest of Moses, was Rameses II who died circa 1213 BC. That means that Jews were enslaved almost 3000 years before the first slaves landed in Jamestown. Another instance from the Bible, there is also the tale of Daniel and the Lion in the Book of Daniel. Daniel was thrown into a lion's den and when the lion didn't eat him, the king of Babylon set him and his people free. Again, it was the Jews who were released from bondage, not Africans. This story is believed to have taken place in the 5th century BC- approximately 2000 years before the first slaves arrived at Jamestown. In fact, Jewish history is the history of slavery because every couple hundred years some other civilization would conquer Israel and enslaves the Jews.

Here's a story which does not use the Bible as a reference. One to which Senator Corey Booker tried to associate himself. The story of Spartacus. His saga of slavery ended in 71 BC when the Roman legions under Crassus defeated him and his army of escaped slaves. His body was never found. Stories of his exploits were recorded by the Roman historians, Plutarch, Appian and Florus. Not only did Spartacus live and die 1,690 years before Jamestown received its first slaves, but Spartacus was not African. This is going to come as a shock to many people, but it cannot be assumed that throughout history all slaves looked like African Americans. Spartacus was Thracian. Yes, Senator Booker was appropriating a culture that was not his own. Spartacus was captured in battle and as was the custom of the time, he became a slave as a spoil of war. His homeland of Thrace includes parts of modern-day Bulgaria and Turkey.

Let's look at the history of slavery in other parts of the world, in particular the far east countries of China, India, Mongolia. Before he died in 1227 A.D., Genghis Khan conquered most of Asia, and parts of Europe making his empire the largest ever. When he conquered a village, if they didn't readily submit to his rule, he enslaved much, if not all of the population. Even the people Genghis Kahn didn't conquer, but who openly resisted his rule had slaves. One of these rulers was an Indian named Alauddin Khilji. In an effort to prevent him being overthrown by people sympathetic to Genghis Kahn, not only did he order the massacre of 20,000 men, but he had their women and children enslaved.

Chinese history too, is a veritable list of the different Chinese States trying to conquer each other. Even after the first emperor united the different states, they still had disputes amongst each other. If they were successful, they would take people as slaves. Not only that, but when one dynasty was overthrown, the next dynasty enslaved its political rivals. For instance, the Ming Dynasty took control of China in 1368 wresting it from the Yuan Dynasty. Guess what the Mings did to the Yuan, they hunted them down, enslaving their political rivals.

Fear not though, the Ming Dynasty gave us things other than a legacy of slavery. The pretty looking brick structure we picture in our heads when we think of the Great Wall of China, was built by the Ming emperors. The Ming Dynasty also gave us the ever-present movie prop, the Ming Vase that is always being broken or is the center piece of a negotiation. The Ming Dynasty ended in 1644 AD, having been defeated by the Shun. The Shun after a brief rule of 30 years were defeated by the Qing with the help of the Manchu. Every conquering dynasty made slaves of the vanquished. Look at paintings depicting scenes from 16th and

17th century China. The people whose heads are bald in the front and not the back, those are slaves.

The point is that slavery was a world-wide norm. It was everywhere. It was not defeated because people found it to be a despicable practice. Slavery was an economic necessity. Today when we think of farms, we think of huge tractors doing in one day what would take a hundred men a week to do. Let's throw out the stereotype of what a slave looks like. Let's also throw out the stereotype of a slave living on the Master's Plantation, in a collective hovel, it too being on the master's plantation.

Now, let us answer this question. In medieval Europe, who farmed the fields? The kings and queens of England didn't, nor did their subservient barons, dukes and knights. The German Kaiser didn't farm the land, neither did any count or countess. The people that farmed the land, the people that worked from sun-up to sun-down, day-in, day-out were the peasants. Serfs. Peasants were, for all intents and purposes, slaves of the aristocracy. Yes they did get paid, but it wasn't in the form of a paycheck. It was in the form of being allowed to keep some of the crops they grew on the land they were allowed to farm with the blessing of the Big Guy living in the castle. European nobility did not have a need for slaves from Africa they had their serfs. Importing other people to work the land would have been economic suicide.

In the New World slaves became a necessary evil simply because there was no one else available. In the beginning, when Spain and Portugal were still dividing up the New World, Native Americans were present, but 25 years after Columbus landed the Native American population had been thoroughly decimated by disease and warfare. Depending on which scholarly study a person reads, by the time the English settled Jamestown, disease and enslavement by the Spanish had killed off 50 to 90 percent of the native population. This was continent wide, not just along the eastern seaboard of the United States. Even if the number is towards the lesser amount, there still wasn't enough indigenous manpower available to make large plantations economically viable. There was barely enough manpower to operate small, individual farms.

If the plantations of the New World were going to out produce the slave plantations in India, China, and Indonesia, they needed a huge workforce. One that wasn't susceptible to European and Asian diseases. They couldn't import peasants from the "old country" because if they did, there would be no one to farm the land in the "old country." Yes people- Africans and Europeans- could be brought over and paid for their work, but operating a plantation had a small profit margin. Profits weren't made by sending one ship loaded with raw materials back to Europe. Profits were made by sending a hundred ships loaded with raw materials back to the European markets. And the only way to keep up with demand was by farming hundreds of acres, not tens of acres.

Yeah, yeah, yeah, I hear you. It is true that cotton and sugar cane could have been sourced from the traditional suppliers in Asia, as was the status quo at the time. However, those sources have one huge problem, they were in Asia. Can you hear that? It's the sound of the smug, righteous voices of the moral crusaders. They are saying something. Let's listen closely and see if we can make out what they are saying.

(sounds of people chanting)

If I...

(sound of chains dragging on the floor)

If I were...

(More chanting, more chains. Getting closer and closer, louder and louder.)

If I were a...

(More chanting, in harmony with each other for a change. Cue the organ and the violins. Holy righteous music plays in the background. The devout begin their cadence.)

If I were a merchant at the time, I would have taken any economic loss and continued to purchase raw materials from my Asian sources. I am a moral person. I am an honorable person. I am an ethical person. I am virtuous.

To which I say, "Horse pucks!" Not just horse pucks. Horse, cow, goat, and guinea pig pucks. Big steaming piles of them. Remember, not only would the Suez Canal not be built for another 300 years, but it would be 200 years before even the most rudimentary of steam ships plied the oceans. These two facts by themselves ensured slavery would exist in the New World.

Think about this for a minute. Prior to the Americas becoming an agricultural alternative to India, a person wanting to go to India had to either walk- WALK, not drive- 2,500 miles overland via the Silk Road or sail- SAIL, not steam- 13,000 miles around Cape Horn. Going to China was an even longer trip. A round-trip journey to India and back via the Silk Road spanned 2 years. A round-trip journey on a sailing ship took one year. This is just traveling time. This doesn't count the amount of time it took to source the supplies, load the cargo, etc. It doesn't even count the amount of time it took to get the ship back on course if the ship was blown off course, or if the ship needed to stop and be repaired.

When the Americas were discovered and it was realized sugar cane and cotton could grow equally as well in the Americas, the amount of time it took to get cotton and sugarcane to the European market went from one or two years down to one or two months. Not only that, but now that the crops were much closer to the market, in the year it took a ship to sail from England to India and return, a ship traveling between England and Jamestown could make 6 round trip journeys. Further, in the amount of time it took to walk the Silk Road, a ship making the Jamestown run could make 12 round trips.

Basic economics states that when there is high demand but low supply, the price increases. The discovery of the New World didn't decrease the demand, but it did increase the supply. Europe went from only having enough spices to meet the demands of the aristocracy, to having such vast quantities of spices, peasants could afford these same exotic spices. No, the spices weren't grown in the Americas but now ships making a run to India and Indonesia, could completely fill their holds with spices and forgo the textiles. Once the Americas were brought online economically, everything became affordable. It's the colonial equivalent of what Henry Ford's assembly line did for the automobile.

Prior to Henry Ford, cars were so expensive only the well-to-do could afford them. After the assembly line, well, look out the window.

Aside from the distance to market being whittled down to a 12th of what it was at the time, and the labor force needed being almost nonexistent, there are two additional items that ensured the existence of slavery in the New World- The entire New World not just the British Colonies.

Fact number three, the Silk Road facilitating trade between Europe and the Far East, for all intents and purposes had been severed by the Ottoman Empire. Once under the control of the Ottoman Turks, anyone transporting goods was required to pay extravagant duties, taxes, and other fees. These taxes drove up the cost of goods exponentially, thus making the already out of reach spices even more out of reach. There were taxes that had to be paid at almost every waypoint along the way. Think of modern-day toll roads. There's never just one toll booth. We won't talk about the ever-present threat of highway robbery bringing an element of danger to the journey. Even the less fortunate members of the aristocracy were becoming unable to afford spices and such. And it wasn't one tax for the entire journey.

The fourth fact that ensured slavery would be present in the New World was that prior to Columbus sailing the ocean blue in 1492, the slave trade was already in full swing, as I mentioned. Yes, you read that correctly. The slave trade pre-dates Columbus. Allow me to rephrase that sentence. The Africa slave trade pre-dates Columbus. The slave trade started on the east coast of Africa, not the west coast. By the time the Dutch brought the first Africans to the Americas, the Arabs had been bringing African slaves to the Middle East for centuries. The Muslims of North Africa and the Ottoman Empire were the first to sell Africans to Europeans. The Muslims, the conquerors of Africa, were the originators of the European slave trade.

Contrary to what most people probably believe about the slave trade, the crews of European slave ships weren't trekking into the wilds of Africa kidnapping people. Most Africans were brought to the slave ports by their own tribesmen. Their own families traded their lives for European firearms and trinkets. Funny how that works isn't it? First, the Africans trade their own relatives for firearms, then the Native Americans trade land for firearms and trinkets. No one ever mentions that Europeans *bought* a good portion of the land from the Native Americans. It's only considered stolen land. It is always *automatically* assumed that the land was stolen.

Economics beget slavery, not a lack of morals. The reason there isn't a major African population in the Middle East even though the slave trade flourished for centuries, is because when African men were brought to the Middle East, the Sheiks, Emirs, and other Arabs to whom they were sold castrated their newly acquired African slaves. This made them less likely to run away or cause trouble. It's the same reason we neuter dogs and cats today. When the subject of reparations rears its ugly head again, let's have an honest discussion about it and have the descendants of those who started the slave trade and who did the kidnapping pay reparations too. Hey, all is fair in love and equity.

It's a common theme for me that slavery was the norm, not just in the United States, but throughout the entire world. Not only that, once again in sharp contrast to what the race hustlers want us to believe- the US Civil War only brought slavery to an end in the United States. For nearly half a century following Lee's surrender at Appomattox Courthouse, the slave trade continued to thrive off the east coast of Africa. A different war, a bloodier war, would have to be fought before slavery would end. Before the RHIC gets their paws on this inconvenient factoid; this war was not fought to end slavery. The eradication of slavery was a side effect. World War One was not only *The War to End All Wars*. It was the war that brought slavery to an end. Why? Mechanization!

Not only did the Industrial Revolution make slavery obsolete, but it also made it economically unviable. Had the US not fought its Civil War, had Abraham Lincoln not been elected the 16th President of the United States, slavery would have fizzled out with a whimper by the turn of the century.

Having entered the Industrial Age (Revolution) over a decade previous to the American Revolution beginning, England was fast becoming an industrial powerhouse like no other country on the planet. The advancements in industrial technology weren't enough to turn the tide of the Revolution in their favor, but following the war, industrialization exploded. The steam engine and other industrial machines were so state of the art that the British government considered their export to be a matter of national security. For national security reasons, the fledgling United States wouldn't enter the Industrial Age until the early 1800s. What we do with computers and electronics today is what was done with James Watt's steam engine in the late 1700s. This was not a technique unique to England. The Chinese did it with the silkworm. The rulers of Ethiopia did it with the coffee bean. The Indians did it with the tea plant. Anything that was new, anything that created an economic advantage for the "inventing" country became a matter of national security.

Why do I say slavery in the United States would have fizzled out by the turn of the century (1800s into 1900s)? Mathematics! *Oh no, not math. You're going to make me think, aren't you?!?!* Yes, but not too much. Follow me on this.

In 1765, James Watt made changes to the steam engine that revolutionized industrial production. It was these changes which made it possible for factories to be built anywhere. Factories could now be built closer to the raw materials, saving money. Prior to Mr. Watt's advances, a factory could only be built near a river so that the kinetic energy of flowing water could be harnessed using large water wheels. Water wheels were the engines of their days. They could be connected to other machines via shafts, pulleys, rudimentary gears, and belts. Yes, at one time water wheels were state-of-the-art.

Many times, rivers were diverted from their natural channels to places where a water wheel could be employed. They were the personal computers of their day. If a factory owner could find a plot of steeply sloped land, he could build multiple factories at different levels, each with a water wheel. Water would flow through one water wheel and power its factory. The water would then flow to the next water wheel in line and power that factory. If the hill was long enough, and the drop was great enough, a line of factories a mile long could be built. I don't know if any were built, but under the correct conditions it is plausible. (The ancient Romans did this.)

Watt's steam engine replaced not only the water wheel, but the windmill too. The most significant advantage a steam engine has over windmills and waterwheels is that a steam engine produces more reliable power. A windmill operated flour mill could only grind flour when the wind was blowing, and at certain speeds. If wind velocity wasn't great enough, it wouldn't have the necessary force to turn the millstone. If there was a drought, or if the river jumped its banks up stream of the mill, the mill wouldn't operate. The steam engine changed that too. So long as someone kept feeding it fuel and water, it would rotate the machinery. The added power also allowed for more machines to be added. A flour mill with one millstone prior to the installation of a steam engine, after upgrades might find itself with not only a steam engine, but five additional millstones.

The steam engine's ability to do ever increasing amounts of work by fewer and fewer men is why the British Parliament was able to ban slavery throughout Her Majesty's (Queen Victoria's) Empire in 1837- Seventy-two years into the Industrial Age. After seventy-two years of making improvements to crude industrial machines, enough technological advances had been made to make slavery obsolete. However, this was just in the United Kingdom. The industrial revolution didn't begin to take hold in the United States until Thomas Jefferson's Administration. The steam engine itself wouldn't make its first appearance in the US until 1801.

Had the US Civil War not ended slavery in 1865, would slavery had ended in 1909, approximately seventy-two years after the British outlawed slavery? I believe slavery would have ended earlier than 1909 because the seventy-two years starts with Watt's improvements to the steam engine. If we add 72 years to the first appearance of the steam engine in the US 1801, slavery in the US could have ended in 1873 of its own accord. The major flaw in my contentions is that the parts of the United States still practicing slavery- the Southern States- were not industrialized on the same level as the northern states. (I know, right, duh!)

The northern states at the outset of the civil war could boast about having over 20,000 miles of railroad tracks. This is in sharp contrast to the southern states which combined had *less than* 10,000. The south would have to lay more rail lines to properly industrialize. The good news is that it wouldn't take too long to lay down additional rail lines to support industrialization. I figure about 25 years to industrialize. This would put the end of slavery in 1890 or thereabouts. It might have been even sooner if tractor development proceeded faster than it did. That is unless one believes that the racist, southern democrat, plantation owners would, with benevolence in their hearts, put their additional profits towards improving the lives of their former slaves, even though they hated the African race with a passion and considered it to be less than human. There you have it, slavery disappearing in the US not to loud explosions of cannons, but with the quiet whisper of a sigh.

CHAPTER EIGHTEEN

REPARATIONS

I broached the subject earlier. Let's discuss this controversial (?) subject now. I will make this quick. No one alive today, who is descended from U.S. slaves, is entitled to reparations. I'll say that again. No one is entitled to reparations! Period. End of sentence!

That should be all I need to type, but it's not. It's shocking to many people, but it is a fact. Here's why. And we will assume out of the goodness of our hearts that all reparations programs would not simply be the big extortion scams everyone knows them to be. Follow me on this! Reparations are billed as the country's big mea culpa for slavery. It is a mea culpa intended for those people who were slaves. Not their descendants! I'll type that differently. I'll also type it really, really slow, in case some people can't read very fast. No one alive today is entitled to reparations because THEY WERE NEVER SLAVES!!!

Not only were they never slaves, if they were born after 1965, they never met anyone who was a slave. If they did meet someone who was a slave, they most likely don't remember the encounter. If they do remember the encounter, they didn't grasp the situation at the time it was happening. It is possible that someone born after 1965 did meet a person who was born into slavery, but the number of former slaves still alive in 1965 was small. They would have numbered in the low 1000s if not low 100s. Think about it!

If someone was born on December 6th, 1865, one second before the final state ratified the 13th amendment, making them a slave for one second of their life, they would turn 100 years old on December 6th, 1965. Even today living to be 100 years old is rare. How rare? Consider this, Queen Elizabeth could command, at the drop of a hat not only hundreds of footmen but also some of the smartest doctors in the world. These doctors in turn had, with no questions asked, access to the most state-of-the-art medical equipment. With all of these benefits, none of the Queen's men and none of the Queen's women were able to extend the life of Queen Elizabeth II so that she could count herself among the exalted centenarians. She fell short by three and a half years.

Imagine how rare it was to live that long in the 1960s. Especially considering that many of the diseases a person could catch prior to the 1940s drastically affected one's lifespan. The average lifespan of a person living in the United States in 1965, was 70 years. That year, the number of centenarians would probably be in the low hundreds. This is counting the entire population, not just former slaves. In case you are curious, the average lifespan of an American in 2023 is 79 years. In 2023, almost every day there is a news story somewhere in the United States celebrating not just people turning 100 years old, but people turning 101, 102, 103 years old, etc.

So, what does that mean for reparations? It means if you were born after 1965, not only were you never a slave, but your parents were never slaves either. Your grandparents could claim to have been slaves, but that would require your grandfather and your grandfather's father to have sired a child around the ripe old age of sixty. Over the course of the next decade, the number of people able to claim to have met a former slave will slowly, with no pomp and circumstance, tick down inevitably to zero. Time might heal all wounds, but it also makes a person's claim to reparations more and more absurd.

I took a roundabout way of getting to this point. This is the part where I reiterate my original statement. No one alive today was born a slave. Therefore, no one alive today is entitled to reparations. If people wish to continue with this absurd notion that they are entitled to receive reparations for something they never experienced, then we need to extend reparations to all people, for all atrocities committed. Let's institute this *social justice* rule:

> *If you or one of your ancestors were ever convicted of murder, you and your descendants need to pay reparations to the descendants of your or your ancestor's victim for 158 years. (Direct descendants, not cousins, aunts, uncles, etc.)*

158 years is the amount of time that has elapsed since slavery was abolished and when the outcry for reparations turned into overt vote buying by corrupt politicians wanting to be elected in the next election. Just to be nice, we can start counting the 158-year sentence on the day the crime was committed, not the day the court verdict was handed down. The only things left to debate now is whether there should be back pay, and if one murder releases a family from their obligations stemming from another.

I am repeating myself again because the following sentences cannot be over emphasized. No one alive today is entitled to be paid reparations by either the United States of America, or any of the many States. Why? Because they were never slaves.!

Any judge, lawyer, or justice who would give any consideration to this matter or who allows someone to extort reparations from any person or organization is themselves a practitioner and connoisseur of Yellow Judicialism. Yellow Judicialism being when a court, or other entities within the justice system goes out of its way to find a reason to either not take the case outright or to find an obscure reason to continue the status quo, etc. so that they don't have to make difficult decisions. In other words, making rulings by running away in cowardice-Yellow Judicialism.

A modern example of Yellow Judicialism is the 2020 election. *Every* case brought before the various courts was either dismissed for lack of standing, or because judges ruled there was no evidence of voter fraud without officially hearing the evidence. True, no evidence of fraud was presented in court, but the reason fraud was never presented in the various courts of law is because the lower-than-excrement judges overseeing the cases would not allow the evidence to be presented. They were cowards!

SECTION 5

AND IT'S NOT JUST RACISM

CHAPTER NINETEEN

LGBTQ ISSUES

Let me start this section by pointing out what should be blatantly obvious. In the abbreviation, LGBTQ, only one sexual orientation is referenced. However, it is referenced twice- The homosexual community. Lesbians are homosexual women. Gay- the G- is a slang term for homosexual. Homosexual includes men and women. Therefore, the proper abbreviation for this group should be HBTQ, or GBTQ not LGBTQ. All the other letters from B to infinity are abbreviations for other things, not a sexual orientation, and not a gender.

With that out of the way, let's talk about what it means to be gay; To be a homosexual. It is simple. It means a person is sexually attracted to people who sport around the same equipment as themselves. That's it! It does not mean they suddenly take on womanly traits. It does not mean they walk around town in their underwear. It simply means that when they, ironically, get the urge to reproduce, they want to reproduce with someone of the same sex. I say it is ironic because if you mate with someone of the same sex, you can't reproduce. Two men can't consummate their relationship and nine months later have a baby.

Is homosexuality normal? No! When I say normal, I simply mean it is not the sexual orientation of most of the population- national and international. Homosexuals comprise less than 5% of the population, therefore homosexuality is not normal. This *does not* mean homosexuals are somehow less than human. This runs contrary to the talking points of the self-anointed, more-moral-than-thou, leaders of the gay community who want people to believe the homosexual population, and all the other current manifestations of non-heterosexuality, combined make up 49% of the population. If not more.

Is homosexuality a modern construct? Again, no! Homosexuals have been part of human existence for ages. It is only recently, within the past fifty years, that the stigma has been removed from the community. The problem that plagues the gay community now are the people who claim to be the spokesmen for the gay community. No one elected them, but for some reason a good portion of the gay community are having to distance themselves from their spokesmen. Not only that, but for some reason the people who are held to be role models, those who have streets named after them, in many cases would not be quite so revered had proper vetting been performed on their past beforehand. The activists that control the gay community are so desperate to have "heroes," they simply latch on to anyone who is gay and who has died of unnatural causes. Case point: Harvey Milk!

Harvey Milk's, for now let's just call them indiscretions are well documented but not well known. If you don't believe me, read the Harvey Milk biography, The Mayor of Castro Street, by Randy Shilts. Also, do a deep dive into the complaints made by the parents of one of Milk's victims to the Attorney General of Minnesota. The *teenage* boy's parents intercepted the letter Milk had sent him and in it he- Milk- convinces his victim, again a *teenage boy*, to run away and join him in San Francisco. Had this only been done in Minnesota, it would only be considered soliciting a minor. However, Harvey Milk, genius that he was, did this from California. Had this been a heterosexual relationship the perpetrator would have spent 50 years in federal prison for soliciting a minor across state lines for the purposes of sex. Yes, Harvey Milk was a pedophile. There is no other way to label him. Being homosexual does not mean it is okay to have sexual relations with anyone under the age of 18- consensual or not!

There are plenty of homosexuals from the past that could be placed on a pedestal. Most of whom are far more accomplished than Mr. Milk. Had Milk not been assassinated, he would have found his way into the "big house" and died an anonymous death. Milk's *only* claims to fame were that he was openly gay, and that he was elected to public office. He was assassinated less than eleven months after being inaugurated so his accomplishments in office were few, if any.

One such person who could honorably be placed on the pedestal is Alan Turing. A genius mathematician who is credited with inventing the first computer which in turn was used to crack the German Enigma code during World War Two. There was even a movie about his accomplishments during World War 2, The Imitation Game, which we discussed briefly earlier.

Another person who could assume the mantle of honorable gay person, Winnaretta Singer. She was one of the children of Issac Singer who is credited with inventing the modern sewing machine. Upon her father's death, and once free of her first marriage, Winnaretta used her inheritance to advance the performing arts. I won't even mention her work with soldiers wounded in France during World War One. I will also neither talk about her philanthropy towards the poor, nor her developing one of the first public housing projects in Europe.

If it is a warrior hero you want, I'll give you a thousand. The Sacred Band of Thebes! These homosexuals of note defeated the much-vaunted Spartans on numerous occasions. The fact that they defeated the Spartans makes them worthy of admiration, as the Spartan army was the world's *first* professional army. Prior to the Spartans, when a city-state went to war, they didn't send an army as we know it today. They sent farmers, artisans, and politicians who had to close their shops, to go and fight. The only military training conscripted soldiers had was when they survived the previous year's war and went again the following year. That was it. The ranks of the Spartan Army were filled by men and boys who had been training for war since they were seven years old. They might not have gone to war until they were eighteen, but prior to going to war, they were trained on how to use weapons, and fight as a unit. That is what the Sacred Band of Thebes defeated on more than one occasion.

Yes, the Sacred Band was a military unit whose ranks were filled entirely with homosexuals. The next couple sentences will show how people, for ages, have not understood homosexuality and how it is as natural as heterosexuality. Not only did the Sacred Band consist solely of homosexuals, but they were homosexual lovers. That is to say, you couldn't be part of the Sacred Band of Thebes unless you had a lover. Why? Because when they went into battle they were chained to their lovers. It was thought that they would fight that much harder if they were faced with the prospect of their lover being killed. This shows how perplexing homosexuality was to people 2,000 years ago. No one would ever think of chaining husbands to their wives and sending them into battle using the same reasoning.

If you wish to have an American war hero to place upon the pedestal, here's one whose identity has only recently been confirmed- Casimir Pulaski. Pulaski is a hero of the American Revolution. Yes, here is a person that can be place upon the LGBT pedestal with a caption under his name, "Hero of the Revolution." or "Literally helped found the nation." Casimir Pulaski is celebrated in Chicago as an icon of the Polish community. He participated in and was a force to be reckoned with in the Battles of Brandywine Creek, Germantown and Savannah, just to name a few. Casimir Pulaski is the father of the United States Army's Cavalry. It has been proven through DNA analysis that he was a hermaphrodite. He possessed both male and female chromosomes- XXY.

Everyone, heterosexuals and homosexuals alike, need to realize something about the self-elected activists claiming to be the voice of the gay community. (If you are standing near one of them you may want to take a couple steps back because this is going to destroy their egos.) They aren't trailblazers. They aren't the ones making a difference. By nature, they aren't the people who do the fighting. They are the people who show up after the fight and then claim to have been part of the fight. Or they are the people at the fight, but their involvement is little more than a town crier. In high school, instead of watching the fight, they were the ones running around screaming, "Fight, fight, fight" in the quad.

There are homosexuals who claim they are the focus of unwanted attention. This may very well be the case. However, there might be an explanation for this which is the opposite of what they claim to be the reason. It might be because they are doing everything they can to be the center of attention. As they plod through their day-to-day lives, most people don't realize it when they interact with a homosexual. Why? Because once again, being homosexual only means a person is attracted to someone of the same sex as they. The people who get instantly recognized as homosexual are probably only recognized as such because they are displaying the stereotypes of homosexuality; A certain walk; a certain lilt in the voice; a certain way of interacting with others; a certain way of dressing oneself.

It is true that in the past, as they will probably be in the future, homosexuals have been discriminated against. It is unfortunate. They have been subjected to absurd, and many times vile and dangerous medical procedures people were convinced would "cure" them of their homosexual tendencies. But thanks to time and the general apathy of the American people, we have come to accept the fact that homosexuality is as natural as heterosexuality.

Here is another myth that needs to be dispelled. Those homosexuals, and other sub-groups of civilization, live in the same neighborhoods and apartment buildings because the government or society is forcing them to live in certain areas. They live together because they have shared values and experiences. Think about modern-day communities like the Chinatowns found in every major city. Who lives in these communities? Mainly the people after whom the communities are named. The Chinese immigrants live in Chinatown. Little Italy is populated by people of Italian descent. Little Havana is mainly populated by Finns and Swedes. That's just a little bit of levity. I purposely inserted the Little Italy as an example to show that the phenomenon of "like" individuals living amongst people whose racial makeup matches their own is not limited to only certain groups.

When people immigrate to the United States or move to other parts of the country they are allowed to live anywhere. The only thing that is stopping them is the housing they can afford. They can move to any community and live in any building. We are a free society. Yes there are places where some *individuals* will do all they can to keep out people they consider undesirable. In decades past, they didn't want anyone living near them who did not resemble them. Thankfully, as time went on, and due in no small part to American society being an open and free society, their numbers are dwindling. The point is that it is human nature for like-minded people to cluster together. Nerds hangout with nerds, jocks hangout

223

with jocks. Diverse communities develop, but it takes time, sometimes generations.

Now, let's talk about the subject which, because no one was stating the obvious, was the impetus for me to need to write this section. Gay Marriage!

The whole controversy surrounding gay marriage has *nothing* to do with love. Absolutely nothing! When asked, a gay couple will say they want to get married so they can celebrate the love they have for each other in front of family and friends. However, do they need to get married to do that? No! If they want to celebrate their love in front of family and friends, it would be cheaper- a whole lot cheaper- to go to a family reunion or to have a backyard barbeque. With this controversy, as it is with all controversies, the people screaming the loudest can't differentiate between what they want and what they think they want. Marriage isn't what the activists want, it's the wedding ceremony they want. More specifically than that, they want the witnesses and the certificate. Why? Because the true reason gay people want to get married is money. That's it! Money. Money, money, money! Moolah, cabbage, the green stuff, wampum!

That's it! There isn't a deep seeded reason. There's no romance. There's no grandiose conspiracy. It is the same reason that has been causing angst for eons. It is the same reason heterosexual couples have been getting married. Money! I can't make it any simpler. The marriage ceremony, the certificate, the witnesses! It all boils down to a financial transaction. Everyone knows it, too! Now don't confuse my reasoning with that of the feminists. They are four square anti-marriage. The feminists scream and shout about marriage being nothing more than a financial transaction hoping to dissuade women from getting married. I am arguing for marriage. I am pulling the wool out from everyone's eyes so they can see the true reason gay couples want to get married.

Think about the ceremony. If you are in love with someone and want to spend the rest of your life with them, how is a wedding ceremony going to make that possible? How is not being able to get married going to prevent a couple from spending the rest of their lives together. A person can rent an apartment and have a roommate. Real life isn't 1970s television. Providing they don't violate occupancy codes, a person can have 10 roommates and all eleven people can split the rent, the bills, and sleep in the same bed, one on top of each other like a momma bear and her cubs during hibernation season. This can continue until the cows come home. No one can say they can't. If someone says they can't and then tries to enforce what they are saying, there are discrimination laws.

An unmarried couple can still have children and raise a family. How is having a wedding ceremony going to make life different? It's not going to make life with children easier. Getting married doesn't instantly entitle a couple to a discount at the farmers' market or gas station. If a gallon of milk costs three dollars prior to the wedding, after the wedding it will still cost three dollars. Being married doesn't get children into special schools unless it is a private school whose faculty frowns on unwedded couples. The only benefit to having a wedding ceremony is the certificate that comes with. It is the certificate that holds all the power. This certificate is what saves money. Again, yes, the argument for gay marriage- as in all marriages- is not about love, it's about money. Money! Money! Money!

A married person can take their new marriage certificate to work, and the very next day have their significant other on their employer sponsored health insurance plan. As a member of a country club whose members enjoy special privileges and benefits, once that certificate is in hand, a wife or husband can instantly enjoy those same perks. There are countless benefits to having a marriage certificate, especially if the marriage goes south. Think about what happens if two roommates who claimed to be "life partners" suddenly split up, but there is no marriage certificate. The wife in the relationship gets nothing. If these "life partners" have a marriage certificate and they get a divorce, the wife, in most states, not only gets half the assets, but is also entitled to alimony. Divorce is the greatest proof that marriage, marriage of any type, is all about money.

To an employer, and in the eyes of the law, a marriage certificate is one way to minimize fraud. I can't add my hypochondriac, chronically out of work best friend to my employer sponsored healthcare plan. Why? Because believe it or not, employers are trying to make money. They aren't wanting to pay the medical bills of every person with a sob story. If we remove the legal contract binding one person to another person, then *anyone* could be placed on the insurance. It would be the insurance equivalent of a marriage of convenience, where a couple wed just to get benefits. Those benefits being an increase in pay, or by being claimed as a dependent or in some cases citizenship.

Side note, in case I didn't mention it in the medical section, there's another kerfuffle which sends people into orbit every election year. It's the scam commonly referred to as healthcare. No one ever takes issue with these activists either. Call it what you want, universal healthcare, healthcare for all, free healthcare. It won't change the fact that it too has absolutely nothing to do with healthcare. It's about health *insurance*. It's about getting one group of people to pay the medical bills of another group of people. There isn't a medical doctor in the country who would deny someone healthcare. The insurance portion only rears its ugly head when the people providing a service dare to want to be compensated for the services they rendered. Universal healthcare too is only about the money. The only reason people become apoplectic is because the dishonest media types keep using the words "healthcare" and "health insurance" as synonyms when they are not. Healthcare is what medical doctors provide. Health insurance is what pays for the doctors. And before you say it, yes the *medical industry* loves Obamacare. Obamacare guarantees that they will be paid.

Back to gay marriage!

The sad part is, had the nauseating, loudmouth activists who think they are somehow more righteous than everyone else because they aren't "breeders" had they been honest from the start, gay marriage would have been "legalized" decades ago. But that is not what happened. For decades we were told the reason they wanted to get married is because they love each other and want to celebrate that love. When heterosexual couples questioned why they want to get married, they were demonized as anti-gay. Discrimination lawsuits filed. Discrimination laws were updated to include not only homosexuals, but every possible type of person, classification of people, and sub-group of civilization. Now if someone has blue hair, it is considered discrimination if they are told their hair color goes against company dress code. People were told to pay thousands, if not millions of dollars. (There's that money thing popping up again.)

The thesis that gay marriage needs to be legalized so that the ceremonies can be performed is as preposterous as the other arguments. Especially in the Internet Age. Follow me on this. Over the past few millennia, the *idea* of two people solely devoting themselves to each other isn't what has changed. It is the ceremony, and the reasons for the ceremony, that has changed. At one time, in the Egypt of the Pharaohs, if a man and woman wished to get married, all they had to do was tell each other that they were married. That was it. There wasn't a five-year engagement period. There wasn't a lengthy negotiation process between two patriarchs. With a quick and simple, "I wed you," it was wham-bam-thank-you-ma'am, abracadabra they were married. Divorce was just as simple, just in the opposite direction. "I divorce you." No judges, no preachers, no commotion. It is only when we see civilizations becoming more developed that we see wedding dogmas becoming more complex and complicated. So, if a couple wishes to marry, why can't they simply put a ring on each other's fingers and call it a day?

The argument that people can't get married because they can't find anyone to perform the ceremony is a crock of horse dung too! Thanks to the internet anyone who wishes to perform a ceremony can go online and become a wedding officiary. No special qualifications required. This means anyone- and I mean anyone- can perform the ceremony.

People claim that homosexual marriage needs to be legalized to force churches to recognize gay marriage. This is B.S. too! If a church doesn't want to join in holy matrimony two people who have the same type of wedding tackle, then those people can simply go to a different church. If they can't find one, they can start a new church. It doesn't have to be a church based on the Christian Bible or the Jewish Torah. A brand-new church can have brand new and wholly original holy scripture. It happens every day. It might take a few months to get the organization recognized by the government as a church, but while that happens the preacher can still marry people. The US government recognized Jim Jones as someone who started his own church and therefore, he could legally marry people.

227

Guess what happened to him, he and 900 of his congregation committed mass suicide.

Yep, starting a church is super-duper challenging. The only reason the government cares about a church is yet another matter of money. They don't check up on churches to make sure they are preaching the correct gospels. They check up on them because churches don't pay taxes. Damn there's that money thing again. I'm sensing something, but I can't put my finger on it.

Let's talk about the third, fourth and the other letters that follow L and G in LGBTQ.

There are three genders and two sexual orientations. That is it! There aren't 57. A man can't magically change into a woman by de-nutting himself. A woman can magically become a man by sticking a kielbasa in her panties. Until a couple years ago, the terms man and woman were defined as they have always been defined. They were sacrosanct. No one ever objected to the widely known definitions of those words. For millennia, across hundreds of languages, the meanings of these two words were held true. These days, however not only have the definitions of those terms changed, but we are required to believe that mother nature does *not* determine who is which. That people can change from one to the other at will and that being a man or a woman is "fluid."

We have been talking about the two sexual orientations for the past few pages. They are homosexual and heterosexual. Now allow me to school the retarded activists about sex. There are three genders, three, not two, not fifty-seven. Three! They are, in no particular order, male, female and hermaphrodite. In terms of chromosomes, they are XY, XX, AND XXY, respectively. That is it! If a man has "transition" surgery to remove his cack and balls, he isn't magically transformed into a woman. He has simply turned himself into a eunuch. So too with a woman. People whose sexual organs have been removed are eunuchs. It doesn't matter how many extra surgeries they have in order to have a wiener-like object sewn on to them, they are still the same gender they were at birth.

Should their remains be exhumed a thousand years after they die, and providing their bones don't completely decompose, the very first thing an anthropologist will do is determine gender. That is done by looking at the pelvis. The pelvis of a man looks different than that of a woman. The pelvis of a woman who has given birth looks different than the pelvis of a woman who has not. In preparation for childbirth, a woman's pelvic bones will spread apart. Sometimes after the birthing process the pelvis returns to its prenatal size, sometimes it stays as it is. This is Anthropology 101 stuff.

A brief digression here.

I am about to tell a story involving someone with no sense of wrong. I don't mean they don't know right from wrong; I mean even when *facts* are presented that disprove their hypothesis, they are incapable of admitting they are wrong. Instead of admitting to being wrong, these people become ever more rabid believers of their faith. Being unable to determine whether or not they are the sole congregant of their faith in the room many times is the only factor keeping many of these people from turning violent.

One day an anthropologist transfixed by the transgender theology, whose devotion to the religion of transgenderism was so fervent, publicly stated that it is impossible to determine the gender of a cadaver by examining the bone structure. Without batting an eye, he said this. He brought up his Ph. D in Anthropology to let people know that what he had just said was on par with the holy words of God, and any dissension towards what he had just said was blasphemy and should be treated as such. There are videos of it happening. There is no contriteness in his presentation, only smug arrogance. His devotion to his religion is so thorough and so utterly unwavering, when he finds himself face to face with people who do not worship at the same altar, the intellectual thinker's equivalent of muscle memory takes over. In this case, without needing an order to be issued, he showed his devotion by lying. And that is what it was, pure and simple.

There is no other way to describe what he did, he lied! He lied in obedience to his religion. He lied for the cause. He lied to vainly prove that of all the people in attendance, he is the most intelligent; That he must be believed at all costs. This is what his religion demands of him, and this is what he demands of others. No one is smarter than him. Liberal activists are today what bible thumpers were in years past; Unable to accept anything but what their religion demands. The institution of higher learning who bestowed upon him a doctorate should be embarrassed and should rescind his doctorate. Again, being able to identify gender by looking at skeletal remains is rudimentary.

I once watched an Egyptologist determine that the excavated mummified remains were the bones of a woman. After 3,000 years of decomposition, and God only knows how many graverobbers, only three of this woman's bones survived. Yet this Egyptologist was able to make the determination in the field. There were no expensive machines. It was done by simply looking at the bones. As an added bonus, the woman's age when she died was also determined.

Yes, gender is *not* determined by how a person feels, it is determined by chromosomes. Excising one's genitalia does not miraculously turn a person into the opposite sex. Further, the semantics behind the words "sex" and "gender" is just another way for debate to be shutdown. If a person uses the wrong word, the opposing arguer will point to that supposed "mistake" and claim the argument lacks merit because "gender" was said not "sex." Or vice versa. These two words *are* synonyms when used as nouns. When they are used as verbs they are not. If a person is engaged in the act of fornicating, they are having sex, they aren't having gender. If a person can change their sex by having an operation, that must apply to all species of life. Therefore, once you castrate your male dog, your dog is now a female dog.

Since pundits are fond of comparing apples and oranges or pointing out how two things can't be compared as if they are apples and oranges, let's talk about transgenderism using apples and oranges. Everyone agrees that apples and oranges are not alike in any way. One has red skin, the other has orange. One tastes sweet, the other citrusy. One has seeds which taste bitter, the other no one seems to know because when they are bitten into, the taste isn't different enough from the fruit to cause a definite change in thought. *This orange is really good...OMG I just bit into an orange seed, man it's nasty.*

If you take the seeds out of an apple, does the apple become an orange? If you take the seeds out of an orange, does the orange become an apple? Do they become bananas? How about coconuts? No, they are still apples, and they are still oranges. There are seedless varieties of fruits. Watermelons for example. Watermelons have been genetically modified and now they don't have seeds. (Thank goodness, that was the *only* drawback to eating watermelon.) We didn't make a new type of fruit by removing the seeds. In terms of reproduction, we only removed the ability of the watermelon to reproduce. Yes, that does raise the question of how seedless watermelons are grown, but if you remove the seeds from an apple or an orange, they still look like an apple or an orange. Having seeds has no bearing on the fruit's taste. The apple doesn't instantly start tasting like an orange nor does the orange turn red. They do not suddenly transform into another fruit. I could go on. But, after using the apples and oranges analogy, if you still don't understand here is what you need to do:

Step 1: Stop what you are doing.
Step 2: Go home,
Step 3: Get in the shower,
Step 4: Turn on the water,
Step 5: Curl up on the floor in the fetal position,
Step 6: Stick your thumb in your mouth,
Step 7: Commence sucking,
Step 8: After 10 minutes of thumb sucking:
Step 9: (If you feel like you can safely rejoin a world where 99.999999999999% of its inhabitants neither know you nor care about your feelings) you may return to your previously scheduled activity.
Step 10: If after 10 minutes you can't think of what I just told you without bursting into tears again, continue sucking your thumb until someone comes to check on you. (Hint: No one is going to check on you for a very long time

so get comfortable. They have better things to do than to wipe your runny nose, call you precious, and tell you everyone is being mean.)

CHAPTER TWENTY

SEXISM AND OTHER 'ISMS

Ladies, you need to cut the crap, too. You really need to shut up. I don't mean you need to shut up because women should be seen and not heard. I mean shut up, as in give it a rest. Your constant need to have the last word in every conversation or to be the one who is all knowing, is blinding you to reality. Especially when women are going on television, pompously preening for the camera as they state, "Men need to stop *'Man-Splaining'* to women because it's sexist." Allow me to explain.

Man-Splaining is a survival technique developed by men over thousands of years, a result of having to back track, re-do and fix things that weren't broken until a woman got her mitts on it. Men don't explain things to women because they want to. They explain things to women because they need to. If you have ever been on a multi-vehicle road trip where one of the cars is driven by a woman, you know what I am talking about. I was once on one of these trips. The men were in one vehicle and the women were in another. When the men were 20 miles from their final destination, they had to back track almost a hundred miles, because none- None- not a single woman in the car was smart enough to look at the fuel gauge prior to departing.

Yes, *the men* had to back track almost a hundred miles to bring the women five gallons of gasoline so they could drive to the next gas station. On top of that, *the men* first had to find a store with a five-gallon gas can and fill it up before driving back. It is instances like this that prompt men to tell women, "Make sure you have gas." To which the reply from the woman is always, "I will, I'm not stupid you know!"

When those women tell their friends the story of what happened, who do you think they blame for there not being a full tank of gas in the car? I can guarantee they don't blame each other.

Another thing, if you want men to stop *Man-Splaining*, you need to stop Woman-Splaining. Ladies, I can tell you this with 100 percent accuracy that women *woman-splain,* more than men *man-splain.* It's a well-known, and unspoken fact. Men don't discuss how and why it's true that women *woman-splain* more than men *man-splain,* because it will inevitably lead to, you guessed it, more *woman-splaining.* I can hear the women now, "We don't do that!" Oh, yes you do. Sometimes the entire conversation you have with men is nothing more than a woman telling a man how to do stuff. Here's are a few examples of everyday *woman-splaining.*

1. You need to put the toilet seat down.
2. You aren't loading the dishwasher correctly.
3. You need to separate the clothes before you put them in the washer.
4. Turn right at the next street.
5. .
6. .
7. .
8. .
9. .
10. .

Guys, I left a few lines available so that you can list all the ways, you have been subjected to *woman-splaining* today.

To keep it simple:

A conversation that begins with a woman using the phrase, "We need to talk," is a conversation in which the guy will be subjected to lively session of *woman-splaining.* And,

The phrase, "Yes, dear," notifies any passerby that the man who sheepishly uttered those two words was the most recent victim of *woman-splaining*.

'Nuff said on that.

Ladies, your ancestors- your female ancestors- would be ashamed of you. You complain like you are about to die at any moment. The few times when your complaining doesn't result in you getting your way, is not sexism. It's simply people standing their ground. Having a dripping slit, and not a swinging dick, doesn't give you the right to get your way all the time. So, shut it.

There was a headline in the news recently which told how a woman was driving in the carpool lane, and she was the only one in the car. She was pulled over and issued a ticket. Her defense was to point out to the officer that she wasn't the only one in the car and she pointed to her pregnant belly. If you want to go down this road, fine. If a fetus, zygote, or baby in the womb can make it legal for a woman to drive in the carpool lane by herself, then abortion *is* murder. You can't have it both ways. You can't scream that it's. "…your body therefore your choice …" for one argument and exploit your body for the next argument.

I recently went a supermarket and when I was looking for a parking spot, I noticed there were spots reserved for pregnant women. Ladies have become so weak and/or so lazy it is apparently impossible for them to walk an extra fifty feet to the store's entrance. These parking spaces are absolutely ludicrous. Why? Because once a woman gets inside the store, she is going to walk close to half a mile while she shops. Think about it, a woman can spend half an hour walking down every aisle in a store, but she can't be expected to add an additional 30 seconds to her walk from her car to the entrance door? Did I say ludicrous? I meant to say, retarded!

Ladies, women have literally been getting pregnant since the dawn of human civilization. You having a bun-in-the-oven in these trying times is nothing special. Stop the bed rest. Be the boss lady you want everyone to believe you are and sack up! Women not being able to walk easily when they are pregnant is a direct function of a sedentary lifestyle prior to pregnancy. It is difficult for women to walk while they are pregnant because their bodies haven't yet compensated for the additional load. If people, all people not just pregnant women, would just walk a couple miles a day, many of their aches and pains would go away.

Furthermore, ladies when it comes to all stages of pregnancy and childbirth, quit using television shows as reference material. I specifically refer to the scene where a woman is giving birth, and she is screaming the entire time. It has been known for years that screaming makes it worse. It reduces one's oxygen intake, and it saps one's energy faster. *Oh crap, I see what I did. I just told a woman what to do. How dare I! Breathe, ladies breathe. Inhale, exhale. Here, have some ice chips.*

Maybe these ridiculous stories are a good thing. Men should get in the HOV lanes, and claim to not only be women, but claim to be pregnant women. Regarding the "Pregnant Women Only" parking stalls at stores, the same thing should happen. If a man is at the grocery store and he sees an open "Pregnant Women Only" parking stall, he should park in that stall. These parking stalls are not only a form of sexism, but they are a form of discrimination as well. If we were to change the word "woman" to "whites" people would lose their minds. It is my hope that this leads to real women seeing what has become of reality and that they finally tire of liberals and their BS pandering.

I'll say it again ladies, your female ancestors would be ashamed of you. If they could speak to you now, they would direct some *woman-splaining* in *your* direction. They would be yelling at you for being lazy. They would call you big babies. Why? Because your ancestors had to walk everywhere. If they wanted to go to the store, they had to either walk, ride a horse, or ride in a *horse drawn* carriage. If they needed to tend the garden, they had to walk up and down each furrow. There was no mini tractor. If they wanted to move from one town to another, they had to either walk or ride in a horse drawn carriage. In fact, many of your ancestors literally walked- Walked- across the country in search of a better life out west. Understand ladies, your ancestors would be able to survive in your world for decades, but you would not last a single day in theirs. In fact, that last sentence is probably true for all of us.

Now then, let's pretend we are on a game show. It's called sexism, sexual harassment, or being a crybaby. The rules are simple. I'll proffer forth examples and the reader can determine the category into which they fall. For example:

- A man tells a woman that if she has sex with him, she will get a promotion.

Duh! Sexual harassment!

Okay, here we go…

- A woman has decided she doesn't want to do a job she has been assigned. She turns to one of her male colleagues, bats her eyes and flirts with him to get him to do the job for her. Which is it?
- A woman wears a low-cut blouse to work, and yells at people for staring.
- A woman finds out her supervisor likes the smell of roses and suddenly begins wearing perfume that smells like roses.
- A woman, whenever she is scolded, throws back her shoulders to get her breasts to "pop".
- A woman, being an inveterate busy body, constantly harangues one of her male colleagues to date her friend even though her male colleague has told her on numerous occasions he is not interested in her friend.
- A woman after being told she needs to dress more conservatively goes to HR and files a report on her supervisor for sexual harassment because he obviously was watching, and it makes her feel uncomfortable.

Should I go on? I could! The point is ladies; there is no such thing as "sexual politics" it is sexual harassment. Men need to stop doing things for women just because they batted their eyes at them and report them to HR. Don't sit there and explain to the woman how it's sexual harassment, immediately go to HR and report them. Yes, it will suck. Many of the women will go out of their way to find things you did wrong in retaliation. However, eventually the sexual harassment lessons will start to include the things women do as well. The idea that the harassers are solely heterosexual men will ultimately cease. Ladies, you have been screaming for equality in the workplace, how do you like these apples? Sexual harassment lessons will eventually also include homosexual men.

Here's yet more proof that the information media, the entertainment industry, and Washington D.C. don't give a rat's ass about sexual harassment unless they can make money off the story.

In 1986, a bunch of US Navy pilots descended on the sleepy little town of Las Vegas, Nevada. They took over a few floors of a hotel and proceeded to get drunk, get stupid and do things which would make their mothers ashamed to have given birth to them. In short, they sexually harassed and abused some of the women who were there either by choice or who happened to be at the hotel and unknowingly stumbled upon the party. This party was the annual Tailhook convention. It is an annual convention where fighter pilots in the US Navy get together and do stupid things. It's not all that dissimilar to the annual retreats held by doctors, lawyers and politicians. I must state it again because retards walk amongst us, and they can't put two and two together without holding a meeting. It was the *annual* convention. The operative word is "annual." Annual as in, "Not the first time," as in this happens every year. As in it is not a surprise because it has been happening for decades.

I'm not excusing the behavior of those at the party nor am I trying to minimize the pain of anyone who was victimized. As a result of the scandal and its subsequent investigation, the United States Navy was not only given a black eye for the actions of a few, but from that day forward, every year there is a "Standdown Day". A standdown day is a day where all normal, non-emergent work ceases. During which time, the entire navy, yes, the entire United States Navy, all 350,000 sailors and 180,000 Marines, not to mention the active reserve components of each, are required to stop learning how to kill the enemy and instead are told to do a deep-dive and to reflect on social issues, to use today's vernacular. For instance, on a Safety Standdown Day, the only thing that is done is everyone must sit through 8 hours of lessons on safety procedures.

As a result of the Tailhook scandal once a year all work stops and everyone must sit through 8 hours devoted to sexual harassment lessons- Not to find out how to do it right the first time- but for educational awareness, etc. Lessons are designed to show people that certain behaviors are inappropriate, and they will not be tolerated.

Here's what rubs me raw.

I must sadly report to the world that in response to the Epstein-Weinstein sexual harassment-sexual assault incidences, absolutely nothing has changed within the offending industries which employed these two perverts. Hey, if the entire US Navy, and the Department of Defense as a whole can be forced to atone for the actions of a few drunken sailors, so too must the entertainment industry when one of their own does much worse. When will the morally superior figures in the Entertainment Industry introduce their industry-wide standdown? When will the clock start on the *you're-never-going-to-live-this-down-timer*? How much longer must we wait for the media to constantly throw Epstein and Weinstein into the face of *all* members of the entertainment industry whenever a similar incident occurs anywhere in the world? How much longer is it going to be before academia starts teaching students that all actors and actresses are perverts and that they are the reason evil exists in the world as they teach of the military?

Section 6

Shut your pie holes, liberals!

Chapter Twenty-One

Liberals caused WWI and every war since

Beware of Greeks bearing gifts, and liberals claiming to be professors.

Yes, I know, that is an insult to Greeks bearing gifts. For most of the book I have been taking issue with liberals, and their policies, so I will try to make this short. However, I wouldn't hold my breath. Why are liberals always angry? The short answer is because someone told them that they had to be angry. If someone were to track liberals from the moment they graduated from high school until the very first time they came out of the closet and let the world know they are a liberal, a correlation would be discovered between being a liberal and being angry. When was the last time anyone saw a person working for minimum wage in an automotive shop as angry as a liberal? It doesn't happen. Do the people working in automotive repair shops get angry? Yes they do, but not like a liberal.

Liberals get a form of angry that can only be explained by saying their anger is the base on which stands the idea of how the devil was born. Further research into the matter would bring to light that most liberals have no earthly idea why they are so angry. Yes, they can be angry that there are starving children in some faraway land, but why does that make them so angry they resort to physical violence? It will also be revealed that most liberals started out happy-go-lucky, fresh-faced freshmen in college. Then one day in one of their classes, in walked the professor, whom they believed to be the smartest person in the world and the professor started ranting and raving about something in full lunatic liberal fashion. The professor told them they should be angry. The professor backed up what he was saying with half-facts and half-truths. Suddenly, the happy college student became angry over stuff that has been happening for generations, in countries five thousand miles away.

No one has been able to explain why liberals and democrats have been so angry about Trump winning the 2016 election. I'll explain it to you. Liberals aren't upset that Trump won the election. They aren't upset that Hiliary lost the election. They are upset because when Trump won, it screwed up their party. The night of the election was supposed to be the event in their lives they would tell their grandkids about. As soon as they realized Trump was going up against Hiliary, their dreams began in earnest. All year long they were dreaming of Election Day and how they would bear witness to and be part of the historic moment when the US elected its first woman president. This was their Elvis is dead moment. This was supposed to be their Woodstock. This was supposed be their "I marched with Dr. King" moment. This was supposed to be the day their Almighty revealed himself, and all of life's unanswered enigmas were to be answered directly to them alone.

They spent the entire year dreaming of this night. It was going to be the Rapture. They could see it! They could taste it! As the results from each state trickled in, and Hillary started accumulating Electoral College votes (unofficial), they would begin to see that their anger was not in vain. It would liberate their souls. Election night was mere foreplay. As more votes were tallied, their elation would become ever more transcendent. It was to culminate in a world-wide, single orgasm when the magic number of 270 was reached. At that time, Hale-Bop would reveal itself to the faithful. True believers were to be rewarded not by being taken into the comet, but by the establishment of the ever-fleeting liberal utopia the ancients called, "Cloud Cuckoo Land."

But that isn't what happened. What happened was that the big, bad orange man snatched it away. They were relegated, once again, to telling their grandchildren the same mundane stories told to them by their grandparents. Trump took away their meth! Ever since then, they have been revealing the depths of their addiction.

To a liberal, everything is complicated. The more dire the situation, the more complex the needed solution, and only they know how to fix the problem.

242

This is why in the thousands of years of human civilization some problems are never solved- Liberals. If your neighbor's dog keeps crapping in your back yard, the liberal solution is for you to go to therapy to understand why the dog isn't at fault. The quick fix is to build a fence. But a liberal can't simply let you build a fence, nope! The fence must be complicated. They want you to submit plans. They want the village government to hold hearings. They want you to build the fence they would never dream of building for themselves. If you want to build a privacy fence six feet tall, they want it to be exactly six feet tall unless it impairs their view. Then, if you have a plan ready to go, you must build the fence on their schedule. You can't build the fence on weekends after work. Nope, it must be done now before they host their first garden party of the year.

Think about all the problems people have every day. Think about all the problems that have been exasperated and blown way out of proportion because someone needs to put in their two cents. There have been countless times when people complain about road repairs being needed, only for those repairs to be shut down because those same people feel it is akin to torture to require them to drive an extra hundred yards to their subdivision's other exit. If one were to ask, those that complained were probably liberals. They want the road repairs to not only *not* inconvenience them, but to only occur at certain times of the day so they don't have to listen to the noise. Regardless of how long the repairs take, they want to be able to go about their lives as if the repairs aren't happening. It's always about them and how they *feel*.

This brings me to my next point about liberalism.

CHAPTER TWENTY-TWO

LIBERALISM BEGETS COMMUNISM,
COLLECTIVISM, AND SOCIALISM.

Many political science majors and Ph.ds will dispute that statement, but that is because they claim to be liberals. Think about it for a minute. Liberals run around telling everyone that people are starving, or that people don't have clean water, or that people can't find work because of the boogeyman. And what is the solution liberals proffer forth? Do they bring to light the dictators and warlords who are stealing the food shipments? Nope! The solution liberals come up with, the solution they always come up with, is to hold a benefit concert of some kind and ask people to send money. In fact, that is the only difference between liberalism and communism. Liberals ask you to send in your money. Communists, socialists, and collectivists force you to send your money.

Just so everyone knows, in the early 1980s a benefit song "We Are the World," was recorded because Ethiopia was in the middle of a famine. This song raised billions of dollars. No one ever discusses the fact that less than half the money raised was used to feed the starving people in Ethiopia. Most of the money and other supplies, were stolen by warlords, the Ethiopian government, and the United Nations.

Do you know what is wrong with the hypothetical question, *"Would you have dropped the atom bombs on Japan?"*

The problem is that no matter how hard people try not to, they will always use current knowledge and hindsight to answer the question. Today's morality will be used also. We will never know- knock on wood- the feeling of a world at war. We will never know what it is like to read stories talking about how this week alone, thousands of our countrymen were killed. We will never know the utter helplessness a person must feel when after years of actual fighting there is still no end in sight. Unlike in Iraq and Afghanistan, those wars ended up being sporadic ambushes simply because politicians thought they knew how to solve all the problems plaguing those countries. Yes, the day after we got Bin Laden, we should have left Afghanistan.

The atomic bomb question shouldn't be asked simply to find out if someone would have dropped the A-bomb in the past. Asking the question in such a manner only creates a talking point for pundits and gives cause for censorship. The question asked should be whether or not they would drop the A-bomb today. For instance, what would a person think of a presidential candidate if the question were, *"If Russia decided to use nuclear weapons, tactical or otherwise, against the Ukraine, would he or she, as President order the US military retaliate in kind?"*

There's only one answer for that question to any true leader. The answer is a resounding, "Yes!" The answer isn't, "Yes, if...," or "Maybe if I consulted..." It's a one-word answer. Yes! Any answer other than a quick, simple "yes" would show the world that the president isn't serious and is wishy-washy. That is one of the major faults with liberalism. It's wishy-washy at best and it allows politicians to get out of hard decisions by allowing them to attach qualifying statements to everything they say. Liberalism allows people to claim to be smart, but then to do dumb things repeatedly.

I'll give you two recent examples of this professional politician protection racket in action.

Number one: Hiliary Clinton's claim- as a guest professor teaching political science- that she doesn't understand how so many people could have followed Adolf Hitler.

Number two: Benghazi 2012

CHAPTER TWENTY-THREE

WORLD WAR ONE AND THE RISE OF HITLER

Buckle up Hiliary, I'm about to splain it to you. Let us begin with Number One...

Most people have yet to realize this, but World War One was the first major conflict fought on the European continent in almost 75 years. The last major war in Europe prior to WWI was the Crimean War which pitted Czarist Russia and her allies against the Ottoman Empire and its allies. This war lasted three years and resulted in the death of almost a million people both sides combined. Soldiers from the battlefields were returning to their homes maimed by the thousands. The civilians at home were forced to bear witness to the horrors of war. Yes, the war was fifteen hundred miles away, but the dead and the maimed soldiers were returning home every day. Everyone could see what happens when countries go to war. The only good thing to come out of this war was the legendary Florence Nightingale and the Red Cross.

When the war ended, the politicians and diplomats on the winning side, as usual, credited themselves with ending the war. They became full of themselves. Twenty years later, since no wars had been fought in Europe since the Crimean War, they continued believing their delusions. These liberals- top hat and coattail wearing diplomats all- went on the lecture touring circuit. They lectured at Cambridge, the Sommes, Yale, and Humbolt Universities. They began explaining that it was their liberal policies which put an end to wars in Europe. These lessons and beliefs were passed on to the students at those schools. And since European society was still largely rooted in a nobility, they were passed on to sons over cigars and brandy. For decades, every member of Parliament in London, the Reichstag in Berlin, and the National Assembly in Paris, believed to their core that their belief in liberalism is what ended all wars.

What they failed to realize is that liberalism had done nothing. The industrial revolution meant raw materials were needed, and many countries either didn't have the necessary raw materials, or the country did have the raw materials, but not the required quantity. For instance, to this day, Germany is coal rich and oil poor. If Germany wishes to have oil, it must get it from other countries or establish colonies. The Industrial Revolution required countries to go halfway around the world if it was going to improve the overall human condition, thereby making life easier for its citizens. The liberals of the 1850s didn't end war, they merely caused the wars to shift to overseas locations. Locations that were thousands of miles away.

No one at home could understand that wars were still being fought because the industrialized countries of Europe were fighting in Africa and east Asia. And it wasn't a fair fight. The modern British army was literally fighting iron age opponents using modern weaponry. Yes, soldiers were coming home from the Boer War dead, maimed, and wounded. They just weren't coming home dead, maimed, and wounded in significant numbers; not at the same casualty rate of the Crimean War and certainly not in the numbers of World War One. This resulted in the civilian population beginning to believe the liberal myth that warfighting was a relic of the past. Going to war was becoming romanticized throughout Europe.

For 60 years this happened. The elites walked around with their noses turned up, and their chests puffed out. Soldiers from the Crimean War were called to lecture about the horrors of wars, but when they finished, people with degrees in political science approached the lectern, recited Ulysses and quoted Nelson. As time elapsed the veterans went extinct, yet the politicians grew ever more numerous. Politicians are bred in the back rooms of state houses every year. Veterans are forged, tempered, and sharpened in blood, guts and fire. Shellshock prevented many veterans from telling their stories, while insecurities make it almost impossible for politicians to stay quiet. For half a century, to whom was the most attention paid? The foolish politician with a quick wit and snappy, but stolen, pearls of wisdom or the warrior who breaks down crying when he hears a loud bang? Sadly, it was the politician! The politician is always listened to first and is always erringly most trusted.

For sixty-odd years politicians and diplomats traveled the world. Stopping skirmishes by entering into alliances. They ended quarrels by dividing up already claimed territories and defended those treaties by sending other people's children into battle. Sixty years of promising their foes there will be reciprocity if any of their allies are attacked militarily. And what happened, the well-to-do became more well-off and they trod upon the masses. When the masses voiced their displeasure with the elites in power, the elites pointed fingers. The Lords and Ministers continued to believe as they were raised. They elected to continue their charade of being all-knowing to keep from having to concede that their policies have failed. Even after two generations were born, the intellectuals failed to correlate to their policies to the rise in poverty and anarchy.

Am I the only one who finds it weird that between the 1880s and the start of World War One, the number of world leaders who were either assassinated or almost assassinated spiked? And that their assassins or would be assassins were almost always disgruntled anarchists?

Continuing on...

Archduke Frans Ferdinand of the Austro-Hungarian Empire was assassinated by a known anarchist on July 28th, 1914. On this day, there were multiple attempts to assassinate him. This wasn't a lone wolf assassination. It is known that multiple anarchists from the same organization, had gathered to kill the Archduke. The first attempt to kill the Archduke using a hand grenade failed. It was the second attempt which succeeded.

After a brief state visit at the Governor's residence (in Sarajevo), the Archduke and his wife Sophie decided to visit the people wounded during the first assassination attempt. As they were riding to the hospital, Gavrilo Princip broke through the crowd, shot the Archduke and his wife multiple times. Sophie died on the way to the hospital and the Archduke died at the hospital. Gavrilo Princip was also attempting to kill the commander of the Austro-Hungarian forces at the time, General Potiorik, who was a member of the Archduke's entourage. Princip, a South Slav (Yugoslavia), had been trained by a Serbian terrorist organization known colloquially as The Black Hand. It's actual degree of affiliation with the Serbian government can be debated later, but it should be debated to determine who is really at fault for World War One.

Be it known however, The Black Hand was founded by officers from the Serbian Army, and it was actively inciting violence across the Austro-Hungarian Empire. Be it also known that hundreds of members of the Black Hand were also active members of the Serbian Army itself. It ranks weren't merely composed of a handful of disgruntled Serbian Army officers. The assassination of Franz Ferdinand was not a one-off event. The Black Hand was also responsible for multiple assassinations and attempted assassinations throughout the Austro-Hungarian Empire prior to the assassination of Franz Ferdinand.

Try to follow this if you can. (Don't worry, Hiliary, I'll write this really slow just in case you can't read very fast.) Serbia was politically aligned with the Allied Powers- Great Britain, France, Russia, Italy, and the United States. Austro-Hungary was allied with the Central Powers- Austria-Hungary, Germany, the Ottoman Empire, and Romania. The assassination of Franz Ferdinand gave Austria the excuse it needed to quell the activities of the Black Hand and it invaded Serbia. It would be a full month before any army mobilized. Plenty of time for cooler heads to stop hostilities before they start.

However, alliances had been formed over the course of the previous sixty years, and one member had been slighted. In July of 1914, Austria-Hungary not Germany, invaded Serbia to put a stop the terrorism crossing the border into Austria-Hungary from Serbia. Two months later, because Serbia was allied with France, in an alliance dreamed up in a cigar-smoke filled back room populated by liberals wearing top hats, France invaded Germany. The Allied Powers fired the first shots of World War One, not Germany. You might want to remember that. It is important!

Are you still with me?

As everyone knows, World War One ended with the Allied Powers being victorious. The belligerents who started the war won the war. By this time, many of the monarchies of Europe had gone into exile or ceded their powers to their country's parliament to become rulers in name only. As such, politicians and diplomats were sent to negotiate terms of surrender. Because Germany was seen as the greatest of the Central Powers, it was considered to be the most at fault. Even though Germany *did not* fire the first- or second- shots of the war, all blame fell upon its shoulders. The stranglehold the Allied Powers had on Germany meant Germany was unable to prolong the negotiations. This meant that Germany *had* to accept the terms of the Treaty of Versailles as written by the Allied Powers. Germany's ally, the Ottoman Empire on the other hand, was not in such dire straits and *was* able to hold out for better terms. Yes, the Ottoman Empire was sliced and diced into the middle eastern countries which we know today, but they didn't have to pay as dearly as did Germany. More specifically, Germany had to accept the terms of the Treaty as written by smug, top hat and coattail wearing liberals who were raised to believe that their political forefathers had ended wars in Europe.

Many, if not most, Germans alike hated the terms of the Treaty of Versailles and believed them to be unfair. One of these people was a twenty-something corporal in the German army (private in the US Army) named Adolph.

Here is why most of the Central Powers believed the Treaty of Versailles to be unfair. And just so everyone knows, the United States Senate did *not* ratify the Treaty. For the United States, World War One was concluded only with the Armistice that went into effect on Veteran's Day 1918. I wonder if that was a coincidence or if it was planned.

The first reason the Central Powers believed the Treaty to be unfair is because it absolved the Allied Powers of *all* responsibility for the war even though they fired the first shot. Second, it required the Central Powers to pay ungodly amounts of money in reparations for a war they did not start. Third, it essentially stripped Germany of any type of economy other than agrarian.

Back in the day when teachers were teaching- you know old school teaching- everyone was taught that the amount of monetary reparations Germany was forced to pay was enormous. However, no one knew the specific amount. Here is the specific amount- one hundred BILLION gold marks. Yes, 100,000,000,000 gold marks- in 1919! However, it gets worse. Less than a year after the Treaty had been signed, Germany was required to hand over the Allies 20,000,000,000 gold marks. That's 20 billion gold marks by May of 1921 so that the Allied economies could recover as fast as possible. I kid you not! It blatantly says that in the Treaty.

> *"In order to enable the Allied and Associated Powers to proceed at once to the restoration of their industrial and economic life, pending the full determination of their claims, Germany shall pay in such instalments and in such manner (whether in gold, commodities, ships, securities or otherwise) as the Reparation Commission may fix, during 1919, 1920 and the first four months of 1921, the equivalent of 20,000,000,000 gold marks.*
> *"*

Treaty of Versailles
Part VIII, Section I, Article 234

It does not end there. Between 1921 and 1926, Germany had to pay to the allies an additional 40,000,000,000 gold marks so that again, the allies' economies could recover with all due haste. The twelfth paragraph of the second annex of Part VIII of the Treaty of Versailles lays out the stipulations in more detail than any of the preceding Articles. It wasn't enough to be paid in German marks, the German currency at the time, however. The Allies wanted to be paid in *gold* Mark bearer bonds- with interest rates of 2.5% to 5% depending on the bond installment. There were three installments the German government had to pay. The initial 20 billion gold mark bearer bonds installment, two succeeding installments of 40 billion gold mark bearer bonds. The required date of delivery of the third installment was left for "the Commission" to decide. The commission was the Reparation Commission composed of members of *the Allies*. Like I said,

100 billion marks in total. Oops! That should read 100 billion *gold* marks in bearer bonds.

Now then, allow me to put this into a modern perspective because someone is probably whispering in your ear that 100 billion Marks (herein after referred to as Reichsmarks) is nothing. Which is true if one adds the word "today" at the end of the thought. In 1920 however, 100 billion Reichsmarks was an astronomical amount. According to the January 1929 Federal Reserve Bulletin, in 1922 a single reichsmark would cost a person paying in U.S. Dollars, 32 cents. In 1921, the Gross National Product of the United States was 231.8 billion US dollars. This means the dollar equivalent of the amount of money Germany was required to pay was 33 billion US dollars. That's 14% of the US economy at the time. That's 14% of an economy that wasn't in ruins because of the war.

For a modern prospective, the US's 2023 GDP was 27 trillion dollars. 14% of the that number is 3.8 trillion dollars. Imagine what would happen to the US economy if the US was forced, in one year- and on a moment's notice- to handover 14% of its economic output because the World Economic Forum, or the World Bank, or the United Nations said we had too. Imagine what would have happened to the US economy if the US was forced to hand over that amount of money three months after the economic crash of 2009 when the US economy was hurting to say the least. Germany's economy was destroyed by the war, and the Allies were rubbing salt into the wound. Nay, they weren't rubbing salt into the wound, they were using the wound to store salt.

Now don't let your mouth get too far ahead of what you actually know and say that the reparations amount could have been reduced by factoring in the value of all the stuff the Allies confiscated from Germany. While this is true, it's of little help in an economy that is about to go into freefall. Yes, Germany could get credit for the property confiscated, but when a battleship cost $8,000,000 to build, it's no help at all. Yes, little-miss-know-it-all, that is how much it cost to build a battleship. The USS Utah (BB-31) was commissioned in 1911, and its total construction cost was $8,000,000. This is according to contemporary sources, a newspaper article in the Deseret Evening News, dated Thursday, 23 December

1909. Honestly, do you think the Reparations Commission would give Germany credit for the total cost of each battleship? After all, everyone knows that once you drive a battleship off the lot it loses half its value.

So there! Those are the *direct* financial reparations Germany had to bear. This doesn't take into account the material reparations like having to give 8,000 locomotives to the allies and 140,000 head of cattle to France and Belgium alone. Are you beginning to get the picture?

By the way Ms. Hillary, are you aware of the fact that not only was the USS Utah the first ship sunk on 7 December 1941, but it too is still resting where she sank in Pearl Harbor? The USS Arizona gets all the attention because of the number of sailors killed, but the USS Utah is still there too, with 58 souls still on board; 59 souls if one believes the urban legend that a sailor had his daughter's ashes in his locker and was planning to bury her at sea when the ship next got underway.

Back to the Treaty of Versailles' effects on Germany.

There are also territorial losses. Everyone screams about Hitler invading the Rhineland and the Sudetenland, but he didn't invade either. Both of those territories were part of Germany. Germany being forced to cede the Rhineland was especially infuriating. They weren't actually turning control over the Rhineland to the Allies. They were simply forbidden to send, place or have military units- of any kind- in the Rhineland. Germany still controlled the Rhineland. Here is something about the Rhineland that will show the true one-sidedness of the Treaty. Under the Treaty, Germany had to remove and dismantle all *their* military assets in the Rhineland within six months of the Treaty coming into effect. By contrast though, if the Allies had troops in the Rhineland, so long as they were stationed in fortresses, the Allied troops could stay until *the Allies* saw fit to remove them. This wasn't a tit-for-tat treaty. If Germany decided to give the Allies a "tat" for their "tit", then the Allies could unilaterally place even more reparations on Germany. And guess what, they did!

Oh, you want an example?!?!

How does the demise of the German High Seas Fleet that survived the Battle of Jutland strike you? A condition of the *Armistice of 1918* was that the German High Seas Fleet must sail for Scapa Flow, Scotland, and was to wait at anchor *in Scapa Flow* for the Treaty of Versailles to be negotiated and signed. When the Treaty was signed on 18 June 1919, Germany was *required* to hand over to the Allies, her entire navy- surface ships and submarines alike. Three days after the Treaty was signed, in protest of the one-sidedness of the Treaty, the commander of the High Seas Fleet, Admiral Reuter, ordered German sailors to scuttle their ships. And they did!

This it irked the Allies big time! Remember, this happened *after* the Treaty was signed. Seven months later, because of the scuttling of the German ships, the Allies placed additional reparations on Germany as reparations for not being given almost a hundred already built and functioning warships. Warships they would have used to augment their own navies. Look it up! It's called, *"Protocol Signed by Germany January 10, 1920."*

Individual Germans didn't simply suffer a loss in pride with the Treaty either. They suffered economically on a personal basis too. Individual Germans were required to hand over their personal property to the Allies if their ancient family home, as a result of the Treaty, was suddenly within the boundaries of a newly formed or extended country. Sure, they could stay in the country and instantly become citizens of the new country, but that would be like requiring Native Americans and African Americans to simply call themselves Americans.

German citizens wishing to remain in Germany were given a year to settle their affairs, to uproot their families, and to move within the new boundaries of Germany. To add insult to injury, if the Allies desired a family's home which prior to the treaty was deemed to be in Germany but as a result of the treaty is now wholly within the boundaries of the Allied country, when the family "sold" its home, it was the German government that had to pay for the house, not the country that was "buying" the house. And guess what, the German government would have to pay them in Reichsmarks, not gold Reichsmarks; ordinary, printed yesterday Reichsmarks; Ordinary, printed yesterday, valueless Reichsmarks.

And why were Reichsmarks valueless? Because, and I quote the Treaty again, *"…to enable the Allied and Associated Powers to proceed at once to the restoration of their industrial and economic life…"* Remember the whole reparations thing? The Allies wanted gold Reichsmarks bearer bonds. For Germany to have gold bearer bonds, they needed to have gold to back up the gold reichsmarks. In order to have gold, they needed to either mine the gold or buy the gold. I don't care how Herculean a group of miners are, they aren't going to be able to mine 100 billion Reichsmarks worth of gold in three years. Germany had to buy the gold so that they could *guarantee* the bearer bonds. By trading their currency for gold, it told the world that Germany itself didn't trust its own currency. THE ALLIES FORCED GERMANY TO DE-VALUE THEIR OWN CURRENCY.

A family that lost their ancestral home due to a line on a map being moved ten miles eastward, may have been paid one thousand Reichsmarks for their house, but the skyrocketing inflation rate caused by Germany having to de-value their currency meant that the family had to immediately spend the money, because it wouldn't buy a loaf of bread the next day.

In the preceding paragraph, I mentioned Germany was required to mine 100 million reichsmarks worth of gold in three years. This is exactly what happened. Sure, on paper in June of 1920, Germany had at least six years to pay the bulk of the monetary reparations. Well, guess what, Germany defaulted. According to the Allies, Germany wasn't making sufficient progress in paying reparations. This being the case, France and Belgium, as part of the Treaty were now allowed to collect reparations as they saw fit. In January 1923- two and a half years after the Treaty was signed- France and Belgium decided to annex the Ruhr Valley. This too is very significant in answering your question about why so many people would find themselves "blindly" following Adolf Hitler; not because of the territorial loses, but because of the economic losses. Don't forget, France and

Belgium were able to enter the Rhineland unopposed because Germany wasn't allowed to station military units in the Rhineland.

So, let's talk about the economic losses Germany was required to endure. The Treaty of Versailles not only forbade Germany from defending its border with France at the border, but it also ceded to France the Saar region of Germany. The Saar Region was full of ore and mineral mines. The Ruhr Valley was full of ore and mineral mines. The Saar and the Ruhr regions together before the war were responsible for almost half of Germany's GDP. In January 1923, when the roaring 20's were just getting started everywhere else, Germany was being forced to pay extraordinary amounts in reparations after having half its economy stolen, while trying also, to rebuild its own infrastructure, with no money and no other commodities. Guess what, another reparation Germany was forced to pay was in the form of coal ore. Would you like to venture a guess as to where Germany would have gotten the coal under normal circumstances? Yes, after World War One, it was a bad existence to live in Germany, indeed.

How bad? Try to imagine this. You are living in Germany. You are walking the streets of Berlin, and you see a nice pantsuit in the window of a clothing store. You walk up to the window and find yourself staring at the suit. However, you aren't telling yourself how good you would look walking down the street wearing that suit. You are telling yourself that the suit would probably taste good simply because it's green. That was how desperate the German people were. Many times, they opted to walk ten miles to town thereby leaving their emaciated horse at home, to keep their horse from being killed and butchered by another starving family. Life in Germany, thanks to the Treaty of Versailles, economically reverted to being a life of bartering because money was *literally* not worth the paper on which it was printed. So in the early 1930s, when a disgruntled former army corporal who, as most of Germans did, thought that the terms of the Treaty were unfair suddenly realized he had a gift for public speaking, the Germans, even German Jews, listened.

What did this future mass murderer promise the German people? *Hope and change.* My dad and I one day stumbled into this very subject about why

Hitler was so well received even towards the end of his life. My dad told me that one of his college professors was from Germany, and that the professor had lived through the Hitler years. The professor told the class that Hitler, for all his faults, was mesmerizing when he spoke. Hitler, Ms. Clinton, is one of history's greatest orators. Politicians all want to be great orators. Hitler was a great orator. If we are ever able to judge Hitler for his abilities behind a podium and nothing else, we will probably have to admit he is probably the greatest orator to ever walk the face of the earth.

When Hitler spoke, it was only after hours of practice. Everything he did when speaking in public was planned. Hitler didn't blink his eyes until just the right time. He spent hours upon hours rehearsing his speeches. If you ever watch any of his speeches, even for a minute, notice there is no teleprompter. Notice also, he doesn't have notes on the podium. Hitler wrote and memorized his speeches. He choreographed his speeches. Every wave of an arm was to emphasis a point. Every extended silence was calculated to let the point burrow farther into people's consciousness. There were no mistakes! There were no gaffs! He told people what they wanted to hear. They wanted to know that their suffering was about to end.

Then, when he had secured his position, he began to deliver on those promises. He gave them hope and then he gave them change! *Your* political forefathers took everything from Germany and the German people. And then *your* political forefathers arrogantly ignored their suffering. The framers of the Treaty of Versailles should be tried for crimes against humanity because what Israel is being *accused* of doing to Gaza in 2024, *your* political forefathers actually did to Germany in 1919.

That, old girl, is why so many people were enamored by Hitler for so long!

Chapter Twenty-Four

BENGHAZI!

Now, let's talk about number two! Benghazi, September 11, 2012, and how it proves the existence of the professional politician protection racket!

Here are some numbers for you to ponder.

13

4

1

6

10

9

5

4

331

2,039

1,040

577

276

520

2,274

I'm sure you've already figured out what the first two numbers represent. Have you figured out any others? Think about it! I'll wait!

Okay, time's up. As you know, 13 is the number of hours the entire attack on sovereign US soil lasted in Benghazi that night. Four is the number of people killed in the attack. The number 1 represents the number of US ambassadors killed by terrorists while inside the walls of a US Embassy or US Consulate since 1979;

only 6 ambassadors, including Christopher Stevens, have ever been killed in the line of duty. This is according to the State Department website. All were killed in Middle Eastern countries. There seems to be a pattern. This raises a question, with this knowledge, why was our consulate so lightly defended?

If a person does a *quick* search on the internet, the number ten represents the number of US military bases within 2,000 miles of Benghazi. If a person were to do an in-depth query, they would find more scattered everywhere. While doing a reasonable amount of research on the matter, I suddenly realized there is a huge question which must be answered by you and your bosses. Why are there more civilians working on US military bases than there are military personnel? Surely, the military isn't being downsized because people believe that social workers can do a better job of embassy protection than the United States Marine Corps. And a follow up question, how many civilians are being employed for every ground pounder? I digressed again…

The number five represents the number of US military bases within fifty miles of the Mediterranean Sea. Four of the ten bases within 2,000 miles of Benghazi are known to have combat aircraft and personnel available for immediate deployment. Nine of the ten bases are within 1,400 miles of Benghazi. So, what gives?!?!

Allow me to explain this to you.

Hopefully the voices in your head telling you how great you are, aren't speaking too loudly.

Of the bases I am referencing above, the US military base in Djibouti, Africa is the farthest away from Benghazi. It is 2,039 miles away as the crow flies and 2,274 miles away flying a dogleg route over international waters and the Suez Canal. Why is this base so important? Because there are US Marines deployed there at any given moment. Along with flesh and blood marines, there are also the machines required to deploy said marines. The V-22 Osprey can cruise at 276 miles per hour. If it takes a platoon of marines an hour to gather their equipment and board the aircraft, these marines could have been fast roping into the compound 9 hours after receiving orders. And that is the simple-as-can-be way to get Devil Dogs on the ground in Benghazi to help the embattled embassy staff. Oh, I can get more complicated.

If it were decided that the best way to disperse the terrorists attacking the consulate was to have a military aircraft buzz the area, that's even more simple. Aviano Air Force Base in Aviano, Italy is only 1,040 miles from Benghazi. If the air force still had "ready fighters," two F-16s could have been airborne 15 minutes after receiving orders and buzzing the consulate within 2 hours. Why? Because the max speed of an F-16 is almost twice the speed of sound and cruising speed is 577 miles per hour. *But...but...but...fuel...the environment...but...but...but.* This is why I said two hours and not 45 minutes. Everyone knows traveling faster than the speed of sound and using afterburners guzzles fuel. So, the pilots could have flown to Benghazi at 700 miles per hour, just below Mach 1, buzzed the compound, and then rendezvoused with a tanker or landed at a US airbase to refuel. Oh wait, cruising speed of an F-16 is 577 miles per hour, this means the F-16 could been overhead in less than two hours *and* lingered for a while.

If no one is picky about the type of aircraft used to buzz the consulate a C-17, C130, or a KC-130 could have been buzzing the compound within 60 minutes because all of them have a *cruising* speed of approximately 520 miles per hour. If the compound was originally buzzed with a KC-130, it could have buzzed the compound then refueled the F-16s coming in hot right behind it.

However, what do you say we get complicated? I am going to write these next few paragraphs in the present tense because I keep confusing myself and auto correct is driving me crazy.

As soon as the order is received by the commanders involved, four V-22 Ospreys will leave Djibouti each with two separate air crews to operate the aircraft; to extend the range of the Ospreys, they will be configured with 2 extra fuel pods and *no* marines. Shortly after the ospreys leave, a refueling tanker will depart to provide in-flight refueling. The tanker and the Ospreys will communicate in-route to set up a refueling point. If there isn't a tanker available in Djibouti, one will leave from an air base in the Mediterranean, an air base in the Persian Gulf, or one of the aircraft carriers the media is always saying is in the area. Either way, in-flight refueling will be available. The V-22s will fly directly to Souda Bay Naval Air Station. *What? Don't they need to go to Benghazi.* Don't fret none, they'll get there.

While the ospreys are getting prepared for flight, four platoons of Marines will gather their gear, be given a quick 15-minute briefing of the situation, and board a C-130, C-17 or whatever transport aircraft is able to depart within 60 minutes. Once the marines are on board, the transport aircraft will take off and it will head directly for Souda Bay. About three hours after the transport aircrafts with marines departs Djibouti, they will pass the ospreys due to the speed of the transport aircraft being twice a great as the cruising speed of the Ospreys. Approximately four hours after leaving Djibouti, the transport aircraft will land in Souda Bay, taxi to a hangar and disgorge the embarked marines. The marines will wait for the Ospreys to arrive. During the ensuing four-hour layover, the marines will take inventory of the equipment and weapons they brought with them. They will be given up-to-date information, and, most importantly, they will come up with a good plan which they can violently execute once on the ground in Benghazi.

When the ospreys arrive in Souda Bay, the air crews will switch out, and the Ospreys will refuel. Two Ospreys will be designated for marine transport, one will be designated and configured to provide close in air support, and one will be configured for close air support, but held in reserve. Two marine platoons will board the waiting V-22s, one platoon in each plane. Two marine platoons will be held in reserve. As soon as the marines are safely stowed on the airplanes, the Ospreys would take off and head directly to Benghazi. A little over an hour later, after traveling 331 miles, two platoons of heavily armed Devil Dogs will suddenly be seen repelling down ropes out of the aircraft like they are the Archangel Michael come to wreak God's vengeance on the wicked. These men will be dispersed around the consulate grounds to provide security and to kill any person who dares to enter or fire upon *sovereign US soil.*

An hour after the flight of 3 Ospreys departs Souda Bay, the fourth Osprey will depart to provide additional air support as needed and to assist in personnel evacuations. Once the marines have deployed from the two Ospreys, those Ospreys will refuel in flight and stand by to assist in personnel evacuation. Once the third Osprey has been relieved of air support duties, it will refuel and stand by to assist in personnel evacuation. The two close air support Ospreys will alternate as their fuel statuses change.

Yes, in a little over 10 hours- 3 hours before the battle for the consulate will end- fifty marines- count them, one marine, two marines, three marines, four…fifty marines, *could have* been "in-country" providing the much needed support to the five or so *former* soldiers and sailors that comprised the consulate's security detachment and the other State Department personnel battling for their lives with the limited resources professional politicians like yourself deemed sufficient. And in the days that follow, the Marine's Hymn will be modified. The line "…to the shores of Tripoli…" will be struck and will be replaced with the line "… to airspace of Benghazi…" (Hey, it's the same country, whoopee do.)

But…but…but…we didn't know how long the siege of the consulate would last.

Absolutely true! You had no idea how long the situation would last and could not have known how long the consulate would be under siege. It could have gone on for days. During which time the entire staff at the consulate could have been killed. Their bodies could have been desecrated and put on display like trophies of wild game. So, why during the first hour was the order never given to send in the marines? If the order had been given and the situation only lasted two hours, the rescue could have been called off. But because the order was never given, had the situation escalated further and lasted longer, the casualties would have been much higher because the marines were sitting around playing World of Warcraft or watching what was happening on CNN.

But…but…but…the operation you listed above requires a considerable amount of planning; it's not a seat-of-the-pants operation.

Says someone who hates the US military and who thinks the only thing the US military is good for is building hospital tents in West Africa for Ebola patients, so that the *good* soldiers of the United States Peace Corps aren't sent into harm's way to do that which is in their charter- build stuff for humanitarian missions. I notice the Peace Corps isn't being tasked with supplying Gaza with supplies right now, either! I'm sure Hamas would recognize how the Peace Corp presents no threat to them and that they will allow them to remain unharmed as they go about their noble duties of feeding the people who put Hamas into power.

Allow me to explain something to you again.

The United States Military trains for situations like Benghazi. They go on deployments so they can learn and know what they need and don't need when they go into battle. In the amount of time it took you to finally answer the phone and put on your little girl drawers and drive to the White House, and get into the Situation Room or whichever room you were in watching the attack in real time, the US Marines could have hatched a good plan and could have been on their way. Why? Because that is what they do! They improvise! They adapt! They overcome! They fight to protect people who can't protect themselves. They don't sit at the water's edge crying about how they can't go on because they forgot to bring hand grenades. They find a way to move forward. But you and your ilk didn't want them to try. What outcome were you hoping would come to pass? You didn't even give them the chance to help their countrymen in need.

Here are a few scenarios that could have happened. Souda Bay NAS is 300 miles from Benghazi, and Sigonella NAS is 470 miles from Benghazi. These are the two closest US military bases to Benghazi. Of the 10 bases I referenced earlier, all are US military bases. Yes, they are on foreign soil and are also home to the host country's military, but they are US military bases. Should I bring up the fact that there are many other NATO bases scattered throughout the Mediterranean Sea? Well, there are. Bases such as Augusta Bay, Sicily or Rota, Spain (also a US military base), or even the Italian navy base which has the distinction of being the first place in which aircraft were used to sink ships-

Taranto, could very well have at the time had a US military detachment capable of responding. But again, you didn't want them to have the chance, did you!

In 2015 your presidential campaign released a commercial saying you were the only one capable of handling a 3 a.m. phone call saying the world is falling apart. The attack on the Benghazi consulate began at 9:40 pm Benghazi time which is 6 hours ahead of Washington D.C. You weren't awakened at 3 a.m. by a phone call, you were already awake. You were awake and had been awake for hours. You failed!

Chapter Twenty-Five

Closing Thoughts

If people still don't understand how liberals are causing wars to erupt consider this next example.

It's a fictitious movie. Thankfully, I was able to watch it a few times *before* I started noticing the underlying messages. Yes, in high school and junior high my English teachers were constantly trying to get us to think about the underlying messages in books. Well, it can be applied to movies as well. The movie is <u>The Martian</u> with a whole list of wonderful actors and actresses. I have no problem with them and their roles. However, if I worked at NASA, I would consider this movie an insult to my intelligence. If you haven't watched the movie, sorry! Spoiler alert! The movie is about how a mission to Mars went awry and a person was stranded on Mars for a year by himself until a rescue mission was able to reach him.

At every possible point in the movie NASA is failing at something. When NASA should be serious about something, in the movie they are thinking about the feelings of people not involved in the mission of getting the astronaut home. Just to make this easier to write and understand, the name of the astronaut stranded on Mars is Mark Watney. The name of the spaceship, the mothership, is Hermes. The name of the Mars lander depends on the mission to Mars- the first mission where astronauts live on Mars is called Ares 1, the second is Ares 2, and so on.

I will also limit the number of times I bring up ridiculous events in the movie such as the scene where another character in the movie, Vincent, finally figures out Mark Watney's destination in the Mars Rover. Try to follow me on this. NASA is a multi-billion-dollar agency. In the movie, Vincent needed a map of Mars to plot out the information he had in his head to confirm Watney's destination. What did Vincent do to get a map? Did he log in to a computer and pull up one of the multitudes of maps NASA would have of the Mars surface? No! Vincent went to the cafeteria, pulled a picture off the wall and drew on the framed picture with a sharpie. However, he somehow managed to have a ruler with him so he could draw a straight line. I will minimize taking issue with scenes such as that and chalk them up to dramatic license.

I also won't take issue with stuff like there being clouds in the Martian sky even though there is no water on Mars. I will not bring up the fact that with half the atmospheric density of Earth, in the movie Mars, somehow has stronger winds than the earth. Maybe it's possible, maybe it's not. However, for the movie premise, it is required, so I won't take issue with that.

I will allow the fact that in the movie it took the Hermes 209 Mars days (209 SOLS) to travel from Mars to Earth, and then after the Hermes crew decided to disobey orders, return to Mars and rescue Mark, even with gravity assistance from the earth, it took 342 SOLS to go from the Earth to Mars. I certainly will not say anything about the Hermes having to slow down to get into a lower Mars orbit to pick up Mark, but somehow at this slower speed it only took the Hermes an extra thirty SOLS to return to the Earth, again. Yes, they had to accelerate to get the Hermes out of Mars orbit, but one of the dramatic points of the movie is that following the use of their retrorockets to get into Mars orbit, they only had enough remaining fuel to get out of Mars orbit.

I will consider this a function of orbital dynamics and the very likely possibility that the Earth-Mars alignment is the reason for the different travel times. Seriously, it takes the Earth one Earth-year to orbit the sun, but Mars takes two Earth-years. So, if Earth and Mars were ninety degrees apart with the Earth having just "lapped" Mars, the Hermes could only catch up to Mars by backtracking. It couldn't play catch up because the Hermes would essentially have to orbit the sun, and it couldn't make a left turn, so-to-speak, because it would fly directly into the sun. The only way to get to Mars at this point in the Earth-Mars alignment is to get a gravity assist slingshot from the earth and go back the way they came; making a trajectory U-turn so it would intercept Mars as soon as possible but on the other side of the sun.

I won't even take issue with the fact that when he walks on Mars, Mark Watney is walking as he would walk on earth while wearing a space suit. Think about the videos of the Apollo astronauts walking on the moon. They aren't walking, they are bouncing, almost jumping. This is because the moon's gravitational pull is one-sixth that of the Earth. A falling object's terminal velocity on the moon is 1.625 meters per second. On Mars, terminal velocity is one-third that of earth- 3.72 meters per second. Walking across the Martian surface should see Mark Watney skipping not plodding. I will consider this artistic license as well. I mean, if there weren't issues like this in movies, people like me would have nothing to complain about.

I will, however, take issue with the fact that at every possible opportunity, NASA is screwing up something.

The slingshot maneuver that sent the Hermes back to Mars was concocted by the resident genius Rich Parnell. The problem is that no one in NASA appears to have thought about sending the Hermes back to Mars until Rich Parnell thought of it on Martian day SOL 134. The accident that stranded Mark on Mars happened on SOL 18. Therefore, 116 SOLs- 119 earth days- after the accident, someone finally had the idea to send Hermes back to rescue Mark. In the movie it is depicted as being something only an eccentric genius would have thought to do, and it is called the Rich Parnell Maneuver.

Rich Parnell is such an eccentric genius, he lives at NASA in his office, and he has no idea what the Director of NASA looks like. He is literally in the NASA director's conference room, standing face to face with the guy, and does not realize to whom he is talking. And he doesn't know this even though whenever he leaves or enters the building he probably must walk by the guy's picture. The Parnell Maneuver adds anywhere 126 to 141 SOLS to the travel time. It varies because the movie doesn't specifically state when the maneuver is performed.

One of the things that NASA does almost immediately when they finally realize that Mark Watney is alive, is they decide to send a resupply capsule. There are a couple problems here, it took NASA a week of meetings to finally decide to send the capsule, then it took NASA almost half an Earth year to get the resupply mission ready to launch. This is a resupply mission, not a rescue mission. The rocket carrying the resupply capsule launched on SOL 182, and because NASA is incompetent, it exploded two minutes after take-off. *Oh no, now Mark is going to starve to death before we can get a rescue ship (other than the Hermes) to Mars.* The rocket blowing up is attributed to NASA personnel not being able to load a capsule properly. Seriously, we are told that some of the supplies shifted during launch.

Allow me to explain something. If NASA is going to be sending people to Mars, they are going to need multiple rockets of the same type. They are also going to need multiple capsules of the same type that fit on those rockets. AND, when a capsule is loaded, the weight of the objects being placed in the capsule will be known so that it can be placed in a place that does not cause an imbalance. AND since this is a resupply mission for food, NASA will have loading plans which have already been used and ones that are therefore known to work. Everything placed in the capsule will have a designated place that is known to work. But because in the movie NASA is incompetent, the cargo in the capsule shifts, it causes excess vibrations and the rocket blows up. And, as I mentioned earlier, it took NASA six months to load the capsule and affix it to the top of an on-hand rocket.

Here's another thing that shows NASA as being incompetent. Mark Watney was stranded on Mars on SOL 18, eighteen Mars days after arriving. Following the incident, NASA didn't check the ARES 3 landing site until SOL 54- twenty-six days after Mark Watney was stranded on Mars someone at NASA finally wanted to look at the area. But the guy isn't looking at the site to see if Mark is alive, he is looking at the sight to see if there are any salvageable supplies. Apparently, after the accident that stranded Mark happened, they simply thought, "Oh well, let's move on." I should tell you this, what caused Mark to be stranded was a huge windstorm. It was so bad that the mission commander decided to abandon the mission and everyone in the landing party boarded the ARES 3 rocket to go back to Hermes. On the way to the rocket, the wind caused debris to fly around as one would expect. An antenna got airborne, impaled Mark Watney

268

and destroyed his life monitoring unit causing everyone to think he was dead. But no one at NASA thought to confirm this- ever! NASA finding out that Mark was alive was a happy coincidence of someone wanting to know what the ARES 3 site looked like and noticing solar panels had been cleaned off following a windstorm.

Here's another thing. In every movie, in every TV show, or punditry session on the news, people are always using the phrase, "leave no one behind." It is used so much, the general public now believes it is a motto of the United States Armed Forces. I hate to tell people this, but it isn't. Soldiers, sailors, airmen, marines and guardians understand it is impossible to always bring everyone back. If someone doesn't believe me or thinks otherwise, there is a black granite wall in Washington, D.C. they need to visit. That's not to say no one will try to get them home as soon as possible, it's to say that there are times when a handful of people are left behind for the good of the many. These people end up POWs if they are still alive. Because people know they may be left behind, there are standards of conduct. Read the Armed Forces of the United States Codes of Conduct and explain to me why we need this code if no one is ever left behind.

For an industry that injects the line, "never leave anyone behind" into movie scripts whenever possible, NASA was quick to leave Mark behind in this movie.

Once the Hermes crew returned to the Hermes, it immediately left Mars orbit and headed home. Had someone said we don't leave anyone behind, and NASA cared to look, someone would have noticed that Mark Watney *was* still alive, and the Hermes could have stayed in low Mars orbit assisting with the rescue. Had this happened once Mark Watney reached the ARES 4 landing site, he could have simply boarded the ARES 4 rocket, pressed the launch button and joined the crew. He wouldn't have had to somehow disassemble half the rocket capsule to make it light enough so that the rocket could propel the capsule into a higher orbit.

So those are the major instances showing that NASA is incompetent. That is one of the two subliminal or underlying messages of the movie. Would you like to know what the other message is?

China is the greatest. China is the savior of mankind. Only China knows what they are doing. That is the second underlying message of the movie.

Shortly after the resupply rocket explodes following its launch, China offers assistance. By this time the Hermes spaceship is about seventy days from Earth, and it is only now that China builds a resupply mission of its own and *China is able to build a resupply mission in 41 days*. Did you get that? China did in 41 days what NASA couldn't do in 180 days.

China only begrudgingly offers to help NASA because in doing so it would bring to the attention of the world that it has been developing its space program components in secret. In other words, China is more competent than NASA and the proof is that the Chinese space agency personnel wouldn't think of telling, spilling or selling technological secrets to other countries. Take that NASA!

In the movie the Chinese Space Agency allows the technology to be made public by saying this will be a "scientist-to-scientist" transfer of knowledge. Inferring that the Chinese Government isn't involved and will never be told. This also implies a certain nobleness on the part of Chinese scientists.

But this movie doesn't just insult NASA, it also insults the Japanese Space Agency and the European Space Agency. At no point in the movie does anyone contact or ask assistance from allies of the United States. One character in the movie, an astronaut on the Hermes, has the German flag sewn on the sleeve of his spacesuit. This means the ARES 3 mission that took everyone to Mars was a joint venture between NASA and at least the European Space Agency. No one thought of asking them for help. What if the European space agency had a resupply vessel ready to launch? We will never know because the movie was written to show China as the hero.

And it isn't in just this movie where China is portrayed as the hero.

In the Sitcom, <u>Young Sheldon,</u> when Sheldon goes to Germany and needs tutoring to get him up to the same level as his classmates, it is a young Chinese girl that comes to the rescue. Not a young German girl.

In the movie, <u>Mortal Engines,</u> the ultimate hero is a Chinese person with a Chinese crew. No big deal there. However, the salvation of mankind is China. For those of you who haven't seen the movie, the city of London has been placed on a huge platform and moves from place to place on tracks like a tank. Yet in this movie, the city of London, whose tracks sink 10 feet into dry ground as it moves, has somehow manage to end up in China. Did you get that? London has traveled to China. It has managed to cross the English Channel. It has traversed all of Europe and surmounted the Ural Mountains which separate Europe from Asia. It has then traveled the breadth of Asia and all deserts and forests and other flora and it has ended up in China.

Allow me to ponder what manned missions to Mars will entail.

First, the safety of the astronauts will be of the utmost importance. Why? Money! If astronauts keep dying, congress will stop giving NASA money for the missions. Therefore, ensuring the astronauts can get home safely will be the first priority of a manned mission. That's right, all research that is to be conducted on the surface of Mars as part of the mission will take a back seat. NASA will not send astronauts on a long-duration mission without having multiple ways of getting them back on earth *alive!*

Second, saving money will be the second priority. Yes, just as they take a back seat to astronauts' safety, experiments will also take a back seat to the need to save money. NASA isn't going to send a Ferrari to Mars if they can get the same result by sending a Fiat, but for a couple of million dollars less. Yes, being able to drive a Ferrari on Mars would be a dream come true, but if the choice is between saving millions of dollars and a joyride in a sports car...

In the movie, one thing that is depicted that has a high likelihood of coming to pass is NASA prestaging the rockets for getting the astronauts from the Martian surface and back to the mothership in low Mars orbit. The ARES 3 mission had a habitat in which the crew lived, but at the ARES 4 landing site where Mark Watney boarded a rocket, there was no habitat. This means the ARES 3 mission was constantly being built out over a couple years. First, the surface-to-orbit rocket was prepositioned. At some point before humans arrived, the modules that made up the habitat were launched, landed and assembled. Then additional supplies were sent. Finally, once everything was in place and the site was capable of supporting astronauts for the duration of their mission on the surface, the astronauts began their year-long journey to the red planet.

One of the other things that NASA will probably find themselves doing to ensure the astronauts can get home is having a rescue rocket or two orbiting Mars. Their sole purpose being that if the primary surface-to-orbit rocket malfunctions, or if The Martian comes to pass, this orbiting rocket will go down to the surface of Mars and get personnel back to the mothership within a couple days, not a couple years. Along with a prepositioned rescue rocket in Mars orbit, there will probably be an emergency resupply capsule as well. Why? Because sometimes the rescue equipment itself fails. In such a situation NASA will need time to effect a large-scale rescue mission. Remember, all this would be in Mars orbit before any humans launch into space on Earth.

That is just the immediate emergency rockets and resupply capsules for rescuing crews on the ground. In both lunar orbit and Mars orbit, we will probably find emergency propulsion rockets, and emergency supply capsules for the mothership, as well as emergency rescue capsules for the crew. All these supplies would be for the sole purpose of getting astronauts traveling to or from Mars back to Earth alive. If the mothership is on its way to Mars and needs emergency supplies, the supplies in Mars orbit would be sent to the mothership. If the mothership is on its way to earth, the supplies in lunar orbit would be sent.

But why would we put supplies in lunar orbit and not earth orbit. For one, there are thousands upon thousands of objects already in earth orbit and they constitute a collision hazard. The main reason for a lunar orbit, however, is speed. For an object in earth's orbit to break away from earth's gravitational tug, it must travel at 25,000 miles per hour, but a rocket or supply capsule intended for lunar orbit storage does not need to be sent to the moon ASAP. It can be sent to the moon at a leisurely pace- a low-velocity Trans-lunar injection. Yes, the craft will still need to be accelerated to 25,000 mph to escape Earth's gravity, but it can do this over an extended time frame using the Earth's gravity to accelerate it up to the required velocity.

A low velocity TLI will have the benefit of fuel conservation. Huh? What? When the Apollo spacecraft were going to the moon and back, because they had humans on board, the point was to get them to the moon as fast as possible. Thus, the Saturn V rocket was built. The catch twenty-two with the Saturn V is that it had to be big in order to carry enough fuel to get the Apollo spacecraft out of orbit and in a trans-lunar injection flight path. If we were to use a Saturn V in this scenario, we could launch the capsule into earth's orbit then expend a minimal amount of fuel in quick bursts at just the right moment to increase the velocity ever so slightly so that the spacecraft picks up velocity by sling-shotting around the earth multiple times. Using this method, there might be fuel savings of 50 percent. (The 50% is just a guess. Real-NASA can figure out the actual number lickety-split, unlike fake-NASA who would take years, and need a Muppet to do the calculations.) Anyway, that savings in fuel could be used in the future. Six months after the maneuver begins, the spacecraft could decelerate to enter lunar orbit and wait for the need to arise.

When the need arises- when astronauts are in dire need of rescue- the fuel not used in the Trans-lunar injection could be used to send the craft to Mars from the moon directly, accelerating as it went. Or it could be used to send it back to the earth for a quick slingshot around the Earth to build up tremendous speed. I don't know what the velocity would be at this point in this scenario, but it would be greater than 25,000 miles per hour. If Mars and the Earth were at a point in their respective orbits when they are as far apart as they can get, 163 million miles apart, at 25,000 miles per hour, it would take the spacecraft 263 days to get to Mars. If the Trans-Mars injection burn and slingshot around the Earth increased the velocity to 30,000 mph, it would take 219 days to get to Mars. For the history buffs, at its current velocity of 39,700 mph, the Voyager 1 space probe would take 165 days to travel from the Earth to Mars. The difference in travel times of 44 days

273

versus 98 days may not seem like much at first, but to someone who is facing the prospect of starving to death it would give hope.

I hear people asking how the movie <u>The Martian</u> could possibly illustrate how liberals are the cause of all wars since Crimean War of 1853. Simple, propaganda. Liberals are using propaganda to demoralize the populace at-large. Eventually, the people who love the country will disagree with the liberals and the two will meet in battle. Hopefully, it won't be an armed battle. People will choose sides. At this point, all it will take to ignite a shooting war is one soldier drawing his sword to kill a snake and the opposing forces to think the sword is being drawn to attack them. Propaganda has been used to justify going to war throughout history. And because liberals hate the United States, they blatantly endorse Chinese propaganda as being true. And just so everyone knows, the Chinese culture being depicted by traveling dance troupes and in the movies, hasn't existed for a hundred years. That part of Chinese culture went the way of the dodo bird when Puyi, the last emperor of China, was overthrown in 1911.

As a matter of fact, because of the Cultural Revolution, the Chinese people are now forbidden from talking about that part of their history. As far as the Chinese Communist Party (CCP) is concerned, it is a dead history. Displaying that part of Chinese history in movies, is how the CCP gets people to ignore the fact that contemporary Chinese history is a murderous regime. And that the CCP has killed ten times more people than Hitler. Seriously, look it up if you don't believe me. During the 40-year reign of Mao Tse-tung, 100 million Chinese people were killed by the Chinese Communist Party. That's 1.5 million people per year. Hitler wishes he could have killed that many Jews annually. Hitler would have looked up to Mao as he initially did Mussolini; He would have downright worshiped Mao.

'Nuff said?!?!

Turn the page for a glimpse at Part Two coming soon!

Part Two

4. An amendment forbidding Congress from giving taxpayer money to any organization that does not pay income tax; Tax exempt 501.c.3 and 501.c.4 organizations. Regardless of how noble the cause they claim to support.

Section 1:

Neither Congress nor any entity of the United States Government shall distribute any monies collected by the federal government by any means: to any foreign or domestic entity, group or other organization which does not pay income tax to the federal government; to any foreign or domestic entity, group, or other organization considered to be tax exempt by any entity of the United States Government; to any foreign or domestic entity, group, or other organization who is by law, by executive order, or by judicial decree free from tax burdens to the United States.

Section 2:

Distributing monies to established and certified educational facilities shall be allowed only when the receiving facilities are actively performing research on behalf of the Armed Forces of the United States, and said research has been approved by the appropriate committees of the United States Congress, and access to said research shall be directly controlled by the United States Armed Forces.

Section 3:

Congress shall establish an emergency fund which shall herein after be called the Natural Disaster Remedy Fund (NDRF), and Congress shall cause to be deposited into the NDRF and maintained within the NDRF in perpetuity an amount of money not less than ten percent (10%) the annual income of the federal government based on the most recently ended fiscal year.

Section 4:

Congress shall have not less than three full fiscal years (3 years) and not more than four full fiscal years (4 years) to provide the initial monies which will be deposited into the NDRF. If Congress is delinquent in its initial funding obligation, an amount of money equal in percentage to the percentage of money still lacking in the NDRF, based on the most recently ended fiscal year, shall be deducted from the salary of all current and former members of congress who were holding office at the time this amendment was ratified by the required number of states.

Section 5:

Congress shall only draw monies from the NDRF: In response to disasters caused by nature or nature's god where the governor of a state has declared an emergency; In response to other-than-natural disasters where the governor of a state has declared an emergency; To provide for the emergency funding of the United States Armed Forces following an enacted declaration of war against a belligerent nation, entity or other power.

Section 6:

All legislation whose intended purpose is to withdraw monies from the NDRF shall be single-subject legislation and shall require a two-thirds (2/3) majority of both houses of Congress to pass. Overriding a presidential veto shall require a three-quarters (3/4) majority of both houses of Congress.

Section 7:

Every year each United States Senator shall be apportioned 25 million dollars to spend within their state. Every year each United States Representative shall be apportioned 5 million dollars to spend within their respective congressional district. All money spent shall be in accordance with this amendment.

*****

Reasoning behind this amendment:

If you don't take it up the ass like everyone else, you can't have a reach around.

Yes, that is crude and wholly inappropriate in most circles of American society, but it's sound statement. In another section I mentioned my animus towards tax exempt organizations. I wish this amendment was not needed, but it is. Being a tax-exempt organization has become legalized grift. Shady, tax-exempt organizations are the cause of all organizations being punished. Ladies and gentlemen, we are a capitalist nation, not a communist, collectivist, or socialist nation. We are also a compassionate nation. We believe that benevolent causes should not be punished, and truly benevolent organizations should be allowed to retain as much of their income as possible so that they can do as much good as they can.

However, we need to understand that every time someone does something magnanimous, someone else sees that as a way to conduct evil. We must draw the line somewhere. This line must be set in stone to prevent fraud. If people want their money to be sent to organizations that don't pay taxes, then they can send money directly. The federal government, nor any state government, should be sending money to tax-exempt organizations. I know there are people out there who disagree with me on this. However, and keep this in mind, by not having to pay taxes on its income, a tax-exempt organization is getting money from the government. They are simply getting it in the form of a full refund on taxes paid or by not having to send in the money to begin with.

Additionally, and contrary to what the powers that be wish us to believe, most of the money spent by the United States Congress does not go to the Department of Defense. Most of the money is paid to charities, and other tax-exempt organizations. Depending on the amount of money received by the federal government each year, only 10 to 20 percent of the money is allocated to the DoD, and of the remaining money, only about 20 percent of federal spending is used to fund the rest of the government. Most of the money congress spends every year is spent on acts of "benevolence." I have benevolence in quotes because a lot of these acts are, in reality, instances of waste, fraud, abuse, and grift.

I have an idea on how to stop a lot of the grift taking place on an individual level, too.

All of us have interacted with someone who never seems to work; someone who only remains employed long enough to reset the welfare counter so that they can collect unemployment for another few months. Here is my fix to this long-con game. Let me preface what I am about to write by reminding everyone that we are a compassionate nation, not a communist, socialist, or collectivist nation.

First, if a person is in the country illegally, regardless of how they came to be designated an illegal alien, they get nothing. Nothing! Not a damn thing. No social security, no unemployment, no medical. Nothing! Why? Because they are in the country illegally. Yes, a person can come into the country legally with all the proper paperwork, but if they overstay their visa, they become an illegal alien instantly. Illegal aliens get nothing! The only help they shall receive is if they commit a crime and are found guilty by a jury of our peers (their peers being in their home country). In these cases, they will be provided with three meals per day and given a roof over their head. However, they will neither like their accommodations, nor their neighbors.

Second, a person can continue to collect unemployment and Medicaid benefits in perpetuity, but with conditions. Here are the conditions. If a person suddenly finds themselves unemployed, regardless of the reason, because the United States of America is a compassionate country, they can collect unemployment. Out of the goodness of their hearts, their fellow citizens will allow their hard-earned money- money which they are forced to send to the federal government- to be given to those who are newly unemployed with no strings attached for the first two months of unemployment. After that, a person can still collect unemployment, but the balance will be deducted from their social security account. Once the balance in their social security account reaches zero, no more assistance shall be given. So, if a person has 10,000 dollars in their SS Account, and they are paid $1,000 each month for unemployment, they can lounge around for an additional 10 months; twelve months in total.

When a person's social security account is empty, they get nothing. The only way they can collect more money is to find employment, get paid, and pay taxes again. They must do all the things the non-parasitic members of society do to live. The same goes for Medicaid. If a person suddenly develops a desire to perform stupid stunts, the first two months will be covered by the taxpayers, if they are claiming to be unemployed. After that, the payments to doctors, hospitals, etc. are debited out of their Medicaid account until there is nothing left. If they still have medical bills, they can beg for help from the doctor, hospital, or find a good Samaritan to pay the remaining balance. If their injury is such that they can't work, they better be able to show to a court of law that their injuries weren't caused because they were doing something stupid as an unemployed member of society.

The third thing to do to fix the current unemployment and social security problems is to launch a massive, and I mean huge, educational campaign to tell people all about the social security and Medicare programs. Every day, during prime-time hours, a person will appear on the television and explain something many people fail to realize.
In order to collect social security in retirement, you need to have paid into social security.
And….

The amount of money that a person has paid into Social Security determines the amount of their social security check.

That's the entire educational campaign. Nothing else, just that. Why? Because there are people in this country who believe they are going to get paid big money in retirement after having a fragmented employment history in what can only be described as entry level positions.

Fourth, make it impossible for congress to change the conditions by which a person must abide in order to collect unemployment. If there is an economic downturn and a lot of people find themselves unemployed it might be three or more months before many people can find gainful employment. In cases like the Great Depression, it would be prudent for the government to issue a moratorium on conditions so that no one starves. What we don't want is for it be easy for congress to waive the conditions simply because it's an election year and the stock market suddenly dropped 1,000 points in three days. Or for a president to be able to waive the conditions because they are trying to turn the country into a socialist hellhole. I suggest a requirement where it takes a three-quarter majority of each house of congress to waive the conditions, and nine-tenths majority to override a veto. I also suggest there be a line item which prevents the President from doing the same, and if he or she does, then they can be dragged out of the Oval Office and be forced to bathe in a swimming pool full of warm penne pasta.

Hey, Doctors Without Borders, why don't you direct some of your benevolence inward. Travel this country performing free operations for those in need here, instead of prognosticating about how the medical system in the country sucks. Quit blathering on about how everyone with even the slightest bit of extra money needs to pay the medical bills of people who feel they are entitled to never have to work for anything. Here is what I think every doctor should do if they truly believe socialized medicine is the way to go- Refuse to get paid for their services. Not just while working pro bono, but for all their work. It's funny how doctors believe medical care should be free, until it is explained to them that they won't get paid.

Disclaimer: This will not affect the retirement or social security payments of people who are either retired from military service, collecting social security or both. Their payments will continue until such time as they die, they shuffle off their mortal coil, or they succumb to man's inevitable destiny.

Lastly, we must not fall into the trap of believing that the problems with charitable organizations can be solved by limiting the amount of money the government can distribute to a charity based on the organization's annual donation intake. It will only extend the problem or make it worse. Yes, local non-profit organizations will suffer the most. Any cash bailout that Congress legislates into law to help small non-profits will always end up in the hands of the larger charities. Why? Because larger charities have the man-power and financial backing which allows them to find the loopholes in the law and ultimately receive the money. And since the amount of money a charity can receive will no doubt be based on annual income, the larger charities will receive most of the money.

Here is what happened in 2009 following the financial meltdown caused by President Clinton through legislation passed by congress that forced banks to give mortgages to people who had no hope in repaying the mortgage. Ignore the bluster fronted by the media and the criminal politicians. Money was, according to the law, designated to be for small, neighborhood banks so they could weather the financial storm, but most of the bailout money went to large banks. This is what I was told by close relative of mine who had a second job working part time at a bank. After the collapse, the bank went out of business because neither of the two branches of the bank qualified for the economic bailout. What ultimately happened nationwide is that after they fraudulently received the bailout money they claimed to need, the larger banks- national banks- put the smaller banks out of business using age-old monopolistic tactics. This happened! Fannie Mae and Freddie Mac!

Eventually, if the fools who make the laws put a limit on the amount of money a charity can collect and still be eligible for government assistance, the larger charities will split into smaller, quasi-independent charities controlled by a supposedly non-existent central headquarters. The spun-off, smaller, quasi-independent charities will then be required to deposit most of the donations they receive into the financial accounts of these invisible HQs. This will all be done at the behest of the aforementioned, non-existent, central headquarters. Years later, and only when a completely unrelated scandal arises, audits will expose how the smaller charities collect and funnel money into the accounts of the mother HQ, but as I said that will be years later, probably decades later. The findings will also show that the larger charity would have made far less money as a behemoth than they did as a collection of smaller, quasi-independent organizations.

It's the Standard Oil effect. If people considered John D. Rockefeller to be a rich man before the US government forced Standard Oil to be split into smaller companies, after the split they would have considered him obscenely rich. And I mean really, really, obscenely rich. In today's money Rockefeller would have died a multi-Trillionaire. Yes, you read that correctly. In the early 20th century prior to the break-up of Standard Oil, Rockefeller was a multi-millionaire. After the break-up, he ended up being a multi-billionaire because he retained a controlling interest in the smaller companies.